The Fall of Nigeria

The Fall of Nigeria

THE BRITISH CONQUEST

OBARO IKIME

Professor of History, University of Ibadan

HEINEMANN
LONDON · NAIROBI · LUSAKA · IBADAN

Heinemann Educational Books Ltd
48 Charles Street, London WIX 8AH
P.M.B. 5205 Ibadan. P.O. Box 45314 Nairobi
P.O. Box 3966 Lusaka

EDINBURGH MELBOURNE TORONTO AUCKLAND
SINGAPORE HONG KONG KUALA LUMPUR NEW DELHI

ISBN 0 435 94140 2 (Cased)
ISBN 0 435 94141 0 (Paper)

DEDICATION

This book has been written during a year that has been extremely busy for me. In the circumstances my family life suffered quite a bit. In particular the kids saw far less of me than they had a right to expect. I apologize to them for my seeming negligence and thank them for putting up with a daddy so often in his office. As a token of my appreciation of the hardship with which they had to live while I worked on this book, I dedicate the book to our three really delightful children, MAZINO, MAJIRO and MAINO.

Set in 11/12 Baskerville
Printed in Great Britain by Butler & Tanner

CONTENTS

PART ONE: THE BRITISH CONQUEST OF NIGERIA

PART TWO: EPISODES FROM THE BRITISH
CONQUEST OF NIGERIA

35970

Illustrations

Maps

Preface

This book tells the story of the British conquest of Nigeria. The subject here treated is one on which quite a few scholars, both Nigerians and foreigners, have written. What is attempted in this volume is therefore essentially a synthesis of existing works. I have been moved to do this synthesis largely by what I see as one of the crying needs of undergraduates in Nigerian universities studying Nigerian history. At the moment, the undergraduate must read at least ten different monographs and a sizeable number of journal articles before he can get an overall Nigerian view. With the soaring price of books and inadequate library facilities, many of our undergraduates are frustrated in their efforts to get a nation-wide coverage of this and other topics in Nigerian history. In this volume I present them with such a coverage with regard to the British conquest of Nigeria. This work is not meant to provide an excuse for not reading the more detailed and scholarly monographs which exist. Rather, it is meant to give a general picture which, it is hoped, will, by its inadequacies, indicate to which particular monograph the reader should turn in search of more detailed argument and narrative.

Although the needs of university undergraduates have been a major factor in deciding me to undertake this work, it is written in a style which I very much hope will commend itself to the general reader just interested in familiarizing himself with this aspect of Nigerian history. It is for this reason that the book is in two distinct parts. Part One provides the historical setting and handles some of the argument and analysis. Part Two furnishes the reader with 12 episodes from the British conquest of Nigeria, one each from the former 12 states of the country. My choice of episodes, I know, is open to criticism. Many others are no doubt possible, but I doubt if any choice can be *the* choice. My aim here has been to demonstrate that to whichever part of the country one turns, there is some story worth telling within the context of this book. Those not interested in the arguments and analysis of Part One can, I hope, discover some interest in Part Two. I am aware that there are repetitions to which some of my readers may take exception. I have left these repetitions in because I am anxious that those who decide to read only Part

Two of the work, should, nevertheless, find each episode self-sufficient and reasonably meaningful.

The decision not to use footnotes has been deliberate. I hope that by doing so I may have cut down the price of the book. More important, however, is the fact that the subject matter of the book is one of the more thoroughly covered aspects of Nigerian history. The main works I have consulted are listed in the select bibliography which must serve as the main indicator of my source material for this book, though I have also had to use primary sources. The select bibliography must also serve as a token of my indebtedness to the large number of scholars whose works I have used here without specific acknowledgement. I hope that they derive some satisfaction from my open confession that this book would never have been written but for the existence of their own studies. I thank them all.

I am grateful to the University of Ibadan for a research grant which enabled me to visit the Kaduna and Enugu branches of Nigeria's National Archives while preparing this work. Other publications which arose from that grant are two articles, 'The British Pacification of the Tiv' in *Journal of the Historical Society of Nigeria*, VII, 1 (December 1973) and 'The British in Bauchi: 1901-1908: An Episode in the British Occupation and Control of Northern Nigeria' in the same *Journal*, VII, 2 (June 1974).

I thank Major General John Obada of the Nigerian Air Force Base, Kaduna, and Mr Osita Okeke, then Commissioner for Establishments in the government of the East Central State, for their very kind and lavish hospitality during my visits to Kaduna and Enugu respectively.

I owe immense thanks to Mr S. Abu for the very tedious typing and retyping which he had to do throughout the preparation of this work.

As usual I am heavily indebted to my wife, Hannah, who not only has to put up with my increasing absences from home but who also constantly encourages me to write even though she must know that this means long hours at my desk at the expense of our family and social life. I am immensely grateful to her for her support, understanding, and love.

OBARO IKIME

A Note on a Few of the Terms Used

AMAYANABO   Title of ruler of the Ijo states of the Eastern Delta.

COMEY   Dues paid by European traders to Nigerian coastal rulers for permission to trade in the latter's territories.

FACTORY   The on-shore installations (stores and premises) of the European traders in the Niger Delta states in the nineteenth century.

MAN-OF-WAR   An armed ship of (in this case) the British navy.

PUNCHEON   A large cask (of wood held together with metal rings) used for storing and transporting oil (and other fluids) capable of holding some 70–120 gallons.

SUPERCARGO   A European merchant who stayed at the coast and organized the trade of his firm.

The term Nigeria is used in this work to refer to the geographical area which in 1914 became the political entity now known as Nigeria.

PART ONE

The British Conquest of Nigeria

CHAPTER

I

Introduction:
The Suppression of
the Overseas Slave Trade and
New Trends in Euro-Nigerian Relations

The bulk of what is now Nigeria became British territory in the period between 1885 and 1914. It is, therefore, usual when we speak of the British conquest of Nigeria to think in terms of the many military expeditions mounted against various Nigerian peoples during that period. Yet the events which took place between 1885 and 1914 were but a culmination of a series of events, indeed a process, which began early in the nineteenth century.

In terms of Afro-European relations in what is now Nigeria, the nineteenth century was markedly different from previous centuries. From the late fifteenth century, when Europeans began doing trade with the coastal peoples of Nigeria, until the beginning of the nineteenth century, a noticeable feature of the relations between them and our forebears was their complete dependence on the rulers of the coastal peoples not only for the securing of trade but also for the safety of their lives and property. Hence, although European commercial activities had some social impact on the peoples of the coast, they hardly produced any political repercussions in terms of European involvement in Nigerian politics. Throughout the period the Nigerian coastal rulers remained very much in control of their own affairs. Indeed the European traders went out of their way to ensure that they were in the 'good books' of the Nigerian rulers in the interests both of their trade and their lives. In Nigeria, unlike the situation in Ghana, the European nations which engaged in trade with our forebears did not build any forts along the coast. This meant that the traders had really no military base in Nigeria. Therefore, they

3

were anxious to maintain peace with their Nigerian clients since, in the event of hostilities, they would be left completely to their own devices. The Nigerian rulers and peoples for their part, desirous of making as much profit as possible from the trade, were equally anxious to maintain peace between themselves and their European clients. In this connection it should be remembered that for the coastal peoples trade was not only a source of wealth, it was also a source of prestige and, in many cases, served the purpose of enhancing the political authority of the ruling classes. Hence, a continued flow of trade was as much in the interests of the Europeans as of the Nigerian coastal peoples. Both sides, therefore, did all they could to ensure that peace which was so essential for profitable trade.

This even tenor of Euro-Nigerian relations was rudely shattered in the nineteenth century by Britain's decision to put an end to the overseas slave trade. As is well known, in 1807 Britain passed a law against the slave trade. Having done that she proceeded to bully, persuade, or bribe other European nations as well as America to do likewise.

The argument as to why Britain decided to put an end to the Atlantic slave trade cannot be taken up in any detail here. What is clear is that by 1807 the climate of public opinion was such that it made abolition possible. While there is a great deal in the argument that by the beginning of the nineteenth century Britain had made enough money from the slave trade and the ancillary trades connected with it to enable her to industrialize, and that industrialization gradually rendered slave labour less necessary, no one can doubt the important role played by those normally referred to as the humanitarians in bringing about actual abolition. These men, products of the evangelical revival which swept through Britain in the closing years of the eighteenth century, were those who felt, as Lugard once put it, that Britain had 'a duty of expiation to perform towards the African' for her part in depopulating and degrading Africa during the two and a half centuries of the slave trade. Economic and humanitarian reasons thus combined to make Britain the leading crusader against the slave trade. But the road to abolition was far from easy. Even in 1807 there were still groups in Britain anxious and eager to continue in the slave trade. If this was true for Britain it was more so for other European countries and America where the arguments — be they economic or humanitarian — for the suppression of the slave trade had not become equally compelling. This was why Britain had to persuade, bully, or dole out substantial subsidies to some of the European countries. This was why, despite persuasion and subsidies, some of the European and American nations, especially Portugal and Brazil, continued to engage in the slave trade until about 1850.

Britain did, however, succeed in getting the governments of the various European nations to pass laws which rendered the overseas slave trade illegal. Once these laws were passed, Britain could argue that any Europeans caught engaging in the slave trade were breaking the law. However, laws require physical sanctions to make them effective. Hence, Britain instituted the now famous anti-slave-trade naval squadron in West Africa. The duty of this squadron was to chase slavers on the high seas, capture their ships, take them to Freetown, which had been founded by British humanitarian interests as a home for freed slaves from Britain, and there liberate the slaves while seizing the boats. Between 1807 and 1830 British efforts at putting an end to the slave trade were concentrated on the activities of the anti-slave-trade squadron.

On the face of it, it might look as if the situation described above was really a matter between Britain and the other European nations. Far from it. There were two sides to the slave trade: a European side and an African side. Although European slavers continued to defy the naval squadron, there is no doubt at all that the constant harassment of slavers by the squadron led, in time, to a gradual reduction in the volume of the slave trade. This in turn produced an adverse effect on the economy of the Nigerian rulers concerned at the same time as it created political problems for them. Hence, any meaningful study of the British conquest of Nigeria, especially Southern Nigeria, must begin with an examination of how the suppression of the overseas slave trade prepared the way for eventual British occupation.

At first the attitude of the Nigerian rulers to suppression was quite simple: they would sell slaves as long as there were Europeans or Americans to buy them. In the Yoruba country, especially as from the 1820s, there were many slaves available for sale as a consequence of the inter-group wars which plagued that part of our nation for most of the nineteenth century. Lagos, the port of Yorubaland, continued to engage in the slave trade till after mid-century. The greatest slave exporting part of Nigeria was the eastern delta where Bonny was the leading slave trading state. Bonny continued in the trade till the 1840s; so did other eastern delta states. In fact, Brass continued right up to the 1860s. In the western delta, the Itsekiri kingdom, never a great slave trading area, nevertheless carried on the trade till the 1830s. The question then arises as to why these states ever gave up the trade. The answer lies partly in the fact that European nations gradually gave up the trade and partly in the fact that Britain decided that it was not enough to chase European slavers on the high seas; that it was even more effective to ensure that the source of supply of the slaves was blocked. Consequently the naval squadron undertook a blockade of the major slave trading ports of Nigeria.

By this decision the old relations between Europeans and Nigerians were torpedoed. Britain's act in stationing her navy in West African waters was in itself questionable in the international law that governed relations between European powers. The decision to use that navy to blockade Nigerian ports was even more questionable as it represented a deliberate and, from the African viewpoint, an unprovoked infringement of the sovereignty of the various Nigerian peoples concerned who at no time gave their consent to such a blockade. Nigerian rulers did not take kindly to this violation of their sovereignty. In 1836 a British gunboat seized a Portuguese vessel doing trade in slaves off the port of Bonny. The ruler of Bonny was furious. He caused the captain of the British gunboat and other Europeans to be arrested and imprisoned for venturing into Bonny's territorial waters without authorization. In earlier times, when European traders could not count on the kind of backing now provided by the navy, some mutually acceptable solution would no doubt have been found. Now, however, the British merely summoned more gunboats and threatened to blow Bonny up unless the prisoners were released. The ruler of Bonny was forced to release the prisoners to save his state. The era of gunboat politics had dawned. From now till the actual occupation it was no longer 'what is right' but 'might is right'. This was one way in which the British determination to put an end to the slave trade began to prepare the way for the eventual British occupation, by making our forebears lose confidence in themselves in the face of superior military or naval might as in the case cited above.

Partly to cover up the questionable legality of actions like the one above, the British also began to negotiate what are known in our history as anti-slave-trade treaties. Such treaties were signed with Brass in 1834, Bonny in 1839, Calabar in 1841, and Aboh in 1842. These treaties provided that in return for giving up the trade in slaves, the rulers of these states would be paid a certain compensation over an agreed number of years. Usually the agreed compensation was trifling when compared with the revenue hitherto derivable from the slave trade. That apart, the importance of these treaties was that once signed, the British used them as the excuse for bombarding Nigerian states on the grounds that one or other of the articles had been broken. These bombardments had the same effect as mentioned above — weakening the states concerned, forcing them to accept the superior might of Great Britain. It is clear, therefore, that in retrospect the suppression of the overseas slave trade provided an indispensable prelude to the British occupation of Nigeria.

The Growth of Missionary Activity in Nigeria

If Britain found herself using force to suppress the overseas slave trade, that is not to say that she regarded force as the best means of achieving the desired end. In a sense it can be argued that the use of force then, as later in the years of actual occupation, was the direct result of the refusal by our forebears to accept a new order that was obviously inimical to their interests. Britain in fact sought other means to achieve her end. If the slave trade had to end, something had to take its place. The palm oil trade was developed to replace the trade in slaves. This was because palm oil was needed by Britain and other European nations for the manufacture of lubricants, soap, and so on. However, the trade in palm oil raised new problems which also altered the pattern of European-Nigerian relations. Then there was Christian missionary activity. It was felt that if Nigerians were converted to Christianity, they would see the evil in the slave trade and so be more willing to give up that trade. It apparently did not strike Europe that Christian Europe had nevertheless found it possible to engage in the slave trade for three centuries. Connected with missionary activity and the new trade in palm produce and other forest products was the work of the British 'explorers' who sought to unravel the 'mystery' of the Niger. The 'discovery' of the mouth of the Niger by the Lander brothers was the prelude to the rise of Macgregor Laird, and their activities had important consequences for all of the Niger Delta, especially Brass, as well as the Aboh kingdom.

The first batch of missionaries to arrive in Nigeria landed at Badagri in 1841. Four years later another batch landed at Abeokuta. In the same year that the Christian Missionary Society landed at Abeokuta, the Presbyterians, led by Hope Waddel, reached Calabar. In 1857 the C.M.S. established itself at Onitsha and the same mission began operating in the Niger Delta in the 1860s. While it would be interesting to go into the details of missionary activities in Nigeria, space forces us to concentrate instead on a few examples, focusing our attention on why such Nigerian groups accepted missionary activity and what the consequences of this acceptance were. Perhaps the two best examples for this purpose are Abeokuta and Calabar. Calabar is treated in full in Part 2 (Episode 2) so here we will discuss Abeokuta in some detail.

It is impossible to understand why Abeokuta welcomed missionaries except within the context of the Yoruba wars of the nineteenth century. As J. F. Ade Ajayi has pointed out, the Egba were the greatest sufferers from the Yoruba wars at least up to the middle of the nineteenth century. When, with the collapse of Old Oyo, refugees flocked southwards, it was into Egba territory, in the area of present-day Ibadan, that they moved. It was thus the Egba who were dislodged from their original homes by the fleeing Oyo. Over 150 Egba settlements were destroyed by Oyo, Ife, and Ijebu elements in the early years of the Yoruba wars.

It was the insecurity created by these new pressures that led to the foundation of a new Egba town, Abeokuta, in 1830, on an easily defensible spot around the Olumo rock. However, the founding of Abeokuta on this militarily strategic site did not provide an answer to all the problems of the Egba. For one thing, those who founded Abeokuta were not a homogeneous group but rather a motley collection from the pre-holocaust towns and villages. Hence, although Sodeke emerged as the leader of the Egba in Abeokuta, his leadership was circumscribed by the tendency of his followers to look up to their former leaders in the pre-holocaust settlements rather than yield complete allegiance to Sodeke. Politically, therefore, Abeokuta was rather unstable, sharing with other groups, in this respect, the general instability caused by war in Yorubaland.

It was into an Abeokuta in this state that the missionaries came in 1846. By this date, the main preoccupation of the Egba, as of other Yoruba groups, was how to survive in the war situation. To survive, the Egba had to have the means to defend themselves against their enemies: they had to have a constant supply of arms and ammunition. But arms and ammunition came from the coast, especially Lagos. However, between Abeokuta and Lagos stood the Ijebu who had joined the Oyo and Ife in despoiling Egba towns. It was clear that if Abeokuta was to have an uninterrupted supply of arms and ammunition she had to find her own port. Badagri, on the Lagoon, provided the answer. The weakness of Badagri at that point in time made her a suitable area in which to build up Egba influence. But even a weak and politically divided Badagri had to be reached and a working arrangement struck. Between Abeokuta and Badagri were the Egbado and Awori peoples. Under the leadership of Sodeke, the Egba sought to control the Egbado and Awori peoples. Sodeke did not seek to rule these people directly; he merely desired that their rulers should allow his Egba free access through their country to Badagri, afford them protection on their way to and from the coast and give them land on which to farm.

Egba efforts in this direction ran into difficulties because at about the same time that Sodeke was seeking to forge this working arrangement, Dahomey, recently freed from Oyo control, and desperately in search of palm-oil-producing areas, was seeking to expand into the Egbado area. The clash of interests inherent in this situation explains the Egba–Dahomey conflict which lasted on and off from the 1830s right up to the 1870s. Indeed the very year in which the Christian missionary effort at Badagri began, Dahomey intervened in an Abeokuta–Ado war as ally of Ado which Sodeke was trying to reduce, since Ado was 'the last remaining obstacle on the Abeokuta–Badagri route'. Any wonder that when, four years later, the missionaries appeared in Abeokuta, through Badagri, the Egba were disposed to welcome them? The welcome which the Egba accorded the missionaries was no more than another facet of the politics of survival. The Egba saw the missionaries not so much as saviours of their souls, as saviours of their bodies: they knew that white men could get arms and ammunition from their fellow white men in Lagos; they could teach the Egba how to use these arms more effectively, and so enable the Egba to overcome their Ijebu and Dahomey enemies and spread their influence over surrounding areas. In the troubled history of Yorubaland in the nineteenth century, the missionaries often lived up to these expectations. They certainly ensured that the Egba were well supplied with arms and ammunition from Lagos; they did, in fact, teach the Egba how to use these weapons of war and how to improve the defences of Abeokuta. Anxious to secure the goodwill of the Egba leaders, the missionaries did not see any contradiction in 'men of God' trafficking in weapons of death. When in 1850-1 a Dahomey attack on Abeokuta looked imminent, the missionaries got the British consul to send two gunboats to Dahomey to warn the king of that country not to attack Abeokuta as there were British subjects there.

From the above it should have become clear that the Egba attitude to missionaries was dictated by the prevailing political situation in Yorubaland. The immediate result of their accept-ance of missionary activity was a strengthening of their position *vis-à-vis* their immediate enemies. However, the missionaries in Abeokuta were not there just for the purpose of serving the interests of the Egba. Apart from seeking to establish the Christian faith, they were generally committed to the goal of establishing British influence and 'civilization'. This indeed was why the missionaries so often worked in close collaboration with the British consular officials. In the case of Abeokuta, the British used the presence of missionaries there to build up a case against Lagos. How this was done is detailed in the second part of this book where the Lagos episode is described (see Episode 1). Here only the main points need to be stated. The British, anxious to establish their presence in Lagos, began to build up Abeokuta as 'the Niger of the hinterland'. The prospects of Abeokuta as a centre for trade and 'civilization' were seen as limitless. Early in 1851 John Beecroft, the British consul of the Bights of Benin and Biafra, visited Abeokuta. There Townsend, the head of the Christian Missionary Society party, stage-managed the Egba leaders into signing an anti-slave-trade treaty. Armed with this treaty, Beecroft and the British traders and missionaries could now argue that Lagos ought to be compelled to do likewise. In fact the argument was now developed that Lagos was 'the port of Abeokuta' and that unless she was made to give up the trade in slaves (a clever way of saying that unless Kosoko allowed British trade and influence to be paramount there) the trade of Abeokuta and the Yoruba hinterland in general would suffer. Thus did the

Egba allow themselves to be used against Lagos. Yet, it must be clear that the Egba were not just allowing themselves to be used by the British; they were also using the British to further their own interests as they understood these at the time.

Having made the last statement, however, one must hasten to add that for whatever reason the Egba welcomed missionaries, British influence in Abeokuta developed apace as a consequence. From 1851 till about 1862 Townsend served as secretary to the Alake, and used that position to influence the Alake and the Egba in favour of the British. When the Ijaye war broke out in 1862 the Egba found that the British wanted them to seek peace while they (the Egba) saw the Ijaye-Ibadan conflict as an excellent occasion for recovering the homes of their fathers. When, in pursuit of their own interests the Egba declared war on Ibadan, they found that they had offended the British government in Lagos. From this time on relations between the Egba and the British began to deteriorate. The conflict which now developed is easy to explain. The Egba saw the white missionaries and the British government in Lagos as existing to promote Egba interests in Yoruba politics. So long as the British did this, the Egba were quite prepared to let the missionaries teach their children how to read and write, to preach Christianity to the Saros (freed slaves who had returned to Abeokuta from Sierra Leone), or to teach them cotton ginning. The British, for their part, were determined to promote their own interests which included, among other things, the establishment of peace in the Yoruba hinterland for the more effective exploitation of trade.

This aim, as the Lagos example had shown, was beginning to involve the dismantling of African sovereignty and its replacement by British authority. Fears that the British meant to overthrow Egba authority completely as they had done in Lagos were certainly behind Egba hostility to the white missionaries from the 1860s. Certainly that fear explains the *Ifole*, the attack on white missionaries and their property in 1867; it lay behind the welcome given to the French Catholic priests of the Société Missionaire en Afrique who began missionary activity in Abeokuta in 1880; it lay behind the Egba invitation to the French to establish a French protectorate over them in 1888. The Egba discovered, as all other groups did, that while missionary activity might have saved them from their Yoruba enemies, it was ultimately robbing them of their sovereignty. Unfortunately for the Egba, by the time they began to see this and to want to take counter measures, developments in Europe had decided Britain to seek to establish her hold firmly on Yorubaland and the rest of Nigeria. Hence, by the 1880s the Egba were not really just fighting against missionaries; they were fighting against the might of Great Britain. True, the Egba maintained a veneer of independence until 1914. But the Egba United Government set up in 1898 was dominated by the Christian Saros and was very much under the influence of the British government in Lagos. From that date, a British protectorate existed in fact, if not in law, in Abeokuta.

Although space forces us to be content with a discussion of the Abeokuta situation (and even this is not as fully treated here as it is by E. A. Ayandele in his *The Missionary Impact on Modern Nigeria 1842-1914*) it is necessary to point out that in every other part of Southern Nigeria where missionaries were established, they served in the end as the harbingers of British colonial conquest, or else helped to consolidate such conquest. It is equally important to note that in each case the Nigerian group concerned accepted missionary activity for other than religious considerations. Between 1841 and 1857, for example, the Obi of Aboh was anxious to have missionaries in his kingdom because he thought he could use the missionaries to make Aboh a centre of European commercial activity such that Aboh would no longer depend on Brass for trade with the Europeans. Obi Ossai's enthusiasm for missionaries and the white man had, by the reign of Obi Aje in the 1850s, turned into one of acute hatred for the white man because, among other things, the missionaries had preferred Onitsha to Aboh as the centre of activities and, what was perhaps most irritating, Macgregor Laird had established trading stations not only in Aboh as the obi would have wished, but also at Onitsha and Lokoja. Consequently all talk of missionary activity in Aboh ceased. Indeed, missionaries were not to operate in Aboh until the twentieth century.

In the eastern delta, Ayandele has argued that the politics of Bonny are not understandable outside the conflict introduced into Bonny society by missionary activity. He shows that the rulers of Bonny as well as those of Brass, Okrika, and Kalabari accepted missionary activity because they saw it as a means of improving their commerce with Europe, underlining the basic point already made as to why various Nigerian groups welcomed the missionaries. As should become clear from the next chapter Ayandele exaggerates the role of the missionary factor. Even so the fact remains that missionary activity in Bonny emphasized the divisions which already existed in Bonny and affected Jaja's decision to move away from Bonny and to found Opobo. As will be shown later, this development was the immediate prelude to Jaja's conflict with the British which led to his deportation in 1887. Hence, in whatever part of Southern Nigeria one looks, one sees the way in which missionary activity unmistakably prepared or helped to prepare the way for British colonial rule.

BIBLIOGRAPHICAL NOTE

Until the publication of Eric Williams's *Slavery and Capitalism* (first published in 1944 and reprinted in 1964) which places the emphasis on the economic factor in the British abolition of the Atlantic slave trade, the literature on the subject as typified by the writings of the humanitarians themselves or by scholars like R. Coupland in his *British Anti-Slavery Movement* (first published in 1933 and reprinted in 1964 by Frank Cass) was dominated by the 'philanthropic' interpretation. Eric Williams's strongly economic views may have ignored other forces at work, but those views have served to ensure a greater balance in the interpretation of an episode in human history that has had a profound effect on Africa, Europe, America, and Asia. That balance is reflected in the view taken here.

The role of missionaries as harbingers of the British conquest of parts of Southern Nigeria can best be appreciated by reading J. F. Ade Ajayi's *Christian Missions in Nigeria 1841-1891* (Longman 1965) and E. A. Ayandele's *The Missionary Impact on Modern Nigeria 1842-1914*, (Longman 1966). Both K. K. Nair, *Politics and Society in South Eastern Nigeria 1841-1906* Frank Cass 1972) and A. J. H. Latham, *Old Calabar 1600-1891* (Oxford 1973), discuss missionary activities in Calabar as an important factor in the wider historical experience of that state though not as the major theme. In my judgement Ayandele overplays the missionary factor in the work cited above. Especially is this the case in his handling of the Egba, Bonny, and Calabar situations. Nair's work puts the missionary factor in proper perspective with regard to Calabar while a reading of K. O. Dike's *Trade and Politics in the Niger Delta* (Oxford, first published 1956, Chapters IV-VII) provides, to my mind, a far more satisfactory explanation of the tensions in Bonny society than Ayandele's missionary oriented interpretation. With regard to the Yoruba country, Ajayi fits missionary activities more satisfactorily into the Yoruba historical experience than does Ayandele. In his contribution in J. F. Ade Ajayi and R. S. Smith, *Yoruba Warfare in the Nineteenth Century*, (Ibadan University Press and Cambridge University Press 1964), Ajayi provides an excellent analysis of the internal factors operative in the Yoruba country of the time which Ayandele does not, perhaps understandably, concern himself with in his work. By thus not concerning himself with these other internal factors, however, Ayandele leaves the way open for the unwary reader to see missionary activity as the major determinant of Yoruba history in the period. This was very far from the case. I have made this point in my 'Colonial Conquest and Resistance in Southern Nigeria' an article published in *Journal of the Historical Society of Nigeria VI, 3* (December 1972). An important work on an aspect of Yoruba history which is often ignored is K. Folayan's MA thesis, *Egbado and Yoruba-Aja Power Politics 1832-1894* (University of Ibadan 1967) which provides an excellent account of events in the Egbado country and discusses in greater detail than is available elsewhere the Egba-Dahomey conflict.

Works on the Niger Delta like K. O. Dike and G. I. Jones, *The Trading States of the Oil Rivers* (Oxford 1963) do not discuss the kingdom of Aboh in any real detail. Similarly, neither Ajayi nor Ayandele fully discuss missionary activity in the Aboh kingdom. Two recent studies have made up this gap in our knowledge. They are K. O. Ogedengbe, *The Aboh Kingdom of the Lower Niger c. 1650-1900,* (Ph.D thesis, University of Wisconsin 1971), and E. O. Okolugbo, *Christianity and Ukwuani Traditional Religion: A Study in Religious Encounter* (Ph.D thesis, University of Ibadan 1972). I have depended heavily on these two works for the synthesis attempted in this chapter.

CHAPTER
II

The Palm Oil Trade and
the Growth of British Influence
in the Niger Delta

Britain realized that the most effective answer to the trade in slaves was to find a substitute. This substitute was the palm oil trade. Although the rulers and peoples of the delta states were naturally unwilling to give up the trade in slaves at the dictate of Great Britain, they did, in fact, begin to organize for the palm oil trade soon after the institution of the British anti-slave-trade naval squadron in West Africa. By 1840 all of these states except Brass were already fully involved in the palm oil trade.

In a number of ways the trade in palm oil was different from the slave trade which it sought to replace. The palm oil trade required a large capital outlay. The would-be successful palm oil trader required a large labour force for the manning of trade canoes, for the actual collection of the oil from the hinterland producers, and for organizing the sale at the coast. He also, of course, had to be able to procure a large fleet of canoes. To ensure that other traders did not seize his oil on the rivers, he also had to have war canoes to convoy his trade canoes. These had to be properly armed and manned.

The raising of capital thus became a major issue of the trade in palm oil. Fortunately, the system of trade which developed provided the answer. The palm oil trade was organized on a trust system. Although the trust system had been used in the days of the slave trade, its use in the palm oil trade presented peculiar problems. European traders gave various commodities in trust to the coastal traders in return for which the latter supplied an agreed quantity of oil. The coastal traders then gave some of these commodities to the hinterland producers to get them to produce an agreed quantity of oil. Three points should perhaps be made here. One, the trust system, as its name implies, could only work given plenty of goodwill and good faith. Any breach of faith on the part of the delta trader or the hinterland producer was bound to result in complications and bad trade. Two, the trust system gave the European trader a very strong hold over his delta counterpart. Since he was the source of capital, he could, by manipulating his capital, get a number of delta traders so indebted to him that they could trade with no one else. While the European was able to ensure trade for himself, the delta traders were often so tied up that they could not trade with other European traders even if they found any offering better prices. To do so would involve a breach of faith which could, and did, lead to disturbances and armed conflict. Three, it was important for the delta trader to appear to be credit worthy in order to attract trust from the European supercargoes. This often meant competition among the leading delta traders, competition which expressed itself in the type of housing, entertainment and dress styles that the successful trader could afford.

From what has been said above, it must be clear that the trust system had built into it elements of conflict. European merchants sought to use the system to keep newcomers out of the palm oil trade of the delta states. But perhaps the greatest source of conflict arose from disagreements over how much oil was outstanding to the European traders. Quite often the European trader and his delta customer failed to agree on this vital question. In such instances it was not uncommon for the European trader to lie in wait for canoes loaded with oil from the hinterland and to seize such canoes to make up for the debt owed him. This practice, which came to be known as 'chopping', was one of the greatest sources of conflict between the European traders and their delta customers, for the European trader did not always ensure that the oil he 'chopped' belonged to the trader who owed him oil. When he thus 'chopped' oil which belonged to a trader not indebted to him, that trader would seek to recoup his losses by attacking and looting the stores of the European merchant. This tendency on the part of European and delta traders to take the law into their own hands need surprise no one. The men involved in the palm oil trade were the same who had been involved in the rough and tough days of the slave trade. While the commodity of trade changed, neither men, methods, nor morality had changed very much. These men were thus palm oil ruffians as they had first been slave trading ruffians.

Another source of conflict between European supercargoes and delta traders was that of fixing acceptable prices. This was not an easy affair. The European traders were anxious to make a reasonable margin of profit. In fixing what prices they would pay for palm produce they had their eyes on prevailing prices in Europe. The delta traders, not always conversant with prices in Europe, had to do all they could to ensure that they were not cheated. Usually the delta traders refused to engage in trade if the prices fell very low. The European traders also tried to use the same weapon, that is, refusal to do trade to force down the price of oil. In this regard, however, the delta traders, especially in the first half of the nineteenth century, were more successful than the European traders. This was because while the rulers of the delta states could bring various sanctions to bear both on their own peoples and the hinterland producers, the European firms, in fierce competition with one another, did not always succeed in holding out together. Sooner or later one firm or trader offered the prices desired by the delta traders and so broke the ban on trade. This is not to say, however, that difficulties over prices did not constitute a real source of unpleasantness between European traders and their delta customers.

The Palm Oil Trade and the Rise of the Slaves

Perhaps this is the point to draw attention to another development which attended the switch from the slave to the palm oil trade. The slave trade was in many ways the trade of the ruling classes. The various rulers of the delta states were able to keep a very firm hold on the trade in slaves. The trade in palm produce was different in this regard. For one thing, success in the palm oil trade needed the establishment of influential contacts with the hinterland producers. The rulers were usually bound by tradition to remain in their capitals and could not make direct contacts with the hinterland. Ironically, it was the slaves, obtained in the first instance from the hinterland, who, especially in the eastern delta, became the greatest trading agents of the delta in the hinterland. Heads of houses in the delta thus came to depend very much on the trading abilities of their slaves. These slaves were allowed to trade on their own behalf while also trading for

their masters. By the 1840s there existed in most of the houses of
the eastern delta slaves who had become some of the wealthiest
elements in society. In the existing books these slaves are quite
often referred to as 'ex-slaves'. It is open to question whether the
rulers and peoples of the delta states regarded this class of people
as 'ex-slaves'. Surely, they were only 'ex-slaves' in the context of
British law. Be that as it may, the question which arose was
whether delta society could prevent these wealthy, and therefore
powerful, slaves from seeking to wield political authority
commensurate with their economic strength.

In this regard one should point out that in Calabar the
situation which arose was slightly different. Calabar was the first
to organize properly for the new trade in palm oil by establishing
palm plantations in the hinterland (see Part 2, Episode 2). The
slaves who worked these plantations never attained the wealth of
those slaves who stayed in the towns to organize the trade of their
masters. For the plantation slaves, then, the question of seeking
political power commensurate with their wealth did not arise.
What did arise was the degree of social justice which these slaves
could enjoy. It was, for example, from their ranks that
sacrificial victims were chosen when important personalities died.
They laboured to ensure the wealth of their masters and the town
slaves. Left on their own they might never have found a
satisfactory answer. Fortunately, the presence of missionaries in
Calabar as from 1846 altered the situation. The missionaries
preached against human sacrifice and got the leading rulers of
Efik society — Eyamba V and King Eyo Honesty II — to sign
agreements banning human sacrifice. The slaves responded to
this development by organizing themselves into the Order of
Bloodmen pledged to save their members from human sacrifice
and other degradations. The Order of Bloodmen then did not
seek political power but social justice. Even so, its very existence, made possible by the missionary presence, was a major
social revolution in Efik society. That Eyamba V and Honesty II
signed the agreement banning human sacrifice and that they put
up with the Order of Bloodmen showed how by mid-century
various developments attendant on the suppression of the overseas
slave trade and the switch to palm oil trade were beginning to
affect the powers and authority of the rulers of the coastal states of
Nigeria.

One of the states which felt the impact of these developments

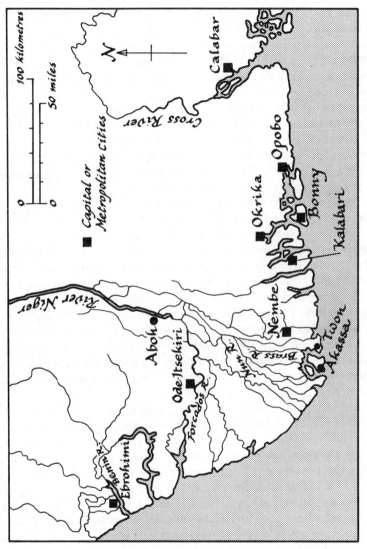

Map 1   States of the Niger Delta in the nineteenth century

most was Bonny. Opubu the Great who ruled Bonny during the opening years of the century was quick to see the need to organize the palm oil trade on an effective basis. While he reigned, he was able to keep Bonny strong and united. By the time he died, the stresses and strains in Bonny society brought about by the new situations already indicated were ready to break into the open His heir, William Dappa Pepple, was a minor. It is instructive that Madu, who became regent, was a slave of the royal house who had become head of the Anna Pepple house when Opubu became king. Madu died and was succeeded as regent by his own son, Alali, in 1833. Two years later William Dappa Pepple attained majority and became king. The new king resented the prominent position occupied by the slave class and was anxious to secure full powers for himself. The very next year, 1836, an opportunity presented itself. In that year a British gunboat seized a Portuguese ship loading slaves within Bonny's territorial waters. Alali, the ex-regent, was affronted by what was clearly a travesty of Bonny's sovereignty. He therefore ordered the arrest and imprisonment of Tyron, captain of the British gunboat, as well as other British subjects in Bonny. As has already been stated in the last chapter, the British reacted by bringing more gunboats into Bonny waters and using this show of force to get Alali to release the prisoners. Fortunately for the British, the king, resentful of the power and influence of Alali and his supporters, was disposed to side with them in their disgrace of Alali. Not only was Alali made to release the prisoners, he was made to sign an agreement to the effect that such an outrage on British subjects would not be repeated.

The 1836 agreement contained other clauses as well. Bonny authorities were forbidden to imprison, detain, or in any other way maltreat British subjects. Disputes between the British and Bonny elements were in future to be settled by a mixed committee of English traders and Bonny gentry. The Bonny authorities were to be held responsible for any loss or damage to British property or persons on the Bonny river. If any Englishman offended a Bonny man he was to be handed over to the captain of his vessel. Bonny authorities were warned that any infringement of any clauses of the agreement would qualify them to be declared enemies of Great Britain, meaning that Bonny would be liable to bombardment. It is obvious that the Bonny authorities could only have signed such a document under duress, for the agreement was openly one-sided. While it made provision for protecting the lives and property of British traders, it made no similar provision for the protection of Bonny citizens against the frequent misdeeds of the European traders and sailors. Rather it denied an essential ingredient of Bonny's sovereignty by requesting that Europeans who offended in Bonny be handed over to European authorities who could decide to take no punitive action against the offender. No one can question Professor Dike's conclusion that 'the treaty of 1836 signalized naval power as the new and disintegrating [also decisive] factor in Delta society'. As will be shown later, similar treaties were to be forced on the Itsekiri and the Efik later in the century.

If Dappa Pepple rejoiced at the disgrace of Alali in 1836 he too was soon to be disgusted with the British. He saw clearly that the main cause of unrest between his people and the British lay in the trust system. In 1838 he proposed a treaty which would put an end to the trust system and so remove the source of conflict which was the justification for naval interference in the affairs of Bonny. Advised by the British traders, the commander of the naval squadron refused to entertain such a treaty. The next year Bonny signed an anti-slave trade treaty by which she agreed to give up the export of slaves in return for 2,000 dollars a year for five years. This treaty was never ratified and the promised compensation was not paid. In 1841 another such treaty was signed, with the compensation fixed at 10,000 dollars a year for five years. Once again the promised compensation was not paid. Meanwhile, Calabar and various groups in the Cameroons which had signed similar treaties were being paid the agreed compensation. Naturally, William Dappa Pepple felt insulted, and relations between him and British traders deteriorated. In 1844 war broke out between Bonny and the British traders. King Pepple had the better of the fighting; not only did he damage British shipping, he seized many of the traders and locked them up threatening 'to roast them alive' if they did not hand in all their munitions of war. At the same time, Bonny's high priest sent his men into the rivers to kill Europeans and loot their property. Awanta, the high priest, was ultimately seized and deported. That Pepple won in the conflict of 1844 was the direct result of the refusal of the naval authorities to intervene in the conflict. These naval authorities could see that King Pepple had good reason for taking the line he took. However, British prestige had to be defended. The navy was ordered in 1848 to put an end to the continued destruction of British property in Bonny. The navy did not, however, resort to bombardment. Rather, yet another treaty was signed by which Bonny promised to protect the lives and property of British subjects. Once again another slave trade treaty was signed with the compensation fixed at 2,000 dollars a year for five years. Once again the compensation was not paid. King Pepple naturally remained anti-British.

It was not only in Bonny that conflict was developing between delta traders and European supercargoes. In the Itsekiri kingdom in the late forties similar tensions developed. Soon after the death of Olu Akengbuwa I in 1848, the factories of a number of European firms were looted by aggrieved Itsekiri traders. The European traders in the Itsekiri kingdom, like their counterparts in Bonny, sent memoranda to Great Britain praying the government to take steps to ensure the protection of their lives and property. It was lucky for these traders that Palmerston, the British Foreign Secretary at the time, was committed to the promotion of British prestige overseas. It was his view that British trade in the Niger delta had developed to a volume and value which justified protection. Consequently, to protect the lives and property of British subjects in the Bights of Benin and Biafra, Palmerston appointed John Beecroft as British consul for that area on 30 June 1849.

Beecroft's Consulship and the Courts of Equity

The appointment of John Beecroft, a British trader with many years' experience in the parts to which he was appointed, was a major step in the process which was to end with the imposition of British rule on what became known as the Niger Coast Protectorate. Beecroft was determined to further the cause of his fellow traders. He was a firm believer in the use of force or the show of force for the furtherance of British interests. Soon after his appointment he received letters of complaint from British traders in the Itsekiri kingdom as well as Bonny. The Bonny traders complained that the king had stopped all trade as a consequence of the non-payment of the compensation promised him. Beecroft visited Bonny in 1850 in a man-of-war and invited the king to go on board it to settle the 'palavers' between him and the European traders. Pepple stood on his dignity and refused to go on board Beecroft's boat, arguing that it was against custom. Ultimately, the two did meet at the king's house. Pepple requested that the treaty of 1848 be abrogated and that the situation should revert to what it was before the treaty of 1836 was signed. Beecroft would not hear of it and accused the king whom he described as a 'subtle rascal' of wanting to revive the trade in slaves. The reference to the revival of the slave trade was no more than an excuse. By mid-century Bonny was making more money out of the palm oil trade than out of trade in slaves. The issue which had arisen was that of where ultimate authority was to lie. Beecroft was anxious to establish his authority. King Pepple was even more anxious to regain the authority he had lost to the British through the gunboat politics of naval officers since 1836. The balance was, however, already heavily weighted against the king.

Beecroft also had to deal with the Itsekiri. During his visit there in 1851, Beecroft meant to investigate the complaints of the British traders. While actually in the Benin River, he witnessed yet another manifestation of Itsekiri discontent against the British traders: the people of Bobi, led by Oritsetsaninomi, attacked and looted Horsfall's factory. Beecroft wasted no time in bombarding Bobi and imposing a heavy fine on their leader. 'These scoundrels', he wrote, 'must be well chastised with powder and shot'. Beecroft then tried to get the Itsekiri to appoint an olu. He failed in this regard and only succeeded in getting the Itsekiri elders to appoint a 'governor' of the Benin River — a kind of collector of customs to whom British traders were to pay the 'comey' and to whom they could take their complaints. Beecroft did more. He got the Itsekiri elders on board his man-of-war and imposed a treaty of commerce on them similar to the Bonny treaty in 1836. Like that treaty the Itsekiri treaty of 1851 provided for the protection of the lives and property of British traders, forbade the molestation of British subjects under any pretext whatsoever, laid down the amount Itsekiri traders were to be fined if they stopped the trade of any British subject who had paid his comey, etc; but made no provision enabling the Itsekiri to punish British offenders. As was the case with Bonny, only the presence of the gunboat could have made the Itsekiri sign such a one-sided document.

In Bonny, meanwhile, King Pepple remained sturdily anti-British despite Beecroft's display of power in 1850. The situation which the king now faced was far from easy. While he was at daggers drawn with the British, Alali and the slave class which he represented were building up their position. Through success in trade, Alali had bought up many a weak and poor house and amalgamated these with his own. Pepple countered this by enacting a law forbidding any future amalgamation of houses. No one could fail to see that by this law the king was openly joining issue with the Alali group. The hostility between the two groups broke more into the open as from 1852 when Pepple suffered a stroke and the need arose to set up a regency council to attend to affairs of state. Pepple appointed two of his favourites, Yanibo and Ishacco, to run the government, completely ignoring the Alali group which represented a powerful section of the society. Alali and his group refused to recognize the new regents and disobeyed any orders which emanated from them. The king then sought to strengthen his position by asking all the European supercargoes to join his chiefs in choosing new regents, having made his wishes known. The European supercargoes and the king's chiefs met and chose Yanibo and Ishacco. Alali's group refused to attend the meeting and persisted in their refusal to recognize the regents.

It is ironical that the king, who since 1848 had remained hostile to British efforts at undermining his authority, should have called on the same British to support his nominees against his enemies in the state. Pepple's action on this occasion clearly confirms the fact that his main concern was not morality or fine principles but the strengthening of his own position in the face of fierce competition from the Alali group. That he was not particularly enamoured of the British was demonstrated by a law he enacted at the same time as the one which prohibited future amalgamation of houses, forbidding anyone to trade in Bonny's interior markets unless he took trust from the king. Primarily aimed against the Alali group, this law also struck at the British supercargoes. In 1838 Pepple had sought to abolish the trust system. Now in 1852 he sought to make himself the sole giver of trust in Bonny. He was sufficiently wealthy by now not to take trust from anyone. By converting all customs duties and other public revenue to his own private use, he had built up enormous wealth. Neither the Alali group nor the European supercargoes took kindly to this law by which the king sought to establish a monopoly of trade for himself. Both groups therefore continued to regard the king as an enemy.

King Pepple played into the hands of the British when he decided to go to war against Kalabari in 1853. Relations between Bonny and Kalabari since Pepple's accession had been strained largely because Kalabari was the one state in the eastern delta that refused to accept the ascendancy of Bonny in the area. The king's decision to to to war was ill-advised. The Alali group could not be expected to co-operate. The European traders naturally protested against any measure that was likely to injure trade. More unfortunately for the king, even his own chiefs who set out with him on the way to Kalabari refused to obey his orders. Beecroft, at the invitiation of the traders, steamed into Bonny, summoned a meeting of the Court of Equity and declared Pepple deposed at the request of the chiefs and people. Professor Dike has argued convincingly that by Bonny's law and custom the king could not be deposed by his people and has produced evidence to show that even by Beecroft's own testimony, the chiefs made it quite clear that it was contrary to their custom to depose their king. The conclusion must therefore be reached that the British had tired of Pepple's efforts to re-establish his authority in Bonny and had conspired with the Alali group to remove him. In a manner foreshadowing Harry Johnston's duplicity in his dealings with Jaja, Beecroft got Pepple to go on board his ship promising to return him to Bonny after a few days. The few days dragged on to seven years which Pepple spent first at Fernando Po, then at Ascension Island, and finally in London.

The removal of Pepple was the final proof that the British consul and traders were determined that if they were to control successfully the trade of Bonny and other delta states, they must also wield predominant political power. Following on Pepple's exile, a new treaty was signed with the puppet king, Dappo, installed by the British. This treaty made the Court of Equity supreme in the government of Bonny. The Court of Equity had been established by Beecroft in 1850. It was made up of a majority of European supercargoes and leading Bonny traders. Beecroft was himself the chairman of the court. Its main function originally was to settle disputes arising from trade between the two parties which composed it. If the knotty problem of disputes between European supercargoes and delta traders necessitated some joint tribunal that could ensure equitable and peaceful settlement, there can be no doubt that the establishment of such a tribunal nevertheless derogated from the fullness of Bonny's sovereignty. To make the British consul chairman and to endow the court with a majority of European supercargoes was to make an important inroad into the sovereignty of Bonny. In 1856 a similar court was established for Calabar. The composition of that court was even more un-favourably weighted for although a number of Efik rulers and chiefs sat on it, only the rulers of Creek Town and Duke Town had a vote. The Calabar court was thus, in terms of voting, a British controlled court. In an effort to find a solution to the perennial problem of disputes over trade, the British, backed by superior force, were thus making important inroads into the sovereignty of the delta states.

The treaty also forbade the King of Bonny from participating in trade. He was to depend for his revenue solely on customs duties and such like public sources. Only the Court of Equity was to handle trade matters in the future. The King of Bonny was not to go to war unless the British supercargoes in Bonny approved. All meetings on matters of interest to the two sides were in future to be heard not in the king's house but in the building which housed the Court of Equity. Any Bonny ruler who accepted terms such as these could hardly call himself king.

King Dappo whom the British placed on the throne, was hardly a king during his brief reign (from 1853 to August 1855 when he died). Alali and his group completely dominated the affairs of Bonny. Alali arrested Yanibo and refused to release him on the orders of the Court of Equity. In fact Alali and his group refused to attend the Court of Equity. Suddenly it dawned on the British that Alali had been more anti-Pepple than he was pro-British. His disagreement with Pepple was really over who was to control the affairs of Bonny. In terms of foreign relations Alali was perhaps even more fiercely independent than Pepple had been. Thus, the British discovered that just as they had sought to use Alali against Pepple so had Alali sought to use them in his struggle with Pepple.

The death of Dappo gave Alali an opportunity for seeking to reduce Pepple's followers to impotence. Although a British doctor certified the cause of death as having been due to the effect of bad weather on Dappo's health, Alali and his group preferred to put it abroad that Yanibo and Ishacco, who had been away from Bonny when the king died, had poisoned him. They demanded that these two, who had taken refuge on board the ship of a

British trader, be given up to face trial according to Bonny law. The captain of the boat refused to give up the two men despite the appeal of other supercargoes. Alali put Bonny in a state of war. Thus Alali deliberately provoked civil strife between his group and the supporters of Pepple. Some 300 of Pepple's supporters were reported by one account to have died in the civil war which followed. The British consul had to intervene to bring the war to an end. In doing so he had to dance to the tune of Alali's group. Three of the four regents now appointed belonged to the Alali group. Further, the consul assured Alali that there could be no question of allowing Pepple to return to Bonny.

The regency proved a failure. Bonny was a monarchy; the absence of the 'Amayanabo', as the ruler was called, left society less than complete. The four regents could not work together harmoniously nor were they really acceptable to the people because they were of slave origin. In fact, the head regent had to plead with the British consul to declare him a free man. This the consul did, but the consul's decree could not remove the stigma which attached to slavery in Bonny society. Bonny society therefore remained unstable and trade suffered.

The Return of King Pepple and the Civil Wars in Bonny

This was the background to the demand by the European supercargoes for the return of King Pepple. Pepple was eventually allowed to return to Bonny in 1861. By that time, however, permanent injury had been done to the economic basis of the monarchy. The civil war of 1855 had seen to it that the royal wealth and treasury were looted and destroyed beyond repair. Similarly the trade of the king had been damaged by seven years of absence: he could not now hope to repair it in his old age. Yet no delta king who did not also boast great wealth could hope to command the respect of his people. So, then, the king had lost his wealth to Alali and his supporters at the same time as the British consul had appropriated a great deal of his authority. In the circumstances there was a lot that could not be restored in 1861.

Alali opposed the king's return till the last. When he found that he could not stop it, he fled from Bonny and died soon afterwards. The leadership of his group now fell on yet another trader of servile origin, the better known Jaja. Pepple reigned only for another five years before he died in 1866. Although he had the support of men like Oko Jumbo, also of the slave class, Pepple's last five years as king were uneventful and pitiful as he was king only in name. He was succeeded by his son George Pepple who was educated in Britain during his father's exile there. George had become a Christian while in England. Deprived of the economic basis of the monarchy, unsuited by his new faith to draw on the spiritual unction which did hedge the Bonny monarchy, Pepple was a clear misfit, unable to reach out to the hearts of his people as his predecessors had done. Against this background it is difficult to accept Ayandele's explanation of the divisions in Bonny society as having been based primarily on the fact that Pepple supported missionaries while Jaja opposed them. Undoubtedly this element may have helped to further confound an already confused situation. Yet it must be clear that Jaja represented the same standpoint as Alali and even Dappa Pepple in his opposition to growing European pressures, of which Christianity was but one facet. Conversely, if Pepple found himself supporting missionaries, it must, partly at least, have been because in the hapless position in which he found himself, he hoped that such support would yield political dividends.

Be that as it may, there really was no doubt that the important forces in Bonny society and politics were now Jaja, who became head of the Anna Pepple house, and Oko Jumbo who led the Manilla Pepple house and supported the monarchy. An unknown quantity until the death of Alali, Jaja, an Igbo slave, proved to be the only one who dared accept responsbility for offsetting Alali's heavy debts estimated at £10,000–£15,000 sterling. All the evidence indicates that he was a great organizer and a shrewd politician. With characteristic zeal he established cordial relations with the hinterland producers and the European supercargoes. He selected young men of ability and put them at the helm of his affairs. Within four years of his election as head of the Anna Pepple house he was already buying up weaker and poorer houses — reminiscent of the activities of Alali.

The Manilla Pepple house, frightened at Jaja's success, sought to crush him through civil war. In 1867 some skirmishing took place. King George Pepple intervened and made peace. The poor king realized, however, that unless the British consul stepped in he could not control the situation. The consul, Livingstone, did not see why he should interfere in the internal affairs of Bonny. Civil war looked imminent and was only postponed by a great fire which swept through Bonny in 1868. Unfortunately for Jaja, his people suffered the worst ravages of the fire. His opponents sought to take advantage of this fact by provoking him to war early in 1869, Jaja did what he could to prevent war since he was badly hit by the fire; but his enemies would not let this fine opportunity slip by. Fighting commenced on 13 September 1869. Within a few days Jaja and his men had evacuated Bonny and established themselves on the Ikomtoro river in the Andoni country from where they could cut Bonny off from her Igbo and Qua markets. While Jaja sent messages to the British and his Bonny rivals to the effect that he desired a settlement, he spent his energies building what was to become the new state of Opobo and fortifying the route to the hinterland in such a manner as to prevent Bonny reaching her traditional markets. European traders in Bonny who saw their investments imperilled by Jaja's actions took umbrage at his master stroke and sought to put a ban on European trade with Jaja. But Jaja found other European traders from the Brass area and so ensured that his produce reached the markets of Europe.

The Manilla Pepple house could not be expected to take the new developments lying down. They realized that Jaja had outwitted them and sought an answer in renewed war. This war lasted from September 1869 to May 1870 and Bonny had the worst of it. By the end of 1870 Jaja had most definitely arrived. He christened his new state Opobo after Opubu, the great ruler of Bonny at the beginning of the century, and was himself chosen as king. As nothing succeeds like success, European merchants flocked to Opobo as did 14 of the 18 leading houses of Bonny. Early in 1873 the British formally recognized the new state and its ruler. The rise of Opobo meant the eclipse of Bonny, since no delta state could survive without trade and Opobo had seized most of the trade which had been Bonny's.

The history of Bonny as sketched thus far shows how events since the suppression of the overseas slave trade and the inauguration of the overseas trade in palm produce led to political, social, and economic upheavals in that city state. From the death of Opubu to the rise of Jaja the palm oil trade had produced a situation in which effective political power slipped from the hands of the Bonny monarchy into those of slaves and the British consul, especially the latter's. Jaja had now founded a

new state and European merchants and the British consul had
taken official note of this and actually followed him to Opobo.
The question which was bound to arise was whether the British
consul would seek to undermine Jaja's authority in Opobo as he
had undermined that of the Bonny monarchy. But that is a
question to which we must return later.

Competition, the Decline of 'Trust' and the Growth of the N.A.C.

While the events of Bonny history depicted above were being
enacted, various other developments were taking place. For most
of the first half of the nineteenth century only large or otherwise
well-organized European firms could cope with the cost and
problems of the delta trade. This trade was, in fact, in the hands
of less than a dozen such firms. In 1852, however, there emerged
Macgregor Laird's African Steamship Company which ran a
regular mail service between Britain and West Africa. As a
consequence of this development, many small European traders
as well as Sierra Leonians were to join the delta trade by taking
advantage of berth space offered by the steamers. From the mid-
fifties, therefore, there were many more competitors for the delta
trade than there had been before. While that trade did not necessarily decline, the presence of many more traders led to a fall
in profits for the old European traders. For the delta peoples and
the old established firms, this development ushered in a period of
considerable tension and turbulence. The old established firms
sought to manipulate the trust system in such a way as to keep out
the newcomers whom they regarded as interlopers. The delta
traders were glad to take advantage of the presence of other
traders to whom they could sell their produce, presumably at
enhanced prices. Nor was that all. A major feature of the sixties
and seventies of the nineteenth century was the gradual push of
European traders into the Niger Valley and the delta hinterland.
Macgregor Laird's firm had established trading stations at Aboh,
Onitsha, and Lokoja as from the 1850s. By the 1860s the West
African Company, Messrs Miller Brothers and Co., the Central
African Trading Company, James Pinnock and Co. — all of these
had pushed their way into the Akassa, Aboh, Ndoni, Onitsha,
and other areas of the Niger Valley. This push threatened the very

livelihood of the delta traders and made them determine to obstruct any further penetration of the hinterland. The history of relations between the Nigerian peoples of the delta and of the Niger Valley on the one hand and the European, mainly British, traders on the other from the sixties on, cannot be understood outside the context of this basic clash of interests.

In Calabar the conflict which developed between the Efik and the long-established British traders centred on the manipulation of the trust system by the latter. While the Efik did all they could to take full advantage of the influx of new traders, the British supercargoes sought to push out the newcomers. Ultimately, in 1856, the supercargoes forced an agreement on the Efik. The first clause of this agreement created a Court of Equity. Half the membership of the court was made up of European supercargoes, each of whom had a vote. The other half was made up of Efik rulers and traders but only the kings of Duke Town and Creek Town had voting rights conferred on them. Another clause provided that if any Efik owed any European trader oil, all other Europeans should refuse to trade until the debt was made good. Further, once comey had been paid, the trade of European supercargoes was not to be stopped for any reason whatsoever.

If this were to happen, the Efik kings would be held responsible and would be liable to a fine of one puncheon of oil per day per hundred tons registered to the ship. If the Efik kings refused for any reason to accept the comey paid by any supercargo, the latter could, nevertheless, begin trading. If an Efik trader was summoned to appear before the Court of Equity but failed to do so, the Efik kings were to be held responsible for producing him within eight days. Thereafter, the Efik kings would be fined 20 pieces of cloth every week until the absentee was brought before the court. Appeals against the decisions of the Court of Equity were to lie before the British consul. This agreement, very similar to the 1851 treaty with the Itsekiri, was one-sided in the extreme and was designed to safeguard the trade of the British supercargoes while undermining the sovereign powers of Efik rulers. While the British traders, backed by their consul, were undermining the position of the Efik rulers through agreements of this type, the missionaries continued to create their own problems for the Efik. This was the background to the gradual assumption of sovereign powers by the British in Calabar (see Part 2, Episode 2).

In the Itsekiri country, conflict continued between the Itsekiri traders and the British merchants, despite the 1851 agreement. This need surprise no one as that agreement was far too one-sided to be observed. In 1861 Mr Henry, a British trader, seized oil belonging to Ikebuwa, an Itsekiri trader. Ikebuwa owed Henry six puncheons of oil at the time. But Henry seized 14 puncheons. When Ikebuwa demanded payment for the extra eight puncheons, Henry ordered his boys to put Ikebuwa in chains. When eventually released, Ikebuwa planned an attack on Henry's 'factory' and carried away various stores. As usual the British trader appealed to his consul. Consul Freeman, who investigated the affair, found that Henry was responsible for what had happened to him. Nevertheless, argued Freeman, 'such an outrage [against Mr Henry] would not be allowed to pass unnoticed or unpunished by Her Majesty's Government'. So Ikebuwa was fined 20 puncheons of oil valued at £265. The Itsekiri chiefs were fined 35 puncheons of oil (about £464 worth) for failing to prevent the 'outrage'. The value of stores taken from Henry's factory was estimated at £200 by the consul. Henry who was pronounced guilty by Freeman did not have to pay any fine! Such was British justice in the Niger Delta. Two years later, a similar conflict arose between another Itsekiri trader and the firm of Harrison and Co. Once again the Itsekiri concerned had to pay a heavy fine. In 1871 another dispute over outstanding debt resulted in armed conflict between another Itsekiri trader and the firm of Louch and Co. This time, not only was the Itsekiri trader fined, he was also sentenced to two years' imprisonment in Lagos with hard labour. The lesson of these conflicts and the action of the British consul was clear: it was not who or what was right, it was clearly a situation in which might was right. The Itsekiri were made to understand that in the developing relationship between themselves and the British traders and consul, they could never win. As yet, formal British rule had not been imposed on the Itsekiri; British power was, however, very much in evidence already.

In the Niger Valley, the arrival of European trading firms also began to produce tensions. In Aboh, where Macgregor Laird had set up a trading station in the 1850s, the obi discovered that the British were seeking to monopolize all of his kingdom's trade, at the same time as British activities in Onitsha and Lokoja reduced the volume of trade that came down to Aboh. The obi consequently organized the looting of Macgregor Laird's stores for which the British tried to punish him by an unsuccessful naval bombardment in 1862. The next year the British signed a trade treaty with Aboh designed to prevent future attacks on British commerce. Yet in 1882 the Aboh again attacked the factory of the National African Company which, by driving off other firms from Aboh, had established a monopoly and was able to dictate its own prices. This time, however, the Aboh did not get away with it. A naval bombardment followed during which Aboh lost hundreds of her citizens. Similar incidents occurred in Onitsha, Patani, Akassa, Asaba, and Idah in the 1870s and early 1880s. In 1879 conflicts between Onitsha and the United Africa Company resulted in the bombardment of that town. In 1882, Akassa, Patani, Asaba, and Idah suffered a similar fate.

Increased tension between Nigerian groups and European firms was matched by increased competition between the many European firms which operated in the delta and Niger Valley in the 1860s and 1870s. As has already been indicated, increased competition not only led to declining profits but also weakened the bargaining position of the European firms *vis-à-vis* the various Nigerian groups. It was in an effort to overcome this situation that Taubman Goldie, who arrived in the Niger Delta in the late 1870s, gradually amalgamated various British firms into what by 1879 had become one huge concern, the United Africa Company (which soon became known as the National African Company). Two years later Goldie succeeded in buying off all the French companies operating in the delta and Niger Valley and so made this area a British sphere of influence. In 1886 Goldie obtained a Royal Charter for the N.A.C. which then became the Royal Niger Company. The obtaining of a charter meant that the company was not just a trading concern; it had conferred on it certain powers of government and law making, as well as powers to raise and maintain an armed force for the effective pursuit of its trade as well as for the maintenance of law and order. The appearance on the scene of the Royal Niger Company was to have momentous consequences for this part of Southern Nigeria.

BIBLIOGRAPHICAL NOTE

The period covered in this chapter is that which the late Professor J. C. Anene described in his book, *Southern Nigeria in Transition* (Cambridge, 1966) as that of informal empire. In Chapters III and IV, Anene concentrates on how the British Commonwealth Office saw its responsibilities in Nigeria during that period. The reader interested in this kind of background will find it worth while to read that part of Anene's work which I regard as the best part of the book (see my review article in *Journal of the Historical Society of Nigeria* IV, 2, 1968, pp. 335-44). I have not in this chapter paid too much attention to Commonwealth Office attitudes, my main concern being to see how British authority spread in the Niger Delta, whatever official policy may have been.

Professor Dike's *Trade and Politics in the Niger Delta* remains an invaluable work for this period of the history of the Niger Delta, while K. K. Nair's work on Calabar provides an excellent account of the impact of European trade on the Efik. Dr Nair's work suffers from a number of weaknesses however, which include his understanding of the structure of Efik society. The arrangement of the material is also open to question in part, and his criticism of Dike is not always justified. However, I regard his handling of the effect of trade on Efik politics during the period as very well done. Brass is not discussed in any detail in this chapter because the story of Brass is told in Episode 5. Dr E. J. Alagoa's *The Small Brave City State* (Ibadan University Press and Wisconsin University Press 1964) provides the best reading not only on this period of informal empire but also on the actual Brass-British confrontation.

For Aboh, Dr Ogendengbe's thesis (now being prepared for publication) is clearly the standard work. For the Itsekiri kingdom my *Merchant Prince of the Niger Delta* (Heinemann 1968) contains many of the details which space forces me to leave out in this chapter. Those interested in a fuller understanding of how the various agreements between delta peoples and the British undermined the sovereignty of the former are advised to read Dike, Nair and my *Merchant Prince of the Niger Delta* which treat this subject in detail.

J. E. Flint's *Sir George Goldie and the Making of Nigeria*

(Oxford 1960) discusses comprehensively the activities of the Royal Niger Company and should be read not only for this chapter but also for Chapters Three and Four. The other works mentioned necessarily discuss the Royal Niger Company and the reader would benefit from the varying interpretations of the respective authors.

1 The fall of Burmi, July 1903: the battle of Burmi was the longest and fiercest fought by the British during their conquest of the Sokoto caliphate. Over 100 supporters of the Caliph lost their lives in this battle.

2 British army square formation, 1903. Nigerian warriors found it difficult to penetrate this novel formation.

3 King Eyo Honesty II
of Creek Town.

4 Rev. Hope M. Wadell—
Presbyterian Missionary in Calabar.

5 Attahiru I, who died
in the battle of Burmi.

6 Frederick Lugard.

7   H. H. Johnston. He deported Jaja of Opobo to the West Indies in 1887.

8   Ilorin cavalry charging the British square on the eve of the conquest of the Ilorin by the British — 1897.

9   The Sokoto-British encounter, 1903. Note the Caliph's flag in the background. (See page 204 of the text for the significance of the Caliph's flag in Sokoto's resistance of the British forces.)

10   The Kano expedition:
mounted British infantry pursuing
Kanawa horsemen.

11   A British field gun in action.

12   British attack on Igbo stockade.

13   British attack on Lagos from the lagoon — 1851.

14   A section of the city walls of Kano, showing one of the gates, the Kofar Nassarawa. The British had to storm the Kano gates before they could capture the city.

15   Arewa Bowmen, 1903 — most of the Savannah peoples who fought against the British were armed in this way.

16   3 75 mm gun in action

17   The submission of chiefs, place unknown, 1903.

18   Waiting to attack: the British expedition before the walls of Kano, 1903.

19   View of Kano.

20   Sir Ralph Moor, Consul-General
of Niger Coast Protectorate 1896–1900,
High Commissioner of the Protectorate
of Southern Nigeria 1900–1903.

21   The Emir Aliyu of Kano, after
his capture by Captain Foulkes, R.E.,
1903.

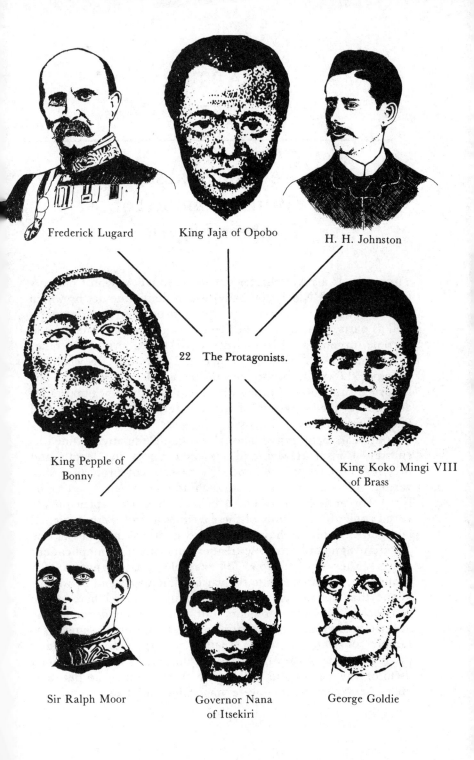

Frederick Lugard

King Jaja of Opobo

H. H. Johnston

22   The Protagonists.

King Pepple of
Bonny

King Koko Mingi VIII
of Brass

Sir Ralph Moor

Governor Nana
of Itsekiri

George Goldie

CHAPTER
III

The New Imperialism and
the British Conquest of
Southern Nigeria

The grant of a royal charter to the National African Company (now the Royal Niger Company) was a deliberate act by which Britain sought to guarantee her interests on the Niger-Benue as well as parts of the delta. The need to guarantee this interest had become urgent as a consequence of the activities of other European powers, notably France and Germany, in what has become known in history as 'the scramble for Africa'. The historical situation in Europe which explains the new importance attached to the possession of overseas territories is by now well known and will not be discussed here.

Four years before the National African Company obtained its charter, Consul Hewett had travelled across the length and breadth of the Niger Delta and signed treaties of 'protection' with various rulers and peoples from the Cameroons in the East to the River Forcados in the West. Much ink has been spent on the vexed issue of the validity of these treaties as well as those signed later on. Historians have raised the query as to whether the Nigerian signatories to these treaties understood the implications of what they signed. How, for example, was the notion of a protectorate translated into the various languages and by whom? While that debate will not be taken up in detail here, I am convinced that our forebears did not fully understand the implications of all the provisions of the treaties they signed (see sample of one of these treaties in Appendix I, noting particularly clauses I-V), for some of the clauses virtually robbed them of any meaningful sovereignty. Yet the men who put their 'marks' to these treaties were men who had had centuries of contact with Europeans; men who, since the 1850s, were witnesses to the gradual erosion of their authority by the British consul. Given these circumstances, has one no right to ask why they should not have been a great deal more circumspect in 1884? Two factors explain the seeming paradox. By 1884 the delta states had become extremely preoccupied with securing their middleman position in the face of the push by Europeans into the Niger Valley. Connected with concern over trade was concern over the labour supply necessary to make that trade profitable. Hence many of the coastal states, notably the Itsekiri kingdom and Opobo, refused to accept the clauses which provided for free trade and for missionary activity. Missionaries were known to preach not only against polygamy but also against slave holding, an important institution in these states. As indicated in Episode 5 in the second part of this book, it was also in consideration of her commercial interests that Brass signed Hewett's 'protection' treaty for a period of only six months. Secondly, there was the fact that the consul arrived in each of these states on board a man-of-war. Many of the states had tasted the fiery justice which emanated from these gunboats and probably felt that provided they could guarantee their trade, it was just as well to sign the treaties rather than face bombardment.

It is significant that while a number of states raised objections to clauses of the treaty which affected trade and labour, only Jaja and Opobo raised the political issue — the meaning of the word 'protection'. Consul Hewett hastened to assure Jaja that all that was meant was that Jaja was not to enter into treaties with other European powers without the permission of Great Britain. As for internal affairs, Jaja was assured that he was to continue to rule his people as before and that Britain had no intention of taking his land from him. Hewett's reply, which apparently satisfied Jaja, represents that duplicity which was to mark Anglo-Nigerian relations throughout the period of colonial conquest. For how could Jaja continue to rule his people as before when he was, by the treaty, denied jurisdiction over Europeans in his own territory? It is a peculiar rule which cannot guarantee protection to the ruled against the depredations of foreigners. How could Jaja continue to rule his people as of old if, as laid down in Article V of the treaty, he was bound to act on the advice of British consular officials in matters relating to the administration of justice, the development of the resources of the country, the

Map 2   Map of Southern Nigeria

interests of commerce, or in any other matter in relation to peace, order, and good government, and the general progress of civilization? Whatever assurances Hewett may have given, there were provisions in the signed treaty which could provide adequate excuse for British intervention in the internal affairs of Jaja's Opobo and the other coastal states. The rulers of these states did not, apparently, grasp this essential fact.

Up to a point discussion of these treaties is no more than an academic exercise, for enough has been said about Anglo-Nigerian relations in the coastal areas to demonstrate that it was not treaties and other agreements which decided what the British did but rather the naval superiority of the latter. Yet these treaties, together with those negotiated by the National African Company were important in the international bargaining that went on in Europe in the years after 1884. The lower Niger and the delta were claimed by Britain as her spheres of influence on the basis of these treaties. And it was on the basis of the same treaties that Britain went ahead, after the Berlin Conference, to announce to the world the establishment of a British Protectorate over what were described as the Oil Rivers.

The late Professor J. C. Anene has set out admirably in his *Southern Nigeria in Transition* the problems which arose with the proclamation in 1885 of the British Protectorate of the Oil Rivers. No attempt is made here to re-state these problems. It is, however, important to draw attention to the major problem: was the British consul to restrict himself to matters affecting the foreign relations of the Oil Rivers or to actively interfere in their internal sovereignty? Legally, the order-in-council which established the Protectorate did not give the consul any authority to intervene in the internal affairs of the Oil Rivers states. These internal affairs included control of trade. It will be clear from the two previous chapters that it was the desire to control the trade of the coastal states that had led the British naval commanders and consuls to get more and more involved in the internal politics of these states. Now that a formal Protectorate had been established, had not the British traders a right to expect that their consul would ensure a regular flow of trade, even if this meant interference in local politics? Only two years after the formal declaration of the Protectorate, Opobo provided a test case.

The Deportation of Jaja

It will be recalled that in 1873 both the British consul and the
merchants had formally recognized the new state of Opobo
created by Jaja; at the same time they recognized Jaja as king of
that state. In Chapter II the question was raised as to whether the
British consul, having been forced by Jaja's cleverness and
obvious military might to accord him due recognition, would
attempt to undermine his authority as he had done in Bonny. The
firmness with which Jaja ruled Opobo and his unquestioned
control of his hinterland markets based on friendships, marriage
alliances, and occasional military demonstrations, soon became a
source of irritation not only to the British merchants but also to
the consul whose business it was to promote and defend British
trade in these parts. It will be further recalled that Jaja was the
only one of the delta rulers who had extracted from the consul a
document which legally guaranteed his internal sovereignty
despite the protection treaty of 1885. His perspicacity in this
regard was a clear indication that he intended to claim his rights
in his relations with the British.

In 1886 a quarrel developed between Jaja and the British. This
quarrel had to do with the British traders' attempts to gain direct
access to Jaja's hinterland markets of Ohambele and Essene. Jaja's
influence in the hinterland was sufficiently strong for him to
frustrate the British traders. In retaliation the British reduced the
comey they paid to Jaja. Jaja replied by banning all trade with the
European firms while he arranged to ship his oil direct to Europe.
He also managed to get one firm, that of Miller Brothers, to trade
on his own terms, and the evidence suggests that that firm did very
flourishing business. The issue which arose, therefore, was really
that of Jaja's determination to control the trade of his Opobo
kingdom and its hinterland markets.

It was unfortunate for Jaja that Harry Johnston, who at the end
of 1886 took over from Hewett (away on sick leave) as acting
consul, was one of those agents of British imperialism who was
not only dedicated to 'painting the map red' but who also had
very little regard for African rulers. Faced with the deadlock
between the British traders and Jaja, Johnston had no doubt as to
who had to go under: Jaja had to be removed in the interests of
British trade. But this aim could not be stated in such stark and
unashamed terms. So Johnston tried to win over the people of

Ohambele and Essene. After some initial enthusiasm these people demonstrated their commitment to Jaja by running away when Johnston arrived a second time to get them to sign treaties. Rebuffed in this manner, Johnston then tried to question the basis of Jaja's claim to these areas. As Anene has shown, the relationship between Jaja and these people was not such as was formally laid down in any legal terms. Nor was there any source to which Johnston could go to determine the exact extent of Jaja's dominion or influence. Johnston could do no more than build the kind of case against Jaja which he hoped would win the sympathy of the British Foreign Office. He accused Jaja of building a large army with which he intended to overawe the hinterland oil producers, of stirring up war and unrest in Kalabari whose ruler was friendly with the British traders; of having sent an embassy to France with a view to selling Opobo to that country despite the British protectorate. The solution, Johnston suggested, was the deportation of Jaja. Johnston's suggestion was acceptable to the officials of the Foreign Office. The only person who refused to be persuaded was Lord Salisbury, then Foreign Secretary. He insisted that the thing to do was to investigate whether Ohambele and the hinterland accepted Jaja's authority. If they did, argued Salisbury, then Jaja was perfectly within his rights to keep the British out.

Neither the Foreign Office officials nor Johnston were prepared to accept Salisbury's stance. In Opobo meanwhile, Johnston had imposed a trade embargo: no European was to do trade with Jaja. Jaja regarded Johnston's action as a breach of existing treaties and actually sent a delegation to Britain to argue his case. Given the attitude of the officials of the Foreign Office, there can be little surprise that the delegation failed to alter the situation. Salisbury's approval of Johnston's trade embargo was mistaken or deliberately interpreted to mean approval of the plan to deport Jaja. Then followed one of the most ignoble acts of the British in Nigeria. Johnston invited Jaja on board the gunboat *Goshawk* for a discussion of the situation. Jaja asked for a safe conduct and got it: he would be allowed to go on board and return to his people without molestation. Once on board, however, he was given what was in effect a non-choice: if he would not accept British terms, he could either go back on shore and face immediate bombardment, or give himself up there and then and be carried away into exile. It was an impossible position to put a ruler in. Jaja's decision, in the circumstances, to allow himself to be taken away into exile must, in fact, be seen as one of his noblest acts. It was an act of self sacrifice, embarked upon, no doubt, to save his people from death and untold suffering. He was taken away to Ghana where he was tried, found guilty, and exiled to the West Indies.

Johnston's act was one of extreme bad faith. Not even his greatest admirers can fail to see that. Yet that event, as later events were to demonstrate, lay in the logic of the new situation. The establishment of a British protectorate on a firm basis was found to involve not only the penetration of the hinterland but the removal of all Nigerian rulers who stood or attempted to stand by their rights like Jaja had done. The immediate prelude to the conflict was reported by Johnston to be Jaja's refusal to allow Europeans to penetrate his hinterland markets. Dr C. J. Gertzel has convincingly shown that after Jaja's removal the British traders who attempted to penetrate the hinterland markets soon discovered that it was more profitable to use the coastal traders than to bear the expense of hinterland installations. While it may be argued that it needed the removal of Jaja before this practical lesson could be learnt, later events justify the conclusion that in the Jaja episode, as in others yet to come, the real issue was what to do with a Nigerian ruler who knew his rights and stood by them and who had the ability and the means to protect his trading interest against British traders. If Jaja had any other fault, it was his acute dislike of missionaries — black or white — whom he saw as collaborating with the white trader and consul in undermining the position of delta rulers. Salisbury regarded Johnston's deportation of Jaja as 'kidnapping'. Yet he did nothing to reverse that action. That this was so must be construed as evidence that even a Salisbury could see that Anglo-Nigerian relations in the years that lay immediately ahead were not likely to be decided by the niceties of the law but by the dictates of the new imperialism of the late 1880s and 1890s. The Jaja episode was but the beginning of the gradual dismantling of the sovereignty of the peoples and rulers of Southern Nigeria in the age of the partition.

It is not clear what the reaction of the other states of the eastern delta was to the fate of Jaja. His deportation left the field free for British economic and political manoeuvres. Bonny, whose economy was all but ruined by the rise of Jaja and his seizure of her markets, probably rejoiced at Jaja's fall. Yet Bonny never again regained any meaningful independence before she passed quietly under British rule. Kalabari, anxious to be seen as the equal of Bonny, actually asked for a British vice-consul to be established in her territory in the early nineties. Generally then, it is fair to say that the Jaja episode served as an object lesson to the states of the eastern delta which, with the singular exception of Brass (Part 2, Episode 5), tended thereafter to accommodate the British without too much ado.

The Macdonald Administration and the Quickening of the Imperial Push

On Hewett's return to the delta after the Jaja episode, he sought to extend British authority from Okrika to the hinterland of Bonny. In July 1888 he signed a protection treaty with Okrika. Only a few months later, however, Okrika went to war against an Igbo village. Hewett regarded this as a breach of the July treaty and tried to persuade the Bonny chiefs to raise a force against Okrika. But they wisely refused to be used as cannon fodder against a commercial ally. Hewett was compelled to leave the Okrika alone. Next he tried to consolidate the British position in Opobo where the chiefs were beginning to clamour for the return of Jaja. Hewett interpreted this clamour as an anti-British demonstration and imposed a heavy fine. This fine was not paid. Thereupon Hewett tried to get the navy to use force against Opobo. The matter was referred to the British Foreign Office which refused to sanction the suggested use of force. It can be said, then, that Hewett's new-found forward policy was singularly lacking in success and imagination.

One reason why the British Foreign Office did not support Hewett's attempted expansion of British authority was that by 1889 that office had decided to send out a special commissioner to report on the future of the Oil Rivers. That special commissioner was Major (later Sir) Claude Macdonald. It is not intended in this work to go into the details of that commission. Only a few points need to be made because of their relevance for what follows. One of these is the unanimous preference of all the delta states for some kind of 'crown' administration as distinct from company rule. The other is that most of the states were quick to point out to Macdonald that they did not intend to give up the institution of slavery. Indeed, it was largely because of this latter point that the Oil Rivers did not become a Crown Colony since slavery could not, by law, exist in a British colony. The upshot of Macdonald's report, therefore, was the establishment of a more effective protectorate over the Oil Rivers with Macdonald himself as commissioner and consul-general. The essential difference between the new adminstration set up in 1891 and the earlier consular authority was that whereas previously there was only one consul and one assistant, now Macdonald established vice-consulates in all the delta states and had in addition customs and other staff. To raise revenue for the administration of the protectorate, he was empowered to impose customs duties on imports. For the first time a constabulary began to be built up, by a soldier of fortune, Ralph Moor, who had come out to Nigeria at his own expense and who was to succeed Sir Claude Macdonald as consul-general. As from 1891 then, the British were clearly determined to formally bring the Oil Rivers and their hinterland under effective control.

The Fall of Nana
and the British Occupation of the Itsekiri Kingdom

As has already been stated, the states of the eastern delta, Brass excepted, tended to accept the Macdonald administration as a necessary evil. Macdonald and his assistants attempted, in the years immediately after 1891, to begin to reach out to the hinterland. Macdonald himself visited Akwete and managed to settle the tensions that had earlier developed between that town and the British as well as to get the chiefs to sign a protection treaty. From his Bonny base Vice-Consul Kenneth Campbell visited Okrika early in 1892 and attempted to move further inland but was, for selfish reasons, dissuaded by the Amayanabo of Okrika. In the western delta Vice-Consul H.L. Gallwey undertook an exploratory tour of the Urhobo hinterland which resulted in the establishment of a vice-consulate at Sapele, others having been previously established at Warri and the Benin River.

Thus far the British had done no more than make tentative moves into the hinterland. Thus far, also, it looked as if the task of extending British rule would be relatively easy and bloodless. But then, in 1894, the British had to deal with the famous Nana, 'governor' of the Benin River since 1883. I have told the story of

Nana fully elsewhere. Only a brief summary is therefore given here. The story of the clash which developed between Nana and the British in 1894 can only be understood against the background of Itsekiri history already given in Chapter II. That story is partly one of conflict between Itsekiri traders and the British traders and consul. In terms of internal Itsekiri history, the period from about 1850 witnessed not only an interregnum which lasted from the death of Olu Akengbuwa I in 1848 until 1936, but also the rise of a number of important trading families. Three important groups of trading families emerged. The royal family had two of these groups. One was based at Ode–Itsekiri and the newly growing trading station of Warri. The other was based at Batere. The leading names in this latter group were Oritsetsaninomi (often shortened to Tsanomi), Numa, and Omadoghogbone (Dogho for short). The third group was the Ologbotsere family (an Ologbotsere is the traditional 'prime minister' of the Olu) with their base at Jakpa. The more important names in this group were Idiare, Olomu, and Nana. Competition for trade in the Urhobo hinterland between these groups was matched by competition for the only executive office in the Itsekiri kingdom during the interregnum—that of Governor of the Benin River. Idiare was the first to hold the office in the interregnum, then Tsanomi held it, and then Olomu, Nana's father. The pattern which had emerged by the time Olomu was Governor of the River was one in which the office rotated between the royal group at Batere and the Ologbotsere group at Jakpa. Apparently this was done to create some political equilibrium between the two most important families in Itsekiriland. This pattern was disrupted when in 1883 Nana succeeded to the office on the death of his father, Olomu.

The reason for this disruption would appear to have been Olomu's phenomenal success as a trader. The consular accounts leave us in no doubt that the Olomu family was the wealthiest and most powerful in Itsekiriland as from the 1870s. Nana, who succeeded to his father's business, was already a successful trader himself. His inheritance put him head and shoulders above others in the kingdom. Success in trade was not achieved by Olomu and his son without making enemies of less successful men. The foundation by Olomu of a new settlement, Ebrohimi, sited on the banks of an easily defensible creek was doubtless in recognition of the existence of jealous rivals who might not scruple to attack him.

Jealousy and enmity arising from success in trade was deepened by Nana's appointment as governor of the River in succession to his father. Numa of Batere who apparently expected to succeed Olomu in that office, brought up his son, Dogho, to avenge the disgrace done to the family. By the time of the Macdonald administration, therefore, Nana was the dominant figure in Itsekiriland both economically and politically. In Dogho (Numa died in 1892 soon after the inauguration of the new administration) he had his chief rival and enemy.

In terms of relations with the British, Nana was the Jaja of the western delta. His hold on most of the Urhobo oil markets was probably even firmer than Jaja's. Gallwey discovered this when he toured the Urhobo areas in 1892. In terms of wealth, Nana was probably much wealthier than Jaja and like Jaja was able to dictate his own trade terms and had no need for trust. Though not an Olu, Nana had a high sense of his position. He saw the British consul as a mere servant of the Queen of England and saw himself more as the equal of the latter than the former. Thus he scolded Consul Annesley for failing to pay his respects when the consul visited the Itsekiri kingdom in 1890. Such a man was bound to fall foul of the British in the new situation of the 1890s as he clearly represented a rival force and authority both at the coast and in the hinterland. It was not surprising, therefore, that only three years after Macdonald's new administration, the British came to blows with Nana. Nana was accused of obstructing the trade of the hinterland, of blocking trade routes and even of human sacrifice. All the evidence suggests that in fact Nana was doing a flourishing business even in the 1890s. It is clear that the stories put abroad by the British originated from the Dogho camp which saw in the British the instrument for their vengeance. The British swallowed the stories because it suited their books to do so: they needed an excuse for getting rid of Nana and so establish their hold over the Itsekiri and Urhobo countries.

The crisis developed in the months of August and September 1894 when Ralph Moor was acting for Macdonald who had gone on leave. Series of letters passed between Moor and Nana in which the former accused Nana of various misdemeanours and the latter denied the accusations. Then Moor tried to get Nana to go on board a British gunboat to discuss the points at issue. Nana refused, obviously remembering the Jaja episode. Events thus reached a stalemate which could only be resolved by force. Moor proceeded to build up a large naval and military force off the Benin River — easily the most impressive collection of British forces up till that date. Hostilities commenced on 25 August 1894 and lasted on and off till 25 September. The length of time involved is explicable in terms of the difficulties which the British experienced in dealing with Nana. All attempts to take Ebrohimi by going up the creek failed. Cutting a path through the dense forest swamp proved an arduous task rendered dangerous by Nana's cleverly masked batteries. In fact it was not till Dogho and his men showed the British the best way to reach Ebrohimi through the swamps that Nana's town eventually fell on 25 September 1894. Nana himself escaped but later gave himself up in Lagos. He was tried for making war against Great Britain, found guilty and sentenced to deportation for life and forfeiture of all goods. With Nana's fall, the way was left clear for the effective establishment of British rule in the Itsekiri kingdom. Dogho, who was awarded a medal for his role in ensuring British victory over Nana, was appointed a British political agent and from that time till his death in 1932 became without question the most dominant figure in the Itsekiri kingdom as indeed in all of what is now the Delta Province. It thus required the British conquest of Ebrohimi to turn the tables against the Ologbotsere group represented in 1894 by Nana.

The Push into the Hinterland of the Western Delta

By the time Nana fell the British had already established vice-consulates at three points in the western delta — Warri, Sapele, and Benin River. Warri and Sapele now became the bases from which the penetration of the Urhobo, Isoko, and Ukwuani hinterland was organized. It will be recalled that Gallwey, Vice-Consul of Benin River, had made an exploratory trip into the Urhobo area in 1891–2. No further effective move was made until 1896. This time-lag requires explanation, the pre-occupation with Nana apart. The fact is that in 1891 there were two co-ordinate British authorities in what used to be the three Eastern States and the Midwestern State of Nigeria. Macdonald headed the Protectorate administration. The Royal Niger Company represented the other authority. A boundary was drawn up between the two authorities in 1891 which put the greater

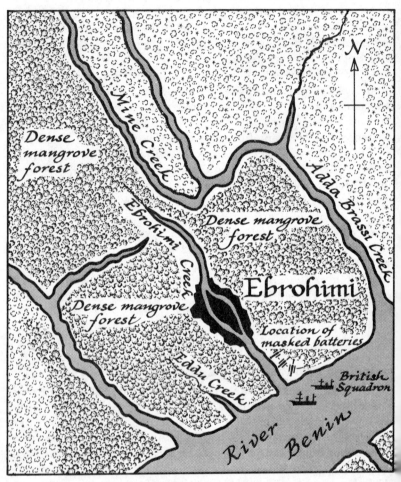

Map 3   Ebrohimi's position on the Benin River

part of the Urhobo and Isoko countries into the sphere of the Royal Niger Company. It was the same boundary which put Brass into the company's area of authority with the consequences discussed in Part 2, Episode 5. Ralph Moor who was acting for Macdonald in 1894 was extremely irritated by the limitations which this boundary placed on his officials. He argued that it was ridiculous that the hinterland of the Itsekiri kingdom under his authority should be placed under a different authority. Thus, when in the first half of September 1894 the Royal Niger Company signed treaties of cession with a number of Urhobo towns in Ughelle, Agbon, and Olomu clans, Moor ordered his men in the second half of that month to sign treaties of protection with some 13 Urhobo towns including quite a number of those with whom the Niger Company had already entered into treaty relations. The Niger Company protested to the Foreign Office which ordered Moor not to make any more treaties. Infuriated though he was, Moor had to obey the Foreign Office injunctions. There was thus a lull in the British push into the hinterland until the end of 1899 when the Royal Niger Company lost its charter and became no more than a trading concern. In the meantime, that lull was used for settling scores with Benin, the story told in Part 2, Episode 6.

The push into the Urhobo, Isoko, and Ukwuani areas, halted in the years 1896–99, began in real earnest as from 1900 and went on till 1914. Although no major wars were fought by the British, the progress of their penetration was slow and agonizing. One reason for this was the fragmented nature of the communities which meant that each village or town had to be dealt with separately. Another reason was that many of these Urhobo, Isoko, and Ukwuani settlements adopted a policy of passive resistance. While they offered no active opposition to British political officers who visited them, they proceeded to act, as soon as these officers had left, as if nothing had happened. Consequently, the British were forced to send a number of military patrols into these areas. A few such examples can be given here — Evhro (Effurun) 1896; Orokpo 1901; Etua 1904; Ezionum 1905; Iyede 1908; Owe, Oleh and Ozoro in 1910 and again in 1911. No account of the British penetration of this area, however brief, can be complete without mention of the British occupation of Uzere in the Isoko country at the end of 1903. Uzere was famous for its Eni cult which had the power to detect and punish witches. As the fear of witchcraft was widespread the Eni cult was widely patronized. The destruction of such cults was a cardinal feature of British penetration, and from 1900 the British began planning to destroy Eni. It took three years and the threat of force to achieve. The Ovie of Uzere, who was high priest of the cult, had to be threatened with force at the same time as he was bribed with the vice-presidency of the Native Court established there in 1904. The British made the occasion of the formal 'abolition' of Eni a grand affair. People from other Isoko towns as well as Urhobo, Ukwuani, Itsekiri, and Ijo 'chiefs' were invited to Uzere and made to put their 'marks' on an agreement formally 'abolishing' Eni. The British regarded this as a major triumph especially as it was achieved without bloodshed and the District Commissioner who presided over the matter earned himself promotion! Needless to say the 'abolition' of Eni did not destroy the belief in witchcraft and new ways were soon found for tackling the old problem.

The British Penetration of Igbo and Ibibioland

Just as the Itsekiri kingdom and Sapele formed the bases from which the penetration of the Urhobo, Isoko and Ukwuani areas was organized, so the eastern delta states formed the centres from which the British pushed into the Igbo and Ibibio hinterland. As for the delta states themselves, none, Brass excepted, gave the British any fight after the Jaja episode. This is not to say that these states willingly accepted British rule. Various aspects of the new situation proved vexatious and produced reactions—some mild, some quite violent. In Okrika, for example, violent resistance to the British occurred in 1893, 1894 and 1895. But not even these disposed Okrika to accept the British whose desire to penetrate beyond Okrika to the Igbo hinterland spelt economic ruin for that state. Moor had to use the threat of force (he actually took over 100 soldiers in a gunboat to Okrika) before Okrika finally submitted to the British in June 1896.

By the time Okrika finally yielded to the British, the latter had hardly started their penetration of the Igbo and Ibibio hinterland. In the same year that Okrika was subdued, the Kingdom of Aboh signed a protection treaty with the Niger Coast Protectorate and so passed formally under British rule. Aboh had, in the period since 1863, experienced the harsh methods of the Niger Company which not only disrupted the Aboh–Brass commercial alliance which had been the main prop of the economy of those two states, but had also encouraged a number of Aboh's tributary settlements to assert their independence. Pushed to the wall, Aboh had revolted in 1882 by attacking the Niger Company's factory. The Company replied by bombarding Aboh, leaving hundreds of her citizens dead on the streets of Aboh itself. That took the fight out of Aboh and the signing of the treaty in 1896 was no more than the final act of surrender to an authority which, it was probably hoped, would be less oppressive than that of the Royal Niger Company.

Two years before the Okrika and Aboh incidents, the British had established a station at Akwete just behind Bonny and on the southern periphery of Igboland. No real push into the Igbo hinterland took place until the beginning of the present century. Detailed research into the British conquest of Igboland as a whole is yet to be done. The material available permits of no more than a bare summary. As is made clear in Part 2, Episode 7, which discusses the fall of the Aro, the British thought that the Aro held the key to Igboland. Once the Aro were defeated all of Igboland would yield up their sovereignty. In 1901-2, the Aro were defeated, but then the British discovered that the Aro were not political masters of the Igbo hinterland and that the many other Igbo and Ibibio groups would have to be systematically brought under control. That task took nearly two decades.

By 1902 the British had established a station at Afikpo. From there they sought to reach the Ikwo, Ezza, and other peoples of the neighbourhood. The Ezza, with an ancient reputation as redoubtable warriors, refused any parley with the British. When, in 1905, a British District Officer with a military escort attempted to penetrate into Ezza country, the Ezza and their Achara allies ambushed and killed some members of the escort. As usual a military expedition was sent against the Ezza to avenge the death of members of the escort. Between 15 March and 16 May the British were engaged in fighting the Ezza and their neighbours. Given the savanna nature of the vegetation, and armed with no more than matchets, the Ezza had no chance of success. They had to yield to superior force.

The Ekumeku Movement in Asaba

Another area of Igboland where the British encountered severe armed resistance was Asaba and its hinterland. Asaba was chosen by the Royal Niger Company as its administrative headquarters. Soon the Company had created for itself what Dr Elizabeth Isichei has described as a 'town within a town' cut off 'by an iron railing nine feet high'. A separate establishment was built for the company's soldiers which numbered some 500 in the late 1880s. Company servants and soldiers alike made life intolerable for the citizens of Asaba. The peoples' farms and houses were raided and produce and property carried away. Young girls and even married women were violated by power-drunk soldiers and company servants all of whom were non-indigenes. As if that was not enough, missionaries who had settled in Asaba began to attack the people's culture and cherished institutions. In 1888 half of Asaba was destroyed by the Royal Niger Company on the grounds that the people practised human sacrifice.

The people of Asaba and the hinterland Igbo towns could hardly have been expected to take the depredations of the Royal Niger Company lying down. Faced with what was a really acute crisis, the people resorted to their own strategy. The young men (*Otu Okolobia*) of the various towns came together and formed the *Ekumeku* secret society. Professor Afigbo has said that the term 'Ekumeku' is untranslatable into English but that it brings to mind such words as 'invisible', 'whirlwind', 'devastating'. It was to this *Ekumeku* society that the task of defending the people was now entrusted. Bound by an oath of secrecy, they adopted guerilla tactics, striking and disappearing in swift movements. The *Ekumeku* so harrassed the Company that the latter took the field against them in 1898. The *Ekumeku* held their own in all of the hinterland areas and only in Asaba did they fail. Eventually the Company was forced to come to terms with the *Ekumeku*.

The settlement which ended the conflict between the company and the *Ekumeku* ushered in no more than a period of uneasy peace. When the protectorate authorities took over from the company in 1900, the hostility of the people of Asaba and the hinterland to the white man, be he trader, missionary, or administrator, remained. The new arrangements worsened the situation by the setting up of native courts and the prevention of the elders from carrying out their traditional arbitrating functions. Discontent with the white man was thus accentuated rather than assuaged. In 1902 the British sent troops against the *Ekumeku*. Some of the leaders were captured and they and many of their followers were imprisoned in Calabar. Yet, two years later the *Ekumeku* rose again, and again they were defeated after severe fighting. But that was not the end. Five years later, in 1909, the *Ekumeku* took what turned out to be their last stand. As elsewhere an unquenchable spirit of resistance was no match for the machine guns of the British. The *Ekumeku* were broken. For a whole decade, therefore, the society had fought to save their people from colonial rule. They fought not only against the British but against their own kind who accepted or benefitted from the new order. The fighting men were indeed the *Otu Okolobia* but there can be little doubt that they had the support of all those elders who lost power and prestige as a consequence of the new developments. That it was a secret organization made it difficult for the leaders to be easily identified and rounded up. Few areas gave the British as much trouble as did Asaba and its hinterland under the aegis of the *Ekumeku*.

The British Occupation of Yorubaland

As was shown in Chapter I, the British, in their dealings with the Yoruba, first established their influence in Lagos and Abeokuta. In 1861 Lagos became the first part of Nigeria to become a British colony. Once established in Lagos, it was only logical for the British to seek to extend their trade and influence into the Lagos hinterland. That hinterland was, however, a very disturbed one. Peace was what was needed in the interests of trade, but peace had eluded the Yoruba since the 1820s. At the time Lagos became a British colony Ibadan was at war with Ijaye. From that time until 1886 most of the Yoruba country was in a state of war. Flushed with her victory over Ijaye, Ibadan attempted to create an empire for herself by carrying war into the Ijesa and Ekiti countries.

The military exploits of Ibadan and her efforts to replace the fallen Oyo as the centre of the Yoruba political system are well known and need not delay us here. What is important to stress is that Ibadan's ambitions gave rise to the Ekiti Parapo — a combination of the Ekiti and Ijesa kingdoms, sworn to resist Ibadan's military aggression. The conflict between the Parapo and Ibadan lasted for 16 years and was thus clearly the one which lasted longest. It was also, as it turned out, the last of the main

Yoruba wars of the nineteenth century. Neither side was able to win a decisive victory and yet neither side would give in. How to win peace with honour became a major preoccupation of the combatants. In the circumstances both sides looked desperately for a third party that would intervene to bring the war to an end. This was where the missionaries came in. Although the missionaries who stepped in to begin the process of 'disengagement' were Saros it was not at all surprising that they looked to the British government in Lagos to bring the war to an end. In a sense that was perhaps the only possible solution, for it was important, if war was to end once and for all, that whichever third party intervened should not only be able to negotiate peace, but should also have the physical force to guarantee that peace. No single Yoruba group could do this in the situation of the 1880s. Thus it came about that it was the British in Lagos who now stepped in to negotiate peace between the warring parties.

The peace treaty was negotiated and signed in 1886. The combatants agreed to put an end to war and to retire to their territories as agreed by the treaty. But they also agreed 'to submit themselves to such directions as may seem necessary or expedient to the Governor of Lagos for better and more effectually securing the object of this Treaty', i.e., peace. Further, any issues which might arise between the late combatants not covered by the treaty were to be referred to Lagos for settlement. Naturally all the signatories promised to promote trade and commerce. Contained in the provisions here indicated were all the excuses the British needed for their future onslaught on the sovereignty of the Yoruba. And these provisions lay in the logic of the prevailing situation: war-weary Ibadan, Ekiti and Ijesa could hardly have refused to sign the treaty. Gratitude to the British for terminating a war that had stretched to the utmost the human and material resources of the combatants overcame for the time being fears of what these same British might do.

With peace now established in the hinterland, the British could at last extend their influence there. The situation as it developed in Egbaland which was briefly alluded to in Chapter I, can now be amplified. But events in Egbaland, especially the acceptance by the Egba of the so-called Egba United Government cannot be fully understood outside the context of the general reaction of the Yoruba to the fall of Ijebu in 1892.

As there exist a number of detailed works on the subject of the fall of Ijebu, no effort will be made here to re-tell the entire story. The Ijebu had managed to escape the worst ravages of the Yoruba wars. Consequently, not only had they enjoyed relative tranquillity, they had also been able to build up considerable wealth through trade. Their pre-occupation by 1886 was how to continue to enjoy this prosperity through trade without allowing their institutions and sovereignty to be eroded by growing British influence in Yorubaland. The Ijebu saw missionaries as the greatest agents of the British and so relentlessly kept them out of their territory. As to be anti-missionary tended to be interpreted as being anti-British, the Ijebu dislike of missionaries singled them out as enemies of the British even though the Ijebu were anxious to do trade with all-comers under their own (Ijebu) terms.

British reaction to what they saw as Ijebu hostility was the opening up of the eastern route which, using the Lagos lagoon, thereby by-passed Ijebu. The development of this route actually led to the Ijebu suffering a fall-off in trade. Directly linked with a decline in trade was fear of political domination by Ibadan. The Ijebu had sought, through control of the trade from Lagos, to starve Ibadan of arms and ammunition. Ibadan could, by taking advantage of the 'eastern route', now obtain arms and ammunition from Lagos which she could use in achieving her ambition of dominating all of Yorubaland. Ijebu thus had no cause to be enamoured either of the British in Lagos or of Ibadan. Yoruba power-politics thus dictated that the Ijebu should be anti-British. It was for this reason that the Ijebu refused to allow missionaries to operate in their midst and it was to counter this anti-missionary, anti-British stance that the British mounted a military expedition against Ijebu in 1892.

In 1889 the Awujale Tunwase at last allowed himself to be persuaded by James Johnson to allow missionary enterprise in Ijebu. Black missionaries were sent to Ijebu, but these were quickly followed by white missionaries. The Ijebu were apprehensive of these whites and put obstacles in their way. They even sought to bring French Catholic missionaries as a counterpoise to the British Christian Missionary Society. In 1890 the Ijebu turned back a white missionary because he could not afford the £50 fee demanded by the former for passing through their territory. At the same time they allowed French missionaries to pass through Ijebu to Oyo without the payment of any fees. By

1891 then, the Ijebu were extremely suspicious of the missionaries. The visit of Acting Governor Denton in 1891 confirmed these suspicions. It was as if the missionaries had brought the Governor. It is therefore understandable that the Ijebu refused to discuss trade with Denton. This refusal became the 'insult' for which the Ijebu had to pay in 1892.

War against the Ijebu might have been averted had 'go-ahead' Carter not taken over the governorship of Lagos from Moloney who was, with regard to the Ijebu, disposed to be peaceful and friendly. On his arrival in Lagos in September 1892 Carter determined that he would break Ijebu. He wrote to the Awujale in December 1892 asking for a deputation to be sent to Lagos to apologize for the 'insult' on Denton. The deputation was sent, the apology tendered. Then Carter went beyond the purpose of the meeting. He spoke about keeping open trade routes, berated the Ijebu for their stubbornness in refusing missionaries and bade them, at gun point, sign a treaty which would guarantee free trade and abolish tolls in return for a £500 annual subsidy from Lagos. The delegation refused to sign the treaty. Carter then got a few Lagos-based Ijebu to sign instead.

It is hardly necessary to argue the point as to whether the treaty was properly executed. It has already been pointed out that might counted for far more than legalities. Carter had obtained a 'treaty' which promised free trade, the kind of document which impressed the British Foreign Office. Both the missionaries and the Ibadan who had always smarted under the stranglehold which Ijebu had over their trade soon sought to take advantage of the treaty. Ayandele has detailed how the missionaries and their Ibadan allies taunted and provoked the Ijebu into attacking certain persons whom he describes as 'wild mission labourers'. The Ijebu also proceeded to close their trade routes both as a demonstration against the British and Ibadan and as proof that they did not accept that a free trade treaty had been signed by any duly accredited representatives of the Ijebu. Governor Carter seized on the opportunity presented by these events to accuse the Ijebu of breaking a treaty they had not really signed in the first instance, and got the Colonial Office to sanction military action against the Ijebu. The Ijebu expedition lasted four days, from 12 to 15 May 1892. The Ijebu performance was described by the British as 'unexpected', meaning that it was stubborn. Like other armed confrontations between the British and Nigerian peoples, there was no doubting which side would win. An Ijebu army estimated by their opponents as over 7,000 was defeated by a British force of less than 1,000 but infinitely better armed and drilled. The Ijebu thus constitute the one Yoruba group that really engaged the British in military combat in defence of its sovereignty which was lost when the war was lost.

It was, perhaps, not surprising that Ibadan soldiers were found serving in the British force that defeated Ijebu. The Ibadan wanted Ijebu smashed so that they could trade direct with Lagos. What the Ibadan did not realize was that by the 1890s the British were no longer just anxious to secure trade: they were also anxious to secure political control. The very next year after the Ijebu expedition, the British stationed a resident in Ibadan and established a garrison there. Captain Bower, the resident, had orders to bring not only Ibadan but also Oyo, Ekiti, and Ijesa under British rule. The Oyo confrontation is discussed in Part 2, Episode 3. Ibadan was powerless to react when her fighting men who terrorized the neighbourhood were arrested and either imprisoned or exiled. In 1897 a resident was appointed for the Ekiti-Ijesa area.

The defeat of the Ijebu thus served as an object lesson to other Yoruba groups and explains what Ayandele has described as the 'peaceful' penetration of the rest of Yorubaland in the years which followed. True, British occupation of Oyo was not achieved without the use of force but the Oyo-British confrontation was not anything on the scale of the Ijebu. Perhaps nowhere did the defeat of the Ijebu lead to such change of attitude as in Egbaland. Throughout the 1880s the missionary party in Abeokuta, led by J. B. Wood, had gradually built up a position of strength at the expense of the traditional authorities. The latter reacted by seeking to use the French as a counterpoise but the Anglo-French agreement over Nigeria's present western international boundary put Egbaland solidly in the British sphere. Unable after 1888 to use the French effectively against the British, the Egba reacted by closing their trade routes against the British. Indeed, Ayandele argues that British traders were infinitely more concerned about the Egba closure of trade routes than they were about the Ijebu. But for the fact that Carter was satisfied that the missionaries in Abeokuta were adequately promoting British influence there, he may well have sought permission to smash the Egba militarily. Egba hostility to what had become overbearing missionary influence was driven underground by the defeat of the Ijebu. The Egba immediately threw open their trade routes. In 1893 when Carter went on a tour of Yorubaland, the Egba signed with him a treaty of trade and friendship. Proof that the Egba were not, even in 1893, prepared to hand over their territory completely to the British was shown in their rejection of the proposals to station a British resident in Abeokuta and to link Abeokuta to Lagos by rail. The Egba also got Carter to include a clause in the treaty which guaranteed their independence.

Despite the events of 1893 the C.M.S. party continued to consolidate its position in Abeokuta. Five years after the 1893 treaty the Egba accepted the so-called Egba-United Government which was set up largely at the instance of the Lagos government and dominated by the C.M.S.: the Revd J. H. Samuel (Adegboyega Edun) was Secretary, C. B. Moore, son of a clergyman, was Treasurer, and the Revd D. O. Williams became 'Prime Minister' to the Alake. A British commissioner was now stationed at Abeokuta, and though in law he was expected to act as an ambassador (in view of the guarantee of Egba independence in 1893 which was still legally in force), the commissioner acted far more like a British resident. More and more the Egba authorities lost effective power to the British and their Saro allies. Yet the Egba had not, technically, lost their independence. When Lugard carried through his amalgamation in the years 1912-14 and sought to introduce direct taxation into Egbaland, he found that the legal if not *de facto* independence of the Egba stood in his way: how could he tax an independent people? Fortunately, events played into Lugard's hands. In 1914, the Egba, in a final stand against British encroachment, took the opportunity of the British pre-occupation with the 1914-18 war as well as a damnable maltreatment of an old and respected chief to rise against the British. Like the Ijebu they were smashed into submission by superior force in August 1914. Thereafter, Egbaland passed formally under British rule. By that time, too, the rest of the Yoruba country had become British territory.

BIBLIOGRAPHICAL NOTE

J. C. Anene (*Southern Nigeria in Transition*) discusses at some length the question of the protection treaties briefly mentioned in this chapter. So do I more briefly in *Merchant Prince of the Niger Delta*. The crucial issue is that there were no interpreters sufficiently versed both in English and the Nigerian languages to really translate the legal jargon of the treaties into the Nigerian languages. Even when the interpreters were competent, as would appear to have been the case in certain parts of Northern Nigeria, they were afraid to tell the rulers that they were yielding up their sovereignty (see R. A. Adeleye, *Power and Diplomacy in Northern Nigeria* (Longman 1971 p. 145). Consequently it can be argued that most of the rulers were not aware of the full implications of the treaties they signed.

There is yet to emerge a full length biography of Jaja. The most detailed study at present available is in J. C. Anene's *Southern Nigeria in Transition*, (pp. 81-97). Ayandele (*The Mission ary Impact on Modern Nigeria 1842-1914*) discusses Jaja's fall on pp. 103-10. Ayandele claims that 'whether the merchants complained or not an open clash between Jaja and Bonny and the consul would have been very difficult to avoid. The missionary forces at work, together with the role of Johnston, ready to act where Hewett had merely talked, were the real determinants of Jaja's fall in 1887' (p. 104). The questions which arise are: what was the basis of the conflict between Jaja and Bonny and what was the aim of Johnston? I fail to see the missionary factor as central to Jaja's fall. While, as Dr C. J. Gertzel has shown in her thesis *John Holt: A British Merchant in West Africa in the Era of Imperialism* (University of Oxford 1959) and her article 'Commercial Organization on the Niger Coast 1852-1891', *Historians in Tropical Africa*, Salisbury, 1962 (pp. 289-304), the issue was not necessarily that of getting rid of the middleman system, it can hardly be denied that the British were eager to get rid of Jaja as a *particular middleman,* economically and politically strong enough to challenge rising British influence in the area. Roland Oliver in his *Sir Harry Johnston and the Scramble for Africa* (Chatto and Windus 1957) valiantly attempts to defend Johnston's action in deporting Jaja. He even argues that the trial of Jaja was 'fairly held' even though Jaja, a non-British subject was tried under British law (pp. 107-23).

The account of the fall of the rest of the eastern delta is based largely on J. C. Anene. Some of the details, however, come from J. B. Anyake's *The Coastal States of South Eastern Nigeria 1891-1939* being prepared for the Ph.D degree of the University of Ibadan.

J. C. Anene (pp. 151-61) also discusses the fall of Nana. His handling of the matter shows an inadequate understanding of the situation in the western delta, and despite the records, Anene seems to have preferred, in part, H. Bindloss's views as expressed in *In the Niger Country*, (first published in 1898 and recently reprinted by Frank Cass1968). Bindloss, who visited the area probably some time after the event, paints Nana as essentially a slave trader who indulged in human sacrifices and other atrocities. My biographical study of Nana as contained in *Merchant Prince of the Niger Delta* is the most detailed work available on the subject and reaches very different conclusions, and I take issue both with Bindloss and Anene. For those interested in the actual military confrontation there is my contribution — 'Ebrohimi' — in Michael Crowder (Ed) *West African Resistance* (Hutchinson 1971) pp.205-32.

The treatment of the British push into the hinterland of the western delta is only briefly presented in this chapter. For detailed studies see my *Niger Delta Rivalry* (Longman 1969), Chapter Four and my *The Isoko People* (Ibadan University Press 1972) pp. 43-84. J. C. Anene briefly discussed the British push into the Ukwuani area (pp. 221-2). The most detailed treatment of this subject known to me is in Okolugbo's thesis already cited, Chapter 4.

A definitive work on the British conquest of Igboland is yet to appear. As of now readers are referred to J. C. Anene's work already cited, Elizabeth Isichei's *The Ibo People and the Europeans* (Faber and Faber 1973) Chapters 8-10 and to F. K. Ekechi's *Missionary Enterprise and Rivalry in Igboland 1857-1914* (Frank Cass 1972) for the missionary aspect.

Isichei's work suffers from her great dependence on written records which never present all the facts as she herself must appreciate from her work on Asaba where she has done some field investigation. Her work does, however, present a readily available summary of events. On the Aro, there is Anene's work and his article on the subject in *Journal of the Historical Society of Nigeria* Vol 1 (December 1965) and Professor A. E. Afigbo's

'The Aro Expedition of 1901-1902, in *Odu* (New Series) No 7 (April 1972). On the *Ekumeku* Isichei's account can be found in her book pp. 139-42. Professor Afigbo discusses the *Ekumeku* in his short but excellent article, 'Patterns of Igbo Resistance to British Conquest' in *Tarikh* 4, 3, (1973). Dr P. A. Igbafe has an excellent article on the subject of *Ekumeku:* 'Western Ibo Society and its resistance to British Rule: the Ekumeku Movement, 1898-1911', *Journal of African History xii* (1971).

The printed works readily available on the British occupation of Yorubaland are Ayandele's *Missionary Impact,* S. A. Akintoye's *Revolution and Power Politics in Yorubaland* (Longman 1971) and J. A. Atanda's *The New Oyo Empire* (Longman 1973). Dr Bolanle Awes's thesis, *The Rise of Ibadan as a Yoruba Power in the Nineteenth Century* (University of Oxford 1964) provides very useful information about the rise of Ibadan and her impact on Yoruba power politics. Although not directly on the subject of the British occupation of Yorubaland, J. F. Ade Ajayi's contribution in Ajayi and Smith (Eds.), *Yoruba Warfare* provides an indispensable background for our understanding of events during the occupation. In his discussion of the Ijebu, Ayandele takes issue with those who argue that the Ijebu attitude to the British was determined by commercial considerations and argues instead that the Ijebu expedition of 1892 was essentially the 'missionary war'. In so far as the attitude of Nigerians to missionaries was, as Ayandele himself makes abundantly clear, determined by political and economic factors, to say that the Ijebu expedition was a 'missionary war' is not to say very much. It is clear from his own evidence that the crucial factor was Yoruba power politics in which economics was an important ingredient. For a good treatment of Carter's role in the Ijebu expedition see, in addition to Ayandele, A. B. Aderibigbe's 'The Ijebu Expedition, 1892: An Episode in the British Penetration of Nigeria Reconsidered', *Historians in Tropical Africa,* (Salisbury 1962). In his article 'The Mode of British Expansion in Yorubaland in the Second Half of the Nineteenth Century: The Oyo Episode', *Odu,* ii 2, (1967), Ayandele discusses not only the Oyo episode but shows how the attitude of the Yoruba was influenced by the British defeat of the Ijebu in 1892. For a military analysis of the Ijebu-British war, see R. S. Smith 'Nigeria-Ijebu' in M. Crowder (Ed.) *West African Resistance,* pp. 170-204.

CHAPTER
IV

Europe and Northern Nigeria in the Nineteenth Century: Prelude to the British Conquest of Northern Nigeria

So far our attention has been focused on events in Southern Nigeria. What, in fact, was happening in Northern Nigeria in terms of relations between Europeans and the rulers and peoples of that part of our country? As we have seen in the case of Southern Nigeria, the suppression of the overseas slave trade and the effort of promoting trade in other products (and missionary activities must be seen as part of this effort), led directly or indirectly to a polarity of interests which, among other factors, preceded and prepared the way for the British conquest. In Northern Nigeria missionary activity may have constituted part of the increasing nuisance that the European presence represented; it can hardly be said to have posed any real threat to the independence of that part of the country. The same cannot, however, be said for European commercial activities which, as in the south, preceded and built up the tensions which erupted in British conquest.

As is well known, the larger part of Northern Nigeria in the nineteenth century was part of the Sokoto caliphate, created as a result of the jihad led by Uthman dan Fodiye. Islam, which became the official religion of the caliphate, influenced to a great extent the relations between it and the Europeans, since Islamic law provided for how such relations were to be regulated. Outside the caliphate was Borno, also a Muslim state but one with which the Sokoto caliphate was hardly on friendly terms. Also outside the caliphate were various communities, like the Tiv for example, which remained non-Muslim and whose relations with the Europeans were regulated by other than the tenets of Islamic law.

In the first half of the nineteenth century it can be said with a fair amount of truth that European activities in Northern Nigeria produced only a minimum of political repercussions. These activities arose mostly from the quest for the Niger. Thus we know of the travels of people like Clapperton and Barth who sought to reach the Niger using the caravan trade routes across the Sahara. In 1824, for example, Clapperton was well received by the caliph, Muhammad Bello, who granted him a commercial treaty. This treaty of 1824 like that granted to Barth in 1853 was essentially a commercial one. The caliph granted Clapperton and his entourage a safe conduct through his domains and laid down the rules which were to govern trade between Europeans and the caliphate. The caliph saw himself essentially as a protector of the Europeans who visited his territory. As Christians (all Europeans were assumed so to be) the caliph regarded these Europeans as infidels, but infidels recognized by the Book which also laid down how they were to be treated by Muslims. While anxious to grant safe conducts and commercial treaties, the caliph was not unaware of the political complications that European activities could involve. While Clapperton's reception in 1824 was decidedly friendly, his reception during a second visit in 1826-7 was noticeably cold. This coldness arose from the fact that Clapperton had, on the second occasion, first gone to Borno where he had not only entered into a commercial agreement but had also, as part of the deal, made a present of arms and ammunition to the ruler of that state. As Borno was regarded as an enemy by the caliphate, Clapperton's activities there made him suspect in Sokoto. In fact, it began to be put abroad that Clapperton might well be a spy. There was thus no lack of political sensitivity in the caliphate's early relations with Europeans.

The Intensification of European Activities and New Trends in Caliphate-European Relations

As was the case in the south, the second half of the nineteenth century witnessed an intensification of European activities in the

Sokoto caliphate. As a result of Dr Baikie's expedition, it is well known, Lokoja became the base of British activities. In 1867 a British consulate was established in Lokoja. The withdrawal of the consulate in 1869 did not in any way represent a waning of the interest of commercial houses even if it can be said to have represented a change in official thinking in Britain. Between 1860 and 1897 a number of British firms established business relations with the Sokoto caliphate, notably with the emirates along the Niger–Benue waterway. The West African Company Ltd, the Company of Merchants Trading to the Upper Niger, Holland Jacques and Co., Miller Brothers — these represent only a selection of the more important firms. Indeed the proliferation of companies was such that by the 1870s cut-throat competition resulting in reduced profits led Taubman Goldie to amalgamate the British concerns into the United African Company, later known as National African Company, which in 1886 became a chartered company with the name of the Royal Niger Company.

The year before Goldie's amalgamation, the French joined the competition for trade in the Sokoto caliphate. The Compagnie Française de l'Afrique Equatoriale which established stations at Gbebe, Lokoja, Egga, Shonga, and Raba on the Niger, and Lokoja and Demsa on the Benue was, from the start, an agent of French imperialism. It was the activities of companies such as this which prepared the way for what, in the 1890s, was to become a major pre-occupation of French imperialism — the building up of a solid block of territory linking France's North African territories, Algeria and Tunisia (with Morocco a much-wanted prize), with her West African territories. In 1880 Germany entered into the picture with Flegel's mission to Sokoto, followed by his hoisting of the German flag on the Benue in 1881. The German effort was, however, short lived as Flegel was soon pushed out of the Benue trade by Britain and France. That left the field for these two European nations which remained the main rivals in the Niger–Benue basin.

Relations between the European traders and the rulers of the riverain emirates were at first friendly. The emirs were happy to receive the European goods brought by the white traders. In particular arms and ammunition were useful as a source of power for strengthening the ruler's position and for war against external enemies. As was the case in the South before the appointment of a British consul, the rulers of the riverain emirates regarded themselves as the protectors of the European traders. In return for the protection they offered, the Europeans paid an annual tribute. Increase in European competition for trade at first redounded to the advantage of the emirs, for the Europeans sought, through offering better prices, gifts and military aid, to win the favour of the rulers. So far were the Europeans prepared to go that rulers like the Emir of Bida used the National African Company and the French company to crush a rebellion mounted against him by the Kede in 1882. There were, however, developments which made it impossible for relations to remain evenly friendly. Increasingly, especially from the 1880s, the European companies, especially the N.A.C. and the French, became committed to the promotion of the imperial ambitions of their respective countries. This meant not only that they sought to monopolize trade where they could, but also attempted to exercise political rights which the emirs did not and would not concede.

In a sense the presence of more than one European power on the Niger-Benue waterway was an advantage to the various emirs with whom the Europeans dealt, since they could play one European group against the other and so seek to retain the initiative. The National African Company, anxious to remove this disability, squeezed out the French from the Niger in 1882. Compelled to leave the Niger to the N.A.C., the French attempted for the next two years to concentrate on the Benue. They obtained a commercial treaty from the Emir of Jibu to trade in his territory. As a result of this treaty a French trading station was opened at Ibi. The N.A.C. responded to this situation by securing a similar treaty from the Emir of Jibu which conferred on it the same rights of trade as had been granted to the French. In October 1884, after some six years of struggle, the French sold out to the N.A.C. and withdrew from the Benue as they had done from the Niger two years before. From that time, therefore, the riverain emirates had to deal not with a number of companies from different European countries but only with the N.A.C. As will be seen, relations between the N.A.C., soon to be the Royal Niger Company (R.N.C.), and these emirates tended to deteriorate after that date. However, the French withdrawal from the Niger-Benue basin must not be interpreted to mean that France had abandoned her imperial ambitions in this part of West Africa. France continued to pursue her ambitions in the

regions that are now Niger and Dahomey as well as in what used
to be the French Cameroons. From these areas France pushed,
from time to time, into the heartlands of the Sokoto caliphate.
Indeed, French and German expeditions in the 1890s explain, as
Adeleye has successfully demonstrated, why the caliphate sometimes adopted a concilliatory attitude towards the Royal Niger
Company.

The Issue of the N.A.C.'s Treaties with the Caliphate

In what has been said so far, reference has been made to treaties
signed between the caliph and some of the emirs with European
travellers and commercial firms. The point has been made that
these treaties were essentially trading agreements and that they
did not, deliberately, concede political rights to the Europeans.
While this position was accepted in the period up to the 1880s, the
Europeans then began, with the increasing tempo of the imperial
push as from that time, to seek to obtain treaties which conferred
on them political rights. In March 1885 the N.A.C. signed a
treaty with Bida. According to Adeleye, the emir gave the
Company 'entire charge of all trading interests in the country; all
foreigners in the country wishing to have the right to trade therein
must obtain permission to do so from the N.A.C. Ltd'. The
Company was also granted sole mining rights. The Company, the
treaty provided, 'agree and bind themselves to allow anyone who
wishes to trade full liberty; always provided it shall be on
equitable terms and according to British laws'. The Company
paid 800 bags of cowries to the emir for the treaty and further
agreed to pay an annual tribute. While the grant of the right to
control foreign trade might appear a major concession, it is clear
from the provision that all who wished to trade be granted 'full
liberty' that the emir was anxious that no monopoly of trade be
enjoyed by the N.A.C. As we shall see later, the Company's
refusal to abide by the provisions of this treaty was to lead to
worsening relations between it and Bida.

In June 1885 the N.A.C. claimed to have entered into
treaty agreements with Sokoto and Gwandu. According to the
Company, Sokoto and Gwandu transferred to it 'entire rights to
the country on both sides of the rivers Benue and Kwarra (Niger)
for a distance of ten hours' journey inland or such other distance
as they may desire from each bank of both rivers throughout their

dominions. The Company was, in addition, to have sole rights over foreign trade and other minerals; Sokoto and Gwandu were not to enter into relations with foreign powers except through them; the Company was to have jurisdiction over foreigners. In return the Company agreed to pay 3,000 and 2,000 bags of cowries annually to Sokoto and Gwandu respectively. If indeed these terms represented what the caliph and the Emir of Gwandu conceded, they would have accepted what was virtually a protectorate. Adeleye has indicated that the originals of these treaties are not available and that therefore it is difficult to be certain what in fact was conceded. He argues further that it is against all the evidence that the caliph would have agreed to sign a document drawn up in English and that if the terms indicated were drawn up in Arabic their implications would have been so clear as to guarantee their rejection. As the Emir of Bida pointed out to Claude Macdonald in 1889 during the latter's inquiry into the activities of the Company, he could not understand how the caliph could have given to the Company political rights over emirates along the Niger and Benue without so much as consulting with these emirates. The burden of Adeleye's argument in fact is that either no treaties were signed at all (in which case Thomson, the N.A.C. agent, deliberately forged the treaties) or that the caliph and the Emir of Gwandu gave no more than commercial concessions which were deliberately magnified to suit the Company's wishes. It is indeed difficult to believe that the caliph would be less politically astute and sensitive than, say, the Emir of Bida, who was extremely careful about what rights he granted to the Company. Yet it was on claims such as this that British rights over the caliphate were based in the purely European bargaining that went on in the age of the scramble and partition. If anything further needs to be said about this matter, it is that five years later another set of treaties was alleged to have been signed between the R.N.C. and Sokoto and Gwandu. Adeleye once again rejects the validity of these treaties, arguing that they did not have the caliph's seal as was customary with properly authenticated documents which emanated from that ruler's chancery. At any rate, the effort of securing a fresh set of treaties would indicate either that there were no earlier treaties which were legally binding or that such earlier treaties did not go far enough.

N.A.C. (R.N.C.)-Bida Relations 1885-1898

In signing the treaty of 1885, the Emir of Bida apparently hoped that other European firms would take advantage of the treaty to trade with him and his people. It would appear that this hope was justified for a short while. To force out such competitors for trade the Company imposed heavy duties on them. In 1887 one German and three British firms were squeezed out of trade with Nupe by what Adeleye has described as 'the strong arm methods' of the Royal Niger Company. The emir naturally reacted to this development. At a meeting in November of that year to which he summoned all foreign traders in his domains, he fulminated against the Company. He made it clear that no one other than himself had a right to receive duties from foreign traders. All were free to trade in his dominions. He emphatically denied having ceded an inch of territory to any European. He ordered the Company to hand over to him all 'tributes' collected from foreigners. The seriousness of the situation was demonstrated by the speed with which the Company raised the annual tribute paid to the emir from £400 to £2,000.

The increase in annual tribute would appear not to have satisfied the emir. Relations between him and the R.N.C. remained tense for the next few years. In 1892 the Emir, Maliki, ordered the Company to leave his territories. In that same year he invited the French to do trade with him and his people. The situation was sufficiently threatening for Goldie and the Earl of Scarborough, the directors of the Company, to rush to Bida in search of peace. Goldie hastened to assure the emir that the Company would observe the 1885 treaty and that it had no intention of exercising any political rights over Nupe territory. Having said that, however, Goldie warned that if Bida for her part broke the treaty, she would be blockaded. It was probably this threat that made the emir invite the French to his territory in 1892, hoping thereby to have a counterpoise to the Company.

The French responded to the emir's invitation by establishing a few trading stations in his territory. However, Bida-French relations were adversely affected by French activities in Borgu which were clearly aimed at territorial acquisition. Playing on the anti-French feeling in Bida, the R.N.C. succeeded in pushing out the French in 1895. The next year the Company proceeded to establish military posts in Leaba, Jebba, and Bayibo. The Company's action would appear to have been in response to pressure from both the British government and public opinion in Britain to demonstrate that it was indeed capable of forwarding British imperial interests in this part of West Africa, the same kind of pressure which forced the Company to take action against Ilorin (see Episode 4, Part 2). The establishment of military posts was seen by Bida as a violation of the 1885 treaty and preparations for war against the Company were set afoot. Towards this end Bida invited Bussa and Ilorin to join her in a joint onslaught against the Company. Though both Bussa and Ilorin were also threatened by the Company, they failed to make common cause with Bida against it. In June 1896 the emir succeeded in withdrawing all Nupe pilots in the service of the company. Soon after, Nupe captured a small R.N.C. force of 45 men with their rifles. This was the immediate prelude to the R.N.C.-Bida war of 1897.

The war which broke out was not just against Bida town but against all territories controlled by the emir. Thus, in January the R.N.C. marched first against Kabba which was then vassal to Bida. For some reason the Nupe war camp in Kabba was deserted and the Company thus met no real opposition. Having informed the chiefs of Kabba that henceforth they were under R.N.C. control, Goldie marched with a force of 32 Europeans and 507 African rank and file against Bida. Open battle was joined on 26 January 1897. Although the superior weaponry of the Company's forces wrought havoc among the Nupe forces, the latter fought back bravely and actually succeeded in forcing the Company to retreat at the end of that day. The emir himself led his men in war and was actually wounded in the fighting. The next day battle was resumed. At 4 p.m. R.N.C. forces entered into Bida town. The Bida army again fought valiantly on that day and it was not until the 28th of January that the town fell and the emir was forced to flee to Kontagora. According to British sources, which may well have been exaggerated, the Nupe lost some 600-1,000 men dead or wounded during the various battles.

Having won the war, Goldie found it difficult to arrange the peace. For days he could find no one with whom to negotiate an agreement. The makum, the next in line of succession, had fled from Bida and was not anxious to reach a peace accord with the British. In fact, it was only the entreaty of his mother that finally convinced him to give himself up to the British and to sign a peace treaty with them. The Company set up the makum as the new

Emir of Bida. The emir then recognized the Company as the new government of Nupe. But having gone this far, the R.N.C. failed to establish any effective administration over Bida town, let alone over the rest of Nupe territory. The makum whose loyalty remained with the former emir, Abubakar, refused to become an instrument of the R.N.C. When in 1898 Abubakar returned to Bida, the makum very gladly handed over power to him. That Bida could not accept the 1897 agreement was soon proved when Abubakar attacked a number of the Company's stations in June 1898. That the Company failed to press home the advantage granted in 1897 would seem to be proof that it did not have the personnel to assume any proper administration of the areas with which it traded, one reason why, two years later, it lost its charter. At that time its relations with Bida remained as hostile as they had been since 1887.

N.A.C. (R.N.C.) on the Benue 1884-1893

As on the Niger so on the Benue, the N.A.C. attempted to consolidate its position in the period after 1884. Treaties were signed with a number of rulers, the more important being those with Muri, Nassarawa, Keffi, and Bauchi. Although all of these treaties granted commercial concessions none was regarded by the rulers concerned as conceding sovereignty to the company. During his mission in 1889, Macdonald was able to talk to some of those who had acted as interpreters for the Company. These men made it quite clear to Macdonald that they dared not tell the rulers, irrespective of what was contained in the printed treaties, that they were handing over political power to the Company. It is thus quite clear that the two parties put diametrically opposed interpretations on the treaties they signed.

In Muri, relations with the N.A.C. soon became strained as the latter proceeded to act as if the treaty with Muri had conferred political rights on it. Late in 1884, for example, the Company burnt the Muri town of Jibu and killed many of its inhabitants. The emir reacted promptly. He led his forces into Ibi and threatened to throw out the Company. The Company, caught unawares by the emir's reaction, promised to be of good behaviour. Yet Jibu was again attacked by it in 1888 and 1891. This time the emir ordered the Company to leave his territory. The Company retired to its base in Ibi. The next year it attempted to conciliate the emir who was flirting with the French expedition led by Mizon which in that year passed through Muri territory *en route* for Adamawa. Not only did the emir refuse to be conciliated, he actually went on to enter into a treaty of protection with Mizon in November 1892. The next month, as proof of the new relations, the French helped Muri fight against Kwana, a traditional enemy. If the emir thought that he had thus thrown off the R.N.C., he was mistaken, for the Company reacted by blockading Muri and forcing the French government to withdraw Mizon in 1893. Needless to say, Muri–R.N.C. relations remained tense thereafter.

The other major area which had to cope with the activities of the Niger Company was Adamawa. Right from the 1850s the Emirs of Adamawa had maintained an essentially hostile policy towards Europeans. In 1852 Barth was turned back from Yola; in 1880 a C.M.S. party was refused entry into that town. In 1882, 1884, and 1886 William Wallace of the N.A.C. was turned back from Yola. In 1888 a German, Zintgraff, visited Yola but was quickly sent away by the emir. When Macdonald arrived in 1889 for his special mission he discovered that Yola was one place where he most certainly was not welcome. In his report he noted that the R.N.C. had very little footing in Adamawa.

What the emir did not know was that as from the late 1880s Britain, Germany, and France were busy signing agreements which would have a major effect on his power over his own territories. In 1886 for example, the British, anxious to create a buffer state between their own and the French sphere of activities, signed a convention with Germany which conceded to Germany the eastern portion of Adamawa beyond Garua. Meanwhile French activity in parts of the Cameroons and what is now Niger were growing apace. The Emir of Adamawa (Yola) found that the only answer to the problem of European pressure was to exploit the existing Anglo-Franco-German rivalry to his advantage. From the 1890s, therefore, he began to adopt a policy of conciliation towards the European powers as it suited his purpose, always ensuring that he did not compromise his sovereignty. In 1891 he entered into a trade treaty with France. Only two years later, afraid of French activities in his domain, the emir turned to the R.N.C. with which he proceeded to reach agreement. He now asked the R.N.C. to protect him against other powers and in return gave the Company freedom of trade within his domains as well as control over other foreign traders. Yet in that same year he entered into another treaty with the French which enabled the latter to establish a military post near the emir's palace. The R.N.C. reacted violently to this development and by the end of the year (1893) succeeded in driving the French away from Adamawa. The Adamawa situation highlights excellently the quandary in which the rulers of the caliphate and other parts of Northern Nigeria found themselves as the European scramble for territory hotted up. Unable to prevent European activity in their respective areas, they sought to play one power off against the other. But then this game could only go on successfully for a brief while, for sooner or later one of the powers established itself as the dominant one in a given area or else, as indeed was the case in Adamawa, an agreement in Europe ended rivalries in Africa. Thus, while the R.N.C. and the French were busy fighting over who should have predominant influence in Adamawa the British government signed an agreement in 1893 with Germany which gave seven-eighths of Adamawa to Germany. The emir in Yola did not know about this agreement which all but gave Yola itself to Germany. The remaining one-eighth was one of the first areas to become British territory in the opening years of the present century.

R.N.C.-Sokoto Relations 1890-1899

As was pointed out earlier, the Niger Company sought in 1890 to enter into treaty relations with Sokoto and Gwandu. Whether or not treaties were actually signed, the fact is that the caliph found that the last decade of the nineteenth century was one of very much increased European activity in the caliphate. French activities, including their conquest of the Tukulor empire in 1889-95, the race between them and the British to Nikki in the struggle over Borgu, (1894) as well as renewed German efforts at digging themselves in at Gwandu (1895) had the effect of making Sokoto and Gwandu harden their attitude towards the Europeans. Nor was the European pressure all that bothered the caliph at this time. There was, in addition, the fear of Rabih Fadlallah who, having overrun Borno by the end of 1893, appeared set to fall on the lands of the caliphate. And, finally, Adeleye lists a large number of internal problems — the fierce war with Kebbi in 1891, the Marafar and Tukulor revolts, the activities of Hayat in Adamawa and of Jibril Gaini in the Bauchi–Gombe region, Kwassau's succession in Zaria in 1897, and the Galadima Ako revolt—which required the attention of the caliph. Adeleye concludes that 'although these problems, with the exception of the Jibril Gaini revolt, were successfully resolved, their existence meant that they, rather than the threat of foreign invasion, constituted the urgent problems facing the caliphate'. One may not necessarily agree with Adeleye's conclusion but the presence of such a long list of internal problems all of which had to be urgently resolved could only mean that the caliph could not devote all of his energies to studying the increasing European pressure with a view to finding an adequate answer.

By 1896 the policy of the R.N.C. was to seek to conciliate Sokoto by posing as the less dangerous of the European powers. This was in reality only a ruse designed to blind the caliph to the Company's determination to conquer Nupe and Ilorin. When in 1897 the Company's conquest of Nupe and Ilorin became a stark reality, the caliph reacted by refusing to recognize these conquests and closing the roads to all Europeans. The next year, however, the attitude of the caliph softened towards the Company in the face of increased French activity in the areas north of the caliphate. Consequently the caliph agreed to receive tribute from the Company which both Sokoto and Gwandu had persistently refused in previous years. Taking advantage of this softening of attitudes, the Company attempted to establish a military post near Sokoto and to persuade the caliph to accept a British resident in Sokoto. The caliph refused to fall for either the establishment of a military post or a residency. Thereafter he was declared an enemy of the British and he responded in September 1899 by breaking off all relations with the Royal Niger Company.

Thus, by 1899 relations between Northern Nigeria and the British had become extremely hostile and uneasy. The rulers of Nupe and Adamawa or Muri could hardly have been expected to be enamoured of the R.N.C. The caliph himself had witnessed the attempt on the part of the Company to dismember the caliphate by the Company's conquest of Nupe and Ilorin. Taking advantage of French pressure the Company had even attempted to station a resident in Sokoto and to over-awe the seat of the caliphate with a military base. So far the caliph and his emirs (including for this purpose even the Emir of Nupe) had succeeded in asserting or re-asserting their authority and retaining their sovereignty. It is clear, however, that this had only been possible as a result of the weakness of the Niger Company both in terms of its fighting machine and its available personnel. This weakness convinced the British government that in the international struggle for territories going on in this part of West Africa at the time, the Niger Company was no longer the best agency to ensure and safeguard British interests. Hence the abrogation of the charter of the Company at the end of 1899 and the decision to establish a British protectorate over Northern Nigeria. That decision meant that Britain was now ready to take a new forward policy in this area. That forward policy involved, as the events proved, the conquest of Northern Nigeria by Britain. And that is the subject of the next chapter.

BIBLIOGRAPHICAL NOTE

There are not too many sources to which one can turn for a study of relations between the Sokoto caliphate and European powers. For the student eager to have some knowledge of the impressions of Europeans who visited the caliphate, a number of works are available like W. Allen, and T. R. H. Thomson, *Narrative of the Expedition to the Niger River in 1841,* 2 vols, (London 1848), W. B. Backie, *Narrative of an Exploring Voyage up the Rivers Kwarra and Benue in 1854,* (London 1836); H. Barth, *Travels and Discoveries in North and Central Africa,* 5 Vols, (London 1857), H. Clapperton, *Journal of a Second Expedition into the Interior of Africa* (London 1829) and other accounts of travellers. There are also available two works by A. F. Mockler-Ferryman, *Up the Niger* (London 1892) and *British Nigeria,* (London 1902) who served as Secretary to Claude Macdonald's special commission appointed in 1889. The bulk of this chapter is based on R. A. Adeleye's *Power and Diplomacy in Northern Nigeria* (Longman 1971) whose account is based in turn on an extensive use of secondary and primary sources in English, French, and Arabic as evidenced in his footnotes. Adeleye's study looks at caliphate–European relations largely from the caliphate's point of view as a necessary corrective to works like H. A. S.

Johnston, *The Fulani Empire of Sokoto* (Oxford 1967) which look at the same subject from a European point of view. J. E. Flint's, *Sir George Goldie and the Making of Nigeria* (Oxford 1960) gives a detailed account of the activities of the Royal Niger Company along the Niger and Benue.

CHAPTER
V

The British Conquest
of Northern Nigeria

By the end of 1899 when the British government abrogated the charter of the Royal Niger Company, it had made up its mind that in order to prevent France and Germany occupying Northern Nigeria, that area must effectively become a British Protectorate. The events depicted in the last chapter show quite clearly that in their relations with Europeans, the rulers and peoples of Northern Nigeria were extremely jealous of their independence. It was thus fairly obvious that if the British aim was to be achieved the rulers of Northern Nigeria would have to be compelled to give up that independence which they had stoutly defended in the face of mounting European pressure. In other words, war between Britain and Northern Nigeria seemed the only logical outcome.

If anything further was needed to ensure war, it was, perhaps, the appointment of Captain Frederick Lugard as the High Commissioner of the Protectorate of Northern Nigeria which the British now decided to announce to the world. Lugard had spent the last few years of the nineteenth century in the service of the Royal Niger Company building up its forces in the expectation of war. This build-up was eloquent testimony to the fact that the Company had become fully convinced that the only way to secure its interests and impose its will was by force. If the Company knew this, then Lugard must have known it even better. In the service of another company, the Imperial British East African Company, just before he took service with the R.N.C., he had played a major role in bringing about the British occupation of Uganda. Despite the internal rivalries and other problems which made it possible for the British to play one African group against another in Uganda, Lugard had not been able to impose British rule without the use of force. Even Buganda, which was to become the greatest beneficiary from the colonial situation had cause to resist the British push by recourse to arms. If that was the situation in Uganda, it was even more likely to be the case in Northern Nigeria the bulk of whose population being Muslim, would naturally reject rule by infidels like the British. If, therefore, the British Colonial Office, which now proceeded to declare Northern Nigeria a British Protectorate, hoped that it might be possible to establish British rule there without war, Lugard, their newly appointed agent, knew from past experience that that was wishful thinking.

Lugard's first act in Northern Nigeria was the formal proclamation of the Protectorate on 1 January 1900 at a ceremony in Lokoja. In the presence of some 1,000 troops commanded by three colonels, Willcocks, Morland, and Lowry Cole, as well as his civilian staff, Lugard read aloud the proclamation and hoisted the Union Jack. The official proclamation ceremony may have been a necessary public act. Lugard knew better than to imagine that that act was in itself of any importance to the rulers and peoples of Northern Nigeria. To bring home to these rulers and peoples what he had done, Lugard sent an Arabic translation of the proclamation to the caliph and his emirs. The impression was given in this proclamation that all that had happened was that Lugard had taken over from the Royal Niger Company which had in the past ruled over the 'territories of the Niger'. However one interprets the 'territories of the Niger', there can be little doubt about the underlying falsity of the claim made by and in the proclamation. It will be clear from the last chapter that the R.N.C. had found itself unable to maintain any rule over the Niger–Benue basin. Even after the successful war against Nupe the Company was unable to establish any effective administration, and by 1898 the returned emir, Abubakar, had become as hostile to the R.N.C. as he had been before war broke out. Neither by the facts of the situation nor by the contents of existing treaties could Lugard legally claim to be the heir of the R.N.C. in terms of rulership over any group in Northern Nigeria. Nor was that all. To call on Muslims, as the proclamation did, to accept infidel rule was virtually to challenge them to war. 'By its contents alone, particularly the breach of treaties implicit in it', writes Adeleye, 'the proclamation could hardly have been better framed to arouse the fear and hostility of its recipients.' Lugard's first act in Northern Nigeria was thus tantamount to a declaration of war on the Muslim peoples of Northern Nigeria.

In the seemingly inevitable clash between the British and the peoples and rulers of Northern Nigeria, it was perhaps understandable that Lugard should have turned his attention first to Bida and Kontagora and then to Adamawa. Bida and Adamawa were emirates which had constantly and successfully prevented the attempt by the R.N.C. to subjugate them politically. If the British were to have anything like a firm footing in their newly proclaimed Protectorate, it was necessary to settle old scores first as it were. Besides, the geography of the situation dictated that the 'southern emirates' should fall first, and fall quickly, if the ultimate British push to Sokoto was not to be hampered by pre-occupation with these emirates. A look at Map 4 will make the point clearer.

Lugard was based at Lokoja. To the east lie what are shown on the map as Bassa, the Upper Benue, and Adamawa 'provinces': to the west, Kabba and Ilorin and to the immediate north of Kabba and Ilorin lie Bida and Kontagora. As is made clear in Part 2, Episode 4, Ilorin did not, after her military confrontation with the R.N.C. in 1897, put up any further active resistance against the British even if a great deal of rancour persisted for many years. Ilorin was thus one of the areas where the British administration first established an effective presence in the opening years of this century. Kabba was, at the time in question, in a vassalage relationship with Bida. British occupation of Kabba thus involved the conquest of Bida. To the east, Part 2, Episode 8 shows quite clearly that the first clash of arms between the British and the peoples of Northern Nigeria was not with an emirate but with the non-Muslim Tiv and related peoples who inhabited the area shown on the map as the Bassa and Upper Benue 'provinces'. Although the British occupation of the Tiv country cannot be said to have been effectively completed until about 1914, their presence there began to be established as early as 1900. Once the British presence began to be established in Tiv territory, it was logical to push on eastwards to Adamawa.

The Fall of Bida and Kontagora

It was clear to Lugard from the very beginning that Lokoja was not an ideal headquarters. It was far too much to the south. As

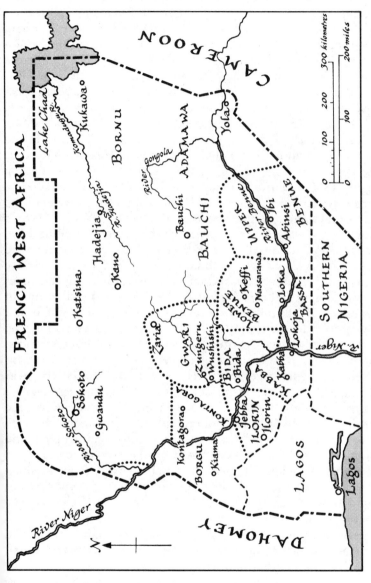

Map 4   Northern Nigeria 1901 : based on Lugard's map of this period

early as August 1900 he had informed the Colonial Office that he
intended to move his base from Lokoja to Wushishi on the River
Kaduna and on territory lying between Bida and Kontagora.
While one cannot quarrel with Lugard's desire to move his seat of
government further north, there remains the fact that he was
moving into an area not yet brought under effective British
control. The lessons of the past should have made it quite clear
that Bida would react violently against any violation of her
territory by the British. Yet without seeking to reach any accord
with Bida or Kontagora, Lugard actually established a military
base at Wushishi under the command of Major O'Neil. Bida and
Kontagora, who felt threatened by this move, reacted quickly to
this unprovoked aggression on the part of the British. Late in
August 1900 Lugard reported that Kontagora had attacked a
British party carrying mail to Wushishi. By November he
was complaining to the Colonial Office that Major O'Neil's
detachment was being constantly harassed by Bida and
Kontagora acting in alliance. Forces of these emirates, reported
Lugard, had closed the Kaduna waterway and fired on British
canoes and 'laid waste a vast tract of country, pillaging and burning the villages and carrying off slaves'. Lugard therefore sought
permission to take military action against Bida and Kontagora.

Anyone who looks closely at the logic of the situation can
hardly fail to see who the true aggressor was in the circumstances.
Not only had a British military base been established at Wushishi,
O.'Neil had been further instructed to establish a similar post near
the Niger (and therefore inside Bida or Kontagora territory) to
ensure the safety of British canoes. Surely it would have been
surprising if Bida and Kontagora did not react to such
provocation. Probably aware that his case against Bida and
Kontagora would be weak if based on the facts alone, Lugard
proceeded to embellish his despatches with reports whose
authenticity was open to serious questioning but of a type that was
bound to produce revulsion both in government circles and the
general British public.

From the very beginning of his case against Bida and
Kontagora Lugard took care to inform the Colonial Office and
the British public that both emirs were barbarous slave raiders:
'Large slave raiding bands have been out devastating the country
during the last month or two and in one direction [Kontagora], I
hear on good authority, destroyed 13 and [Bida] 8 towns. The

populous country to the north of the Niger is rapidly becoming as depopulated as the country to the south has become where, owing to the Nupe raids, a mere fraction of the people now remain.' The Emir of Kontagora, another report claimed, was 'a slave raider of the worst type, and has harried and desolated a great area of the country, and is said to have captured 8,000 slaves this season'. At a time when Britain was committed to the suppression of the slave trade, such reports produced the desired results (even though it is clear they were based on hearsay) and Lugard got the permission he sought to take action against Bida and Kontagora.

The military offensive against Kontagora began on 31 January 1901. The British force of 10 officers, 3 NCOs, and 322 rank and file was commanded by the Acting Commandant of the West African Frontier Force himself, Colonel Kemball. On the first day a British advance party was held up by Kontagora forces for seven hours. The next day the real battle took place with the entire British force in action. The Kontagora forces, estimated by the British at 5,000 and armed mostly with bows and arrows and dane guns fought bravely, but were no match for the 'volley firing' of the British. The issue was, in the circumstances, soon decided. The emir, Ibrahim, fled before the town fell and was to proceed to ravage Zaria territory (see Part 2, Episode 10), until he was captured and exiled by the British in March 1902. Many of his subjects fled with him. In fact, so deserted was Kontagora when it fell to the British that Lugard was unable for some time to find anyone with whom to consult with regard to the appointment of a new emir. The British showed their awareness of the basic hostility of Kontagora by leaving a garrison of 100 troops to hold the town.

While Kemball was leading British troops against Kontagora, Lugard was himself trying to get the Emir Abubakar of Bida to hold discussions with him on the terms on which he could remain emir. It will be recalled that Abubakar had fled when the R.N.C. forces defeated Bida in 1897 but had come back and resumed his throne in 1898. Abubakar now refused to hold any discussions with Lugard. On 19 February Lugard led 'a British force of 300 into Bida. The emir had fled by that time. Although Bida forces were massed just outside the town, they did not, in fact, give battle to Lugard. The makum, whom Goldie had appointed emir in 1897 but who had enthusiastically handed power back to Abubakar, now submitted to the British. Lugard was in some doubt as to the true loyalty of the makum but as he seemed the obvious candidate, he nevertheless appointed him emir on his own terms, that is, readiness to take his orders from the British political officers.

The Fall of Adamawa (Yola)

In the last chapter the point was made that in the last decade of the nineteenth century the ruler of Adamawa tried to safeguard his position by playing the French against the British. This game only lasted for a brief while before the R.N.C. succeeded in pushing out the French in 1893. Meanwhile, Britain and Germany entered into an agreement which made most of Adamawa German territory. However angry the Emir of Yola may have been about the bi-lateral partition of his domains by Britain and Germany, the opening years of the century saw him rather anxious to be on friendly terms with the British. This was because of the depredations of Rabih and his son Fadlallah after him (see Part 2, Episode 9) which threatened the security of Yola. The emir's friendly overtures were soon turned into hostility by Lugard's policy which was clearly not one of alliance but of political domination.

By July 1901 the emir was being accused in Lugard's official reports of hostility to the British as evidenced by his dealings with the Niger Company. Angered by Lugard's attitude, and making no distinction between Lugard's administration and the Niger Company which since 1 January 1900 remained as a trading concern only, the emir, Zubeir, 'forced the Niger Company to pull down their flag and instructed them to quit their station or be prepared to trade from a hulk'. By August the emir was reported to be harassing the British in his domain by refusing supplies to those passing through. William Wallace, one-time agent of the R.N.C. now turned Lugard's second-in-command, urged the Colonial Office for permission to deal militarily with Yola. The Colonial Office, inundated with charges against the emir of slave raiding and obstruction of trade gave the necessary permission. On 2 September 1901, the emir was offered Lugard's terms in a letter sent through a messenger. Adeleye records that the messenger 'was turned out of Yola without the letter he carried having been touched, let alone read'. There followed a military encounter which saw in action a British force of 13 officers, 7

NCOs, and 365 rank and file commanded by Colonel Morland. The British reported that the fighting which resulted was fierce, especially when their troops got to the emir's palace and mosque. Once again, however, the events showed that courage and a stubborn determination were no match for superior weaponry and drill. Yola fell on 3 September 1901. By the time military resistance collapsed, the emir had fled. On 8 September, Bobo Ahmadu, Zubeir's brother, was persuaded to accept the office of emir on Lugard's terms. That a garrison was left in Yola, however, was evidence again that the British did not think that military success meant anything like a full acceptance of the new order.

The Fall of Bauchi and Gombe

The nineteenth century ended with relations between Bauchi and Gombe and the R.N.C. being rather strained. The R.N.C. complained of the refusal of the emirs of these places to co-operate with company teams in search of army recruits. When Lugard sent the translation of his proclamation to these rulers, it failed to evoke any reply. Consequently, Wallace, who ac-companied the Borno expedition (see Part 2, Episode 9) as Political Officer, was asked to deal with both places. It was thus the same expedition that tackled Borno which dealt with the Bauchi and Gombe emirates.

For some reason it would appear that Bauchi did not imagine that the British meant to occupy her territory. Apparently a British reconnoitring party had turned back some 50 miles to Bauchi and this fact had given the Bauchi people the impression that the British had no immediate hostile intentions towards them. The emir must, therefore, have been shocked when he received a letter from Wallace intimating the British intention to establish their political presence in the emirate. With their defences unprepared, the Bauchi people had to reply to the effect that they would accept British terms. Yet Wallace decided that a show of force was necessary to make the right kind of impression. With the troops on the ready, therefore, Wallace marched unopposed into Bauchi town on 16 February 1902. The emir, Umar, escaped from Bauchi that night.

The escape of the emir was not unconnected with Wallace's terms for a peaceful occupation. Put off by Bauchi's apparent willingness to accept what appeared inevitable, Wallace had given as the condition for peaceful occupation the deposition of Umar for allegedly oppressing his people. On the evening of 16 February, the leading officials of Bauchi met with Wallace. They informed him that they had nothing against their emir but that since Wallace would not have him, they wished that the Chiroma (heir apparent) be put in his place. The helplessness of the Bauchi people could hardly be more pathetic. The emir must have escaped as soon as he knew the outcome of the meeting. Concrete proof that his people had nothing against him was shown in the very large number of people who fled the town with him. The British themselves reported that very many houses were completely deserted.

From the time of his escape till August Umar remained free and is, in the British records, presented as a scourge to Bauchi. The present writer does not know how often or determinedly Umar and his supporters attacked Bauchi or otherwise harassed the British. The latter would have us believe that he was a real pest. At any rate the British spread their dragnet for him and in August he was caught and taken to Bauchi. Then, in the comical manner typical of the British in their imperial expansion in Nigeria, the emir, who had been hounded out of his domains by the British, was charged with 'conduct likely to cause a breach of the peace', found guilty and sentenced to deportation from Bauchi for his natural life — another excellent example of British justice!

From Bauchi the expedition moved on to Gombe where it was welcomed because it was seen as an ally against Jibril Gaini, a freelance raider, who had terrorized the locality for some time. The British did no more here then, than to formally recognize the reigning emir.

Having occupied Bauchi town, the British created a Bauchi Province made up of the two Emirates of Bauchi and Gombe and a large number of other groups whom the British regarded as being under the Emir of Bauchi but who in reality had, until the coming of the British, maintained a sturdy independence from, and an attitude of hostility to, Bauchi. A few of these groups were chiefdoms, most were loosely organized, fragmented societies, who had not been conquered by the forces of the jihad and remained non-Muslim. Indeed, if, as the British sometimes put out, Bauchi engaged in raids, it was against these people, many of whom, as the British themselves were soon to discover, were extremely difficult to subjugate. Between 1902 and 1907 the British were engaged on and off in various expeditions against the Dass, Jengre, Shiri, Ningi, Sura, Ziggam, Wajah, Tangale, Angass, and other groups.

While the details of these expeditions make interesting reading, considerations of space prevent a recapitulation here. One major feature of these expeditions, however, requires to be mentioned: they were on the whole much more bloody than those mounted against any of the emirates. Connected with this is the wanton destruction of foodstuff, livestock, and dwellings. A few figures of casualties will prove the point: the Jengre lost 60 killed, the Ningi 50, the Sura 300, the Ziggam 175 and the Wajah-Tangale expedition accounted for 188 killed.

The figures have been culled from the reports of the British military officers. There is thus a possibility that the numbers involved were inflated in self-glorification and in the struggle for medals. It is important, however, to remember that the groups concerned had become accustomed to resisting militant Islam as the means of survival. For them, therefore, resistance had become a way of life, the necessary guarantee of their identity. Tucked away on the Bauchi Plateau, these groups would anyway have had next to no previous experience of Europeans before the invading British suddenly destroyed the rhythm of their lives. To them the British would have been seen as no more than yet another invading force that had to be resisted. However, there was a major difference between this new set of invaders and their traditional enemies. This was, of course, the much greater sophistication of British munitions of war. Unaware of the deadly efficiency of the maxim and other guns, the peoples of the Bauchi plateau took on the British hoping, no doubt, that their familiarity with their own difficult terrain would enable them to hold out against the enemy. Effective and long-range fire, however, turned the tables against them. The surprising thing is that though news of the success of British arms must have travelled quickly, group after group still offered armed resistance, vindicating the point already made that here were people accustomed to fighting for their independence.

While the British were dealing with the peoples of the Bauchi plateau, they were also pushing their way in, in other directions. Thus Zaria (Episode 10) fell to the British in 1902, followed by

Kano (Episode 11) and Sokoto (Episode 12) in 1903. The defeat of Caliph Attahiru at the second battle of Burmi can be said to have represented the final collapse of Northern Nigeria before superior British military might. Between 1903 and 1906 the British engaged in what can be described as a process of consolidation. In 1904 Lugard deposed the Emir of Katsina for persistently obstructing British rule. The process of consolidation naturally brought home to the people the full implications of what had happened in the years 1900-3. Although it is not intended to go into the details here, it is relevant in this context to indicate that in many places these years of consolidation witnessed a rather dogged spirit of passive resistance in most of the emirates. In Hadejia emirate and in Sokoto (the famous Satiru revolt) passive resistance blossomed into open revolt as the people took a last stand against government by aliens and infidels. As during the original clash of arms, so now, these revolts signified the peoples' deep attachment to their independence, their religion, and their way of life. It remains to draw attention to certain features of British conquest and Nigerian resistance, a task taken up in the concluding remarks at the end of this book.

BIBLIOGRAPHICAL NOTE

Until recently the major work which dealt with the British conquest of Northern Nigeria was Margery Perham's, *Lugard: The Years of Authority* (Collins 1960). In 1969 appeared I. F. Nicolson's, *The Administration of Nigeria 1900 to 1960* (Oxford) which called in question many of Perham's conclusions in connection with the conquest of Northern Nigeria. Two years later, in 1971, came Adeleye's work already cited. Other works which deal with the subject include C. Orr, *The Making of Northern Nigeria,* (first published in 1911 and reprinted by Frank Cass in 1965) and D. J. M. Muffet, *Concerning Brave Captains* (Andre Deutsch 1964). Johnston's work already cited also deals briefly with the subject.

Margery Perham's handling of the British conquest of Northern Nigeria reveals that she accepts, for the most part, the views of Lugard on the peoples of that region. Thus she accepts Lugard's pre-occupation with showing that the rulers of the caliphate were barbarous slave raiders who therefore deserved to be divested of authority; she accepts the moral basis for the dismantling of the Sokoto caliphate which Lugard so painstakingly builds up. In doing so, Perham fails to see the real issues from the point of view of the caliphate. Nicolson rejects the Perham view of events which is essentially Lugard's own view, and shows that Lugard was a dyed-in-the-wool imperialist enamoured of military methods. In rejecting Perham's views, however, Nicolson does not give us any detailed account of events in the emirates themselves—that is clearly not his concern in the book. In the absence of such details his castigation of Lugard and Perham while convincing to one who has seen the primary material is not always convincing to the general reader. Adeleye's work makes up the inadequacies of Nicolson's, for Adeleye is concerned not so much with Lugard as with the caliphate. This means that he looks at the British conquest from the caliphate point of view and so provides the kind of evidence necessary to call in question the conclusions of Lugard re-echoed by Perham. In fairness to Perham one has to say that she herself provides the evidence that calls her conclusion in doubt. In other words whatever her own conclusions, she does not attempt to hide or twist the evidence. In my judgement anyone specially interested in this subject should read all three authors as an exercise in comparing how historians handle their material. My own brief interpretation here and in the episodes from the caliphate is based not just on these authors but on my own familiarity with the primary sources and my work on Lugard and the conquest of Northern Nigeria forthcoming as part of a volume on *Lugard in Nigeria*. Most works on the subject tend to concentrate on the Muslim north. For some material on the non-Muslim north, in addition to Part 2, Episode 8 on the Tiv, see my article 'The British in Bauchi, 1901–1908: An Episode in the British Occupation and Control of Northern Nigeria, in *Journal of the Historical Society of Nigeria,* VII 2 (1974). Dr A. Y. Aliyu of the Institute of Administration, Ahmadu Bello University, Zaria, gives a different interpretation of the British conquest of Bauchi in his detailed unpublished thesis on Bauchi.

PART TWO

Episodes from the British
Conquest of Nigeria

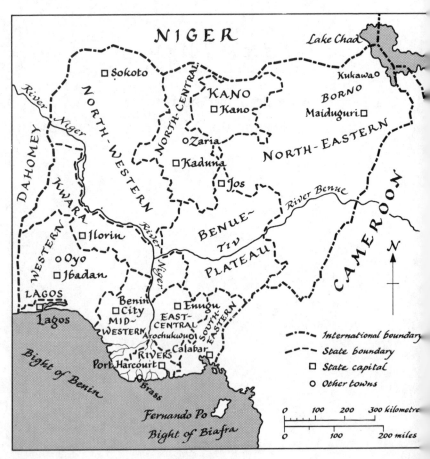

Map 5   Nigeria, showing the twelve states

A Note on the Arrangement

Although each episode in this part of the book is treated separately, the arrangement is designed to tell its own story.

British activity in Nigeria in the nineteenth century began with the suppression of the slave trade. That was used as the excuse for the bombardment of Lagos (Episode 1). Part of the attack on the slave trade was the establishment of missionaries. Missionary activity had quite a lot to do with the building up of British influence in Calabar (Episode 2). The occupation of Lagos was only the prelude to the occupation of the Yoruba hinterland, represented by Oyo (Episode 3). With the British in Lagos and the Yoruba hinterland, the question of Ilorin became a vexed one. Hence, although the Ilorin episode dragged on till 1903, it is here treated as Episode 4.

In the Niger Delta the encouragement of 'legitimate' trade was seen as the best answer to the slave trade. 'Legitimate' trade posed problems of organization and competition which produced the Royal Niger Company, the activities of which resulted in the sack of Brass (Episode 5). Once the coast was under control it was necessary to move into the hinterland. The famous Kingdom of Benin posed an interesting challenge and so had to be demolished (Episode 6). Then there were the Aro who were seen as the 'rulers' of the Igbo and Ibibio hinterland, a vast area which had to be brought under control (Episode 7).

Meanwhile the charter of the Royal Niger Company was abrogated at the end of 1899. Lugard had the responsibility of bringing 'Northern Nigeria' under control. That part of the country could be divided into three broad groups. There were the the non-Muslim peoples outside the Sokoto caliphate represented here by the Tiv. (Episode 8). There was Borno, a Muslim state outside the Sokoto caliphate (Episode 9). Then there was the Sokoto caliphate, which accounted for the greater part of Northern Nigeria. Within the caliphate, Kano was the strongest military power; Sokoto the seat of the caliph. So why not deal with a lesser emirate first? Hence Zaria (Episode 10) before Kano (Episode 11) and finally Sokoto itself (Episode 12). No doubt other arrangements are possible. I hope, however, that the one here adopted does make some sense.

EPISODE

1

The Fall of Lagos

In 1851 the British navy bombarded Lagos into submission. Ten years later (1861) Lagos became a British colony, the first part of what is now Nigeria to become part of the British Empire. Until very recently it used to be accepted that the reason why the British bombarded Lagos was that the Oba of Lagos engaged in the slave trade which Britain was determined to abolish. This explanation, which was given by those who were responsible for the bombardment, is not now regarded as satisfactory. The events which led to the bombardment of Lagos were much more complicated than that.

It is common knowledge that despite British efforts through legislation, treaties, and, in West Africa, the use of force, the overseas slave trade continued into the 1860s. This, as we know, was because other European and American countries did not always co-operate with Great Britain, since each nation naturally pursued its own economic interests. If Europeans and Americans refused to give up the slave trade, there was even less reason why the Africans should give up the trade. So long as there were Europeans and Americans ready to buy, the Africans were ready to sell. Lagos was no exception to this practice. Right up to the 1840s the Brazilians and Portuguese made enormous profits out of the slave trade in Lagos. The British were not allowed to take part in the slave trade or, indeed, in any other type of trade by the Oba of Lagos, Kosoko. Kosoko even refused to allow freed slaves returning from Sierra Leone to settle in Lagos. This was because he was afraid that such freed slaves might introduce new ideas into Lagos which would disturb the society there. The major reason why Lagos was bombarded was that Britain wanted a share, perhaps the lion's share, of the trade of Lagos from which she had been excluded for nearly 40 years. Lagos was a particularly important centre to occupy, because the British saw that whoever controlled Lagos could hope to control most of the trade of the Yoruba country which lies in the hinterland of Lagos.

In their bid to stop the slave trade the British at first concentrated on the high seas. They captured vessels carrying slaves and took these vessels to Sierra Leone where the slaves were freed. They even searched empty ships to ensure that they were not the type used for the slave trade. If they were, such ships were also seized. In other words, during the early period, the British concentrated on trying to stop other European and American traders from engaging in the slave trade. This went on till about 1840. But there was also the need to stop the Africans from engaging in the overseas slave trade. From about 1840 therefore, the British began to sign treaties with African rulers by which the latter agreed to give up the trade in slaves in return for some usually small compensation. These treaties gave Britain the opportunity of interfering in the affairs of African kingdoms on the grounds that the rulers had failed to observe the terms of the treaties. The British were anxious to sign such a treaty in Lagos in the 1840s. It was because they found that the then oba, Kosoko, was unwilling to sign such a treaty that they began to plot against him. It was lucky for the British that there already existed in Lagos a dispute between the different branches of the ruling house which made it possible for them to find a ruler who was prepared to sign the treaty in return for taking Kosoko's place on the throne.

The dispute started as early as 1811. When Ologun Kutere the then oba died, his eldest son, Esilogun was not, for reasons not very clear, chosen to succeed him. Rather the second son, was made oba — Adele I. Esilogun was naturally angry that he had been by-passed. So he and his supporters began to plot how to seize the throne from Adele I. In 1821 Esilogun and his party succeeded in driving Adele from the throne. Esilogun was supported in this coup by the Brazilians and Portuguese which may have meant that Esilogun was a very successful trader at the time. Adele fled to Badagri and from there appealed to the British for help. In 1825 a small British force tried to bombard Lagos but it was too small to have any real effect.

In 1829 Esilogun died and was succeeded by his son Idewu. Apparently Idewu was very unpopular and so Adele was able to return from Badagri and push him off the throne without too much opposition. This was about 1833. But Adele himself died within a year and was succeeded by his son, Oluwole. In 1841 Oluwole died suddenly after a gunpowder explosion. The death of Oluwole produced a succession crisis. Kosoko, Esilogun's second son was anxious to become oba; so was Akitoye, Adele's junior brother. The people of Lagos had not, however, forgotten that Kosoko's brother, Idewu, had been an unsuccessful ruler. So in the new situation, they preferred Akitoye who thus became oba. The defeated Kosoko and his supporters were forced to leave Lagos and go into exile.

The new oba was said to be 'a soft, charming, rather naive character'. His main concern seems to have been to re-establish peace and trade after the crisis. In the process of doing this, he allowed all the chiefs, including Kosoko, to return to Lagos against the advice of some of his closest friends. This was in May 1845. Kosoko showed his appreciation for being allowed to return to Lagos by plotting to overthrow Akitoye. Before long he was successful. He seized the throne and Akitoye was forced to flee from Lagos. He fled first to Abeokuta, then to Badagri. There, like his brother Adele I before him, he appealed to the British to help him recover his throne.

The Badagri to which Akitoye fled was a politically weak and divided town. It had been an important slave trading centre in the heyday of the slave trade. Then the Portuguese and the Dutch traders controlled the activities of the town and both chiefs and people could conveniently be divided into the pro-Portuguese and the pro-Dutch. No strong central authority developed. With the suppression of the overseas slave trade Badagri ceased to be important as a trade centre since it did not have much palm oil to offer. Its harbour was too open for the slave traders to want to use it at a time when the British navy was busy patrolling the West African coast.

But if Badagri was no longer a major trading centre, it was the kind of place which welcomed the British missionaries. Politically weak and divided it could not oppose the coming of the missionaries there in 1842. In fact, the missionaries were invited to Badagri by freed slaves from Sierra Leone who had settled there. Most of these freed slaves were Egba who were not welcome in Lagos and so had taken refuge in Badagri. By the time Akitoye fled to Badagri, the missionaries and the freed Egba slaves had become the most influential group in the town. They were themselves anxious to settle in Lagos because they saw it as a more prosperous trading centre than Badagri. Besides, the missionaries regarded Lagos as the gateway to the rest of

Yorubaland. From Lagos they could hope to spread the Christian faith and with it 'legitimate' trade to the rest of Yorubaland. But Lagos was at the time unfriendly both to the missionaries and to the freed slaves. It was against this background that the missionaries and freed slaves welcomed Akitoye and began to appeal to the British to help restore Akitoye to the throne of Lagos and so establish British power there through him. The arrival of Akitoye in Badagri, however, had the result of further dividing that town, for some chiefs supported him while others supported Kosoko.

Four years after they landed at Badagri, the missionaries moved into Abeokuta (1846). The political situation in Abeokuta was at the time not very stable. The Egba had suffered most from the troubles which followed the collapse of the old Oyo Empire. Over 150 Egba settlements were destroyed by Oyo, Ife, and Ijebu elements in the early years of the Yoruba wars of the nineteenth century. The town of Abeokuta was founded by refugee Egba who chose a site by the Olumo rock that they could easily defend in the troubled years of the Yoruba wars. But even in the new town of Abeokuta, the Egba were not safe.

Dahomey, which had by this time won her independence from Old Oyo, was seeking to control the palmbelt of the Egba and Egbado areas. Besides, the Egba needed to be properly armed to defend themselves against fellow Yoruba attackers. Arms and ammunition came from the coast. Between the Egba and the coast, however, stood the Ijebu, the enemies of the Egba. It was against this background that the Egba welcomed missionaries in 1846. In doing so the Egba were not necessarily eager to become Christians. In fact most of the ruling class did not embrace Christianity. The missionaries were white men who could use their positions to ensure that the Egba got the arms and ammunition they needed. For the Egba, therefore, the matter was more one of politics than of religion.

But we must return to the story of Lagos. The missionaries, once they had established themselves in Abeokuta, began to argue that Lagos was the port of Abeokuta; that the people of Abeokuta were anxious to develop trade in cotton and other products but that to do this Lagos had to be under proper control. Lagos, they claimed, was a notorious slave trading centre and Kosoko an even more notorious slave trader who had to be removed. On the other hand, they painted Akitoye as a lover of legitimate trade who would work with the missionaries at Badagri and Abeokuta to promote legitimate trade and spread civilization. The Egba naturally played up to the British: all they wanted was to have friends in Lagos who would make sure they got a regular supply of arms and ammunition. If the only way to get the arms and ammunition was to help the British remove Kosoko and install Akitoye, the Egba saw no reason to demur.

Meanwhile, in Badagri, Akitoye continued to team up with the missionaries who in their reports to Britain painted him as a man opposed to the slave trade. In Lagos, Kosoko was not taking all of this lying low. He made sure that no trade went to Badagri from Lagos and this produced results. The anti-Akitoye group in Badagri was angry that Akitoye's presence was leading to a loss of trade. They therefore attempted to expel Akitoye from their town. But the missionaries got supplies of arms and ammunition and succeeded in expelling the anti-Akitoye chiefs from the town. After this the missionary party requested the British government to restore Akitoye to the Lagos throne by force.

It was not easy to get the British to act. The government knew that Kosoko was being backed by the Portuguese who were helping him fortify Lagos. To take Lagos by force would therefore need a major and costly expedition. Besides, Britain had no legal grounds for attacking Lagos. Kosoko had very wisely refused to sign an anti-slave trade treaty with Britain. Had he done this, it would have been easy to accuse him of breaking the treaty and use that as the excuse for attacking him. Also, Kosoko had kept out all British traders from Lagos. Britain could not therefore interfere in Lagos on the grounds that she was protecting the lives and property of her subjects there. As if all this was not enough to make Britain cautious, the naval commander in West Africa, Commodore Bruce, advised the government to be careful. In this view Akitoye was not likely to make a very able ruler and if the British put him on the throne by force, they would have to maintain him there by force as well.

As often happens when the British government is not sure about what to do, they asked one of their servants to report on the situation. In 1849 John Beecroft was appointed British Consul for the Bights of Benin and Biafra. He was now asked to visit Badagri and Abeokuta as well as to report on the Lagos situation. Unlike Commodore Bruce, who advised Britain to be cautious, Beecroft accepted the views of the missionaries. Even before he went on his visits, therefore, he had already made up his mind what he would do. When he visited Badagri, Beecroft decided that Akitoye was in danger. So he took Akitoye with him to his base in Fernando Po. The idea was that once Akitoye was with him in Fernando Po, it would be difficult for the British government not to take the next step of reinstating him on the throne of Lagos.

However, Beecroft's action in removing Akitoye from Badagri created complications. The pro-Akitoye group suddenly found themselves exposed to ridicule by the removal of Akitoye. The pro-Kosoko (anti-Akitoye) group was emboldened by the new situation. The resulting tension led to civil war in Badagri. The British navy had to rush arms and ammunition to the missionaries to prevent the pro-Kosoko group from winning the day. The British were getting more and more deeply involved in the Kosoko-Akitoye affair.

Then Beecroft visited Abeokuta. The missionaries had arranged everything before the visit. The Egba chiefs signed a treaty by which they agreed to give up the slave trade. The idea behind getting the Egba to sign the treaty was to make them appear more enlightened than Kosoko in Lagos. But at the time the Egba were not thinking either of Kosoko or of the British. They were worrying about themselves. Dahomey was planning an attack in 1850-1. The Egba wanted the help of the British against Dahomey. Hence they signed the treaty. And indeed, the British did send warships to Dahomey to warn the king that Dahomey must not attack Abeokuta as there were British subjects there, thus preventing the attack of 1850-1. So if Beecroft and the missionaries thought they were using the Egba for their own purposes, the Egba were making similar use of the British.

Beecroft now saw himself in a very strong position. Akitoye was in his custody and the Egba had signed an anti-slave-trade treaty. It was time Kosoko was made to sign a similar treaty. In November 1851 Beecroft, with four British warships in attendance, visited Lagos to persuade Kosoko to sign an anti-slave-trade treaty. Kosoko refused to accept the treaty. Beecroft then decided that he would use force. He ordered the ships to fire, which they did, but Kosoko was ready for this, and he and his men fired back. The British party was forced to withdraw with the loss of two officers killed and sixteen wounded. British arms had been disgraced by an African ruler.

The one thing that the Europeans hated was defeat by an African force. The events of November 1851 was therefore seen as a major disgrace. Beecroft had acted without authority and was later blamed for this. Commodore Bruce had warned the British government that she really had nothing against Kosoko. Yet this disgrace of British arms had to be wiped out: British prestige was at stake. Even Commodore Bruce was now ready to go into action against Kosoko, just to restore the prestige of Britain.

So it was that on Christmas Eve 1851 a British naval force steamed into Lagos. On Boxing Day the bombardment of Lagos began and went on for the whole day. Kosoko met shot with shot and did not surrender as was expected. On 27 December the fighting continued. Unfortunately for Kosoko, a rocket landed in the royal arsenal on that day, blowing up the oba's store of arms and ammunition and this led to great confusion. The oba could not hope to carry on fighting without arms and ammunition and so he fled with his closest supporters. Akitoye was then set up on the throne and on New Year's Day 1852, he signed an anti-slave-trade treaty. In 1861, ten years after the attack, Lagos became a British colony.

The fact that Akitoye signed an anti-slave-trade treaty in 1852 did not in itself mean that he handed over control of affairs to the British. As Commodore Bruce had said, Akitoye was, in fact, a weak ruler. He had regained the throne through British help. He needed that help to run the affairs of Lagos. But his interests and those of the British were not necessarily the same. Soon after 1852, European traders began to flock into Lagos. So did missionaries and freed slaves from Sierra Leone, Brazil, Cuba, and so on. These newcomers had to have land on which to settle. They got this land from the oba, through the British consul, for very little or no payment.

In 1853 Akitoye died and was succeeded by his son, Dosonmu. In that same year the British appointed a separate consul for Lagos. This consul gradually usurped the powers of the oba in Lagos. Especially was this the case in matters of trade and justice. It was the consul who regulated the internal and external trade of Lagos; he began to settle disputes between traders in his own court. By 1860, the British were in fact, if not in law, rulers of Lagos. In 1861 power was formally handed over to the British when Dosunmu was forced to sign a treaty by which he ceded Lagos to the British.

It is important to stress that Dosunmu was *forced* to sign the treaty. The British decision to occupy Lagos formally was taken in view of increasing British activity on the Niger as from about 1854. From that time on there was the hope that there could be developed an overland route from Lagos to the Niger through the Yoruba country. If this route was developed, Lagos would be the centre from which the goods would be exported. Hence Lagos was important and had to be under British control. This was the only way to ensure that British trade would be paramount in Lagos.

If the British thus saw clearly the value of Lagos, Dosunmu must also have seen his own interests. In fact, he was unwilling to sign the treaty. But there was a British man-of-war within shooting distance of the palace. When Dosunmu was first asked to sign the treaty, he asked for time to consult his chiefs. Two days later (1 August 1861), the oba and the chiefs refused to sign the treaty. They were then given three days to change their minds or face bombardment. Meanwhile, British troops occupied key positions in the town of Lagos. On 5 August the oba was again asked if he would sign the treaty. This time he had to say yes, because he knew that to refuse would mean that his people would be bombarded. It was thus it came about that on 6 August Lagos was ceded to the British.

From what has been said, it is quite clear that Lagos was not bombarded in 1851 because Kosoko was a notorious slave trader, nor did the British take over full powers in 1861 because Dosunmu, the oba, had revived the slave trade. The real issue was British determination to control the trade of Lagos and the Yoruba hinterland. It was fortunate for the British that the internal politics of Lagos played into their hands by providing two factions which they could play against each other. It is clear that Akitoye in appealing to the British for help was more interested in regaining his throne than in selling Lagos to the British. In fact, regaining the Lagos throne and selling Lagos to the British were irreconcilable. Yet by regaining the throne through British aid, he found himself unable to be a real oba, with full powers. Here was another example of the problems which African rulers faced in the nineteenth century. Those like Kosoko who tried to be independent were invariably bombarded into submission. Those who tried to support the Europeans soon found that the Europeans gradually took power from them. In other words the African rulers lost whichever way they chose to go. In the final analysis it was an age in which might was right.

BIBLIOGRAPHICAL NOTE

A number of works written by non-Nigerians deal with the British occupation of Lagos. These include W. N. M. Geary (1927), *Nigeria Under British Rule*; A. C. Burns (1929), *History of Nigeria*, A. N. Cook (1943), *British Enterprise in Nigeria*; J. Coleman (1958), *Nigeria: Background to Nationalism*. All of these works take the view that the British occupied Lagos as a result of Kosoko's refusal to give up the trade in slaves. In a very simply written and well argued article, 'The British Occupation of Lagos 1851-1861: A Critical Review', *Nigeria Magazine*, 169 (August 1961), J. F. Ade Ajayi takes issues with these authors and shows very convincingly that the slave trade issue was no more than part of a much more complex situation. I have taken very much after the Ajayi interpretation. Ajayi's *Christian Missions* and Ayandele's *Missionary Impact* provide useful analysis of the situations in Badagri and Abeokuta which affected the Lagos episode, so also does C. W. Newbury (1961), *The Western Slave Coast and Its Rulers*.

EPISODE
2

The Fall of Calabar

The story of the fall of Calabar to the British is in some ways peculiar and different from that of other parts of Nigeria. This peculiarity derives from internal developments in Efik society during the nineteenth century which helped to determine Efik reaction to the British—traders, missionaries, and ultimately consul.

As is well known, Calabar had traded with Europeans for centuries before the nineteenth. The commodity of trade was, of course, slaves. However, by the last quarter of the eighteenth century the slave trade in Calabar was already in decline. This was largely because Bonny was a more successful rival for this trade. When, therefore, the British decided early in the nineteenth century to suppress the overseas slave trade in Nigeria as in other parts of West Africa, Calabar was one area that did not hold out for long against the British. In fact, but for the efforts of the French in the late 1830s and early 1840s to revive the slave trade in Calabar, it can be said that the Efik had given up the overseas slave trade by 1830.

While the slave trade lasted, the Efik nobility had done very well for themselves since only the heads of the various lineages in the Efik towns controlled the trade in slaves. One should say at this point that the Efik are, in reality, a fragmented society broken into various towns. Each town was made up of a number of lineages. While the head of each lineage ordered the affairs of that particular lineage there was usually also a headman of the town who represented its founding ancestors. It was these headmen who began to be styled kings by the Europeans in the nineteenth century. Of great importance in Efik social life was the Ekpe Society, which was originally open only to freeborn Efik. Membership involved the payment of a fee and the performance of certain ceremonies. The Ekpe Society was divided into various grades. The highest title within the Society was the Eyamba title which would appear to have been a monopoly of Duke Town. Because of its rituals and its corporate nature, Ekpe was a most influential force amongst the Efik. In fact, it can be said that each Efik town was governed by the Ekpe. All the kings belonged to it and most effective sanction was the Ekpe sanction. If a king 'blew Ekpe'—that is, if in the name of Ekpe he decreed that certain things were not to be done, none dared go against the decree. Efik nobles, therefore, were invariably members of Ekpe which assumed the role of a ruling caste.

Efik society was very lineage conscious. Birth was thus an important factor in determining the social importance of any Efik. In the days of the slave trade it was possible to maintain this birth consciousness, and membership of the Efik house was usually limited to freeborns. Slaves who traded for the house were not usually fully absorbed. However, the new trade in palm oil radically altered this situation in a number of ways. One, in order to more effectively prosecute the trade in slaves, the Efik established palm oil plantations in the hinterland—in the Akpabuyo and Odukpani areas. To work these plantations slaves were stationed in the hinterland. These became known as plantation slaves. While the Efik stopped selling slaves to Europeans, they, like other Nigerian groups, continued to buy slaves to use locally. In addition to plantation slaves, there were those who could be described as domestic or town slaves—those who stayed in the towns and organized the trade of their masters. So there arose two types of slave within Efik society, the town slaves being much better off than the plantation slaves. This was one new source of tension.

Two, as the palm oil trade developed, so the town slaves began to play a major role in it. Because they were usually bought from the hinterland where the oil was produced, they were extremely useful in the organization of the palm oil trade. At first slaves traded exclusively for their masters. Later on, when they had done a great deal to enhance the wealth of their masters, they were allowed to trade for themselves as well as continuing to trade for their masters. Gradually there arose a class of wealthy slaves in Efik society who even bought other slaves for themselves. They were given land on which to farm in return for an annual payment to their masters. Over the years there were more wealthy slaves in Efik houses than free members. Yet they were theoretically debarred from holding political positions such as the headship of houses. The question which arose was whether this situation could last. What in fact happened was that Efik society responded to the pressure of the times. Slaves began to become advisers to kings and where there were no fit freeborns, slaves even rose to become heads of houses. Sheer force of wealth and merit thus began to create a social revolution. But all revolutions create a discontented group. The poor free could hardly have enjoyed the situation in which former slaves now sat in king's councils. Another area of tension was created.

Three, the slaves who thus rose on the social ladder were the town slaves. The plantation slaves without whose labours the palm oil trade could hardly flourish were kept down. It was from among them that sacrificial victims were selected when a king or some other notable died. The injustice of the situation produced the Order of Bloodmen, made up originally of the plantation slaves bound by an oath of blood to defend themselves against the oppression of the nobility. In particular, they strove to prevent the practice whereby their members were sacrificed on the death of important personalities. So yet another area of tension developed.

Hence, although Calabar was doing well in trade from the 1820s to the 1850s, Efik society was undergoing great internal stress. To the areas of tension already indicated we can now add the rivalry for trade in palm oil which developed between the main groups. Two of these groups are particularly important for our purpose — Duke Town and Creek Town. In the 1840s these two groups were ruled by Kings Eyamba V and Eyo Honesty II respectively. Each of these rulers was anxious to attract as much trade to his town as possible. Great rivalry developed between the two. This rivalry was, however, not played out just within Efik society. It was played out in a situation which included European (mostly British) traders, missionaries, especially Hope Waddel's Presbyterian mission and, from 1849, British consuls. The fall of Calabar to the British can thus only be fully studied against the background of the internal situation among the Efik principalities.

As is well known, missionaries arrived in Calabar in 1846. Both Eyamba V and Eyo II were anxious to welcome the missionaries. Duke Town being much nearer the coast, Eyamba very much hoped that the missionaries would make Duke Town the centre of their activities to the exclusion of Creek Town. For him as for Eyo II the important thing was not Christianity. He hoped that missionaries would help increase his trade. They would teach his people the white man's book and so enable them to develop their commerce even more. Eyamba was so eager to get the missionaries to settle in his town that he used Ekpe sanctions in getting a mission house built.

Eyamba had good reason to seek the support of missionaries as well as the British traders. Apart from the natural desire to increase his trade, there was the instability of the politics of Duke Town. He did not become king without opposition, especially from the Archibong lineage. Consequently, once enthroned, he killed many who were seen as potential enemies. This, of course, merely created other enemies for him. In order to make himself acceptable, he lived luxuriously and became over-generous, distributing presents freely to ensure support. The consequence of this was that he over-reached himself and did not have the means to prosecute his trade satisfactorily. In an age when trade depended on the trust system it was folly to lavish one's wealth the way Eyamba did, for this meant that he was short of goods to advance to the oil producers and so could not always meet his commitments to the European supercargoes. In 1846 he suffered the humiliation of being arrested and put in chains on a British boat because he was in debt. Little wonder that he felt called upon to support the missionaries in the hope that they would help increase his trade with the Europeans.

Eyo II was equally anxious to welcome the missionaries for the same reason of expanding trade. Both he and Eyamba were anxious not to depend on palm oil alone. They pressed the missionaries to establish in their country so as to teach them how to grow coffee and cotton. They even hoped that the missionaries and the traders would bring in equipment to enable them to manufacture sugar from the cane which abounded in their country. Eyo, however, was free from the internal political problems which faced Eyamba and was an even more successful trader who paid his debts promptly. Consequently he was able to deal on a more independent line with the missionaries. He encouraged them; he interpreted for them at their services and yet remained unconverted till his life's end. His interest in Hope Waddel and his team was economic not spiritual.

If Eyamba and Eyo had their own ideas as to what they wanted from the missionaries, the latter also had their own ideas as to what aspects of Efik customs they would not accept. But before we discuss the social reforms which the missionaries brought, we have to introduce the British consul, John Beecroft. Strange as it may seem, King Eyo II actually approached the British about the appointment of a consul. King Eyo had dealt with British traders for so long that he was frightened when the French began to trade actively in Calabar in the late 1830s and early 1840s. Not only were the French seeking to trade in slaves, they talked about hoisting a French flag. King Eyo preferred the British and requested them to appoint a consul. At the same time Hope Waddel was also pressing the British Government to establish its control over Calabar. The appointment of John Beecroft in 1849, for other and weightier reasons than just the Calabar situation, pleased Eyo very much. For one thing, the French could now be kept in their proper place. For another, Beecroft was a trader of long standing, well known to the Efik rulers and traders.

With the appointment of Beecroft there were now three British forces operating — missionaries, traders, and the consul. The traders and the consul were anxious that trade should flourish. The missionaries were also interested that trade should flourish but in addition had the task of converting souls and reforming Efik society. All three groups desired peace. Yet there were factors in Efik society which threatened peace. Like human sacrifice. In 1850 when some notables died slaves were sacrificed. In 1852 on the death of King Archibong the Order of Bloodmen poured into Duke Town and dared anyone to sacrifice their members. By that date, however, traders, missionaries, and consul had got King Eyo and King Archibong to sign an agreement banning human sacrifice and the killing of twins. Beecroft made it clear that if either ruler found it difficult to enforce the agreement he would bring a gunboat into Calabar and ensure that the agreement was kept. Calabar was already beginning to feel the British pressure. The agreement of 1850 did not immediately put an end to human sacrifice in Calabar but it was the beginning of the end for that and other customs disapproved of by the British.

While the consul and the traders thus helped the missionaries in their work, the traders sought to ensure their own interests by attempting to penetrate into the Calabar hinterland. Here, however, both Eyo II and Eyamba, before he died in 1847, combined to prevent the traders from destroying their middleman position. Not even Beecroft was allowed to go beyond a certain point in the hinterland. When he tried to bluff his way through he was sent back by armed men of both rulers. So the sovereignty of these rulers was not yet completely lost.

Even so, however, British influence developed rather strongly in Duke Town. Eyamba died in 1847. After a two years' interregnum during which the usual lineage rivalries further weakened Duke Town, Archibong I was installed as king. His installation was, however, made possible by the missionaries, traders, and the consul. He was told in clear terms that he would be supported only as long as he remained friendly to the British. In 1852, Archibong I died. Once again the consul intervened and secured the election of Duke Ephraim as king. These events reveal how utterly dependent Duke Town had become on the British. The missionaries took advantage of the internal weakness in Duke Town. In 1852, Edgerley, one of the missionaries, went into the Ekpe shrine and broke the sacred drum. Two years later the same missionary broke an egg on the temple of the Efik god of Anansa. That he got away with both incidents reveals that Duke Town was so internally weak that it could no longer ensure that its rights were respected by the British.

At this time Beecroft was not prepared to deal the death blow to the ruling class. When the Bloodmen revolted in 1851 Beecroft presided over the peace agreement. While he warned that no Bloodman must be sacrificed, he made it quite clear to the Bloodmen that he respected the rights of masters of slaves so long as such masters did not sacrifice their slaves. He was thus anxious to maintain the *status quo*. It is, of course, possible to argue that by taking that stand, Beecroft ensured that one area of tension remained in Efik society over which he could always preside as umpire.

Growing British power in Calabar was further demonstrated when Old Town was bombarded in 1855. The town was razed to the ground and its rebuilding was forbidden by the consul. The crime committed by Old Town was that some slaves had been sacrificed. Yet Old Town had not signed any agreement by which it had agreed to give up human sacrifice, that agreement having been signed only by Creek Town and Duke Town. The British government in London had to intervene and permit the rebuilding of the town on condition that Old Town signed an agreement agreeing to give up human sacrifice, twin killing, and trial by ordeal. Old Town had little alternative but to sign.

In 1856 the missionaries in Duke Town declared the independence of the Mission House which had become a refuge for all those fleeing from the legitimate authority of the Efik rulers. So angry was King Duke Ephraim that he 'blew Ekpe' against the mission house. The missionaries were surprised that after eight years of their presence the Efik responded to their ruler. No one came near the mission house. No one attended church. The consul had to intervene and force the king to lift the ban. The event is significant in showing that increasing British pressure had not yet succeeded in killing the customs of the Efik, as indeed it was never to succeed in doing. Meanwhile, in Creek Town, King Eyo II held his own till his death in 1858, bowing to the British when it suited him, maintaining his ground when he realized that fundamental issues were involved.

It was a pity that King Eyo II died at the time he did for the late 1850s and 1860s were very difficult times for the Efik. The situation which arose can be briefly described. Newcomers came into the trade of the area. These were the Sierra Leonians and the independent British traders who were enabled to do profitable trade by the introduction of a regular mail service by the African Steamship Company pioneered by the famous Macgregor Laird. The long established British traders responded by wanting to drive the newcomers off the trade. In the trust system they had a weapon which they could use. They argued that until Efik traders had met all their obligations to them, they could not supply oil to either the Sierra Leonians or the independent traders. The Efik traders were only too glad that another group of traders had arrived with whom they could do business. The late 1850s and 1860s were thus years of considerable insecurity in Calabar. The Efik could not win because the consuls backed up the supercargoes (British traders) and forced the Efik rulers to sign one-sided trade agreements which, while securing the trade of the British provided no security for the Efik (see Part I p. 28). All the Efik could do was to resort to a certain amount of lawlessness—attacking British cask houses on shore in their frustration.

At the same time as the above was happening, the political authority of the Efik rulers was being further undermined by the setting up of the Courty of Equity in 1856. This mixed court was supposed to settle disputes between the British trader and the Efik. Yet although there were quite a number of Efik on the court, only the Kings of Duke Town and Creek Town had voting rights, while every European on the court had a vote. The Efik, hopelessly outnumbered when it came to voting, could hardly hope to get any justice from such a tribunal. The trend of events was very clear.

The next development was the rise of large firms like the West African Company (1864), Miller Brothers (1868), and the United Africa Company (1879), to mention only a few. These companies arose because prices of oil had fallen in Britain while the Efik and other Nigerian traders refused to reduce their own prices. Besides, since the late 1850s the competition for trade in the Niger Delta and Calabar had become very keen. By the seventies it had become quite cut-throat. Only large organizations could cope with these new developments. Calabar was the centre of activity of these big companies largely because the trade of the Cameroons was passing through Calabar and so the companies hoped to cash in on that. Also it was hoped that the trade of the Calabar hinterland itself woud increase considerably. Needless to say, the rise of these big firms merely made things even more difficult for the Efik trader.

Internal developments in Calabar in the 1870s and 1880s were not such as could preserve Efik independence in the face of what was soon to become the new European imperialism. Duke Town continued to be unstable. King Archibong II, who ruled from 1858 until 1872, ensured that he was a friend of the British. After his coronation he wrote asking Great Britain to recognize him so that he could be paid 'comey' by British merchants. He went out of his way to court the friendship of the missionaries. His successor, Archibong III, was a blind ruler who fell out with the British because his physical handicap prevented him from going on board British ships while British traders regarded it as *infra dig* to visit him in his 'palace'. As if that was not enough, the Henshaw lineage of Duke Town rebelled and attempted to secede. It required the aid of the British to foil the secession. But even so, when Archibong III died in 1879, the Henshaw lineage contested the kingship. The acting British consul, Easton, intervened and installed Duke Ephraim Eyamba IX (usually just King Duke IX) as king on 17 April 1880. The British government in London refused to accept Easton's action because petitions poured in from various chiefs protesting against Easton's choice. That Easton was able to do what he did, and that the British government could order its consul to annul Easton's choice and install another King of Duke Town shows to what level the internal affairs of that town had degenerated.

By 1880 events in the Oil Rivers were moving swiftly to the imposition of a British Protectorate. Hewet urged the British government to annex Calabar outright in 1880. But that the government refused to do. In 1884–5 came the spate of treaty making by Hewett from the Cameroons to the Forcados River, designed to keep the French and Germans out of this zone. Calabar had to sign one of these protectorate treaties. From all that has been said above one would expect that the British would have no trouble at all in getting Calabar to sign the treaty. Creek Town, which under Eyo II had managed to balance her interests against those of the British was, in 1885, eager for annexation by Britain. Duke Town, which had been the weaker for most of the century was not at all eager to sign the treaty and was thoroughly opposed to annexation. In fact, when the Efik eventually signed the treaty, they rejected Article VI which provided for free trade just as Bonny, Brass, and the Itsekiri had done. To sign that was to sign their economic death warrant. So even the Efik, harassed by the British for over half a century, put up resistance at this point.

As is well known, the British proclaimed a Protectorate over the Oil Rivers in 1885. Little effective British control was established for the next four years. In 1889 the Macdonald Commission was sent out to report on how best to rule the Oil Rivers. Once again Creek Town was more eager than Duke Town which asked to be left alone to rule itself. Macdonald was quick to tell Duke Town that that was not one of the choices he was offering! He was offering a Protectorate or rule by the Royal Niger Company. The Efik chose a Protectorate. When Macdonald was later appointed commissioner and consul-general of what was to become the Niger Coast Protectorate, he made Calabar his headquarters — perhaps deservedly, for British influence in Calabar had been closer, more intense, than elsewhere in Southern Nigeria. Calabar had at last finally fallen to the British.

BIBLIOGRAPHICAL NOTE

The main sources to turn to for this episode are Ajayi's *Christian Missions*, Ayandele's *Missionary Impact*, K. K. Nair's *Politics and Society in South Eastern Nigeria*, and A. J. H. Latham's *Old Calabar 1600-1891*. K. O. Dike's *Trade and Politics* also has some useful background information.

EPISODE
3

The Fall of Oyo

In the first part of this book quite a bit has been said about events in Yorubaland in the nineteenth century which gave the background to the British conquest of Yorubaland and which explain the differing reactions of various Yoruba groups to the British push. In that context the role of Oyo in the turbulent history of Yorubaland was outlined. It is not intended here to go over the ground again, but the reader will do well to refresh his memory if he is to understand the events about to be described below.

It will be recalled that the Yoruba wars were brought to an end by the peace of 1886, the terms of which have already been discussed. Alafin Adeyemi I of Oyo was one of those who signed the treaty of 1886. Although Oyo was not directly involved in the war which raged between Ibadan and the Ekitiparapo, the alafin had his own reasons for wanting peace to be concluded between the warring parties. As from 1881 Dahomey began to attack the Upper Ogun region of the alafin's territories. These were the areas which Kurunmi had defended in the days of Ijaye. The alafin could not raise an army that would withstand Dahomey. He would have liked Ibadan to fight his wars for him, but Ibadan was busy seeking her own empire in the Ijesa and Ekiti country. That was not all. The Ilorin had spread their influence over Iseyin, part of the alafin's domain, and the alafin was anxious that the Ilorin be driven from Iseyin. Then there was Ibadan which had become so powerful that she hardly respected the alafin. It was against this kind of background that Adeyemi I who became alafin in 1875 thought that the best thing to do was to ask the missionaries to come into his territories.

In asking for missionaries, Adeyemi was not actually saying that he preferred Christianity to the religion of his fathers. In fact, he did not see the matter as religious at all; he saw it as political. The Egba had welcomed missionaries to their land since 1846. And the missionaries had helped the Egba against their chief enemy, Dahomey, by providing the former with arms and ammunition and even teaching the Egba how to use these weapons of war more effectively. Adeyemi hoped that the missionaries would do the same thing for him — help drive Dahomey from the Upper Ogun area, remove the Ilorin from Iseyin and help keep Ibadan under control. What Adeyemi did not foresee was that the missionaries, by seeking to bring him closer to the British authorities in Lagos, would prepare the way for the fall of Oyo as an independent kingdom.

In 1881, Abraham Fasina, a C.M.S. agent in Iseyin, asked the alafin to approach the British government in Lagos to help bring about peace in Yorubaland. This was shortly after Dahomey had attacked the alafin's territory. The alafin was, in the circumstances, only too glad to do so. He got Revd D. O. Olubi and Mr (later Revd) Samuel Johnson to write a letter for him to the Lagos government inviting the British to help negotiate peace between Ibadan and the Ekitiparapo. At that time the British were not ready to act. Failure in 1881 did not, however, stop the missionaries from putting pressure on the alafin and other Yoruba rulers to ask the British in Lagos to intervene and bring about peace. That peace was ultimately signed in 1886. The alafin thus played a full part in getting the British to act.

It has already been pointed out that some of the clauses of the 1886 treaty were against the interests of the Yoruba groups concerned, even though the latter may not have known it at the time. For one thing, those who signed the treaty had agreed that there should be no more war in Yorubaland. Yet the alafin had hoped, in inviting missionaries to his territory, that the missionaries would help him in his wars against his enemies — Dahomey and Ilorin. In that regard, at any rate, his hopes could not be realized. What is more, in the years after 1886 the British gradually began to push their influence and power into Yorubaland — a Yorubaland that was, after nearly a century of unrest, not really in a position to resist this British push. The alafin himself was one of those who felt this push soon after 1886.

Only two years after the 1886 Treaty, Governor Moloney of Lagos persuaded the alafin to sign a treaty with him. By this treaty the alafin was made to agree that he would not give away any part of his domain or enter into any agreement with any power without the permission of the Governor of Lagos. Five years later, in 1893, another Governor of Lagos made the alafin sign yet another treaty by which the alafin consented that the Governor of Lagos was, from then on, to handle any disputes which arose in Yorubaland between any British subject on the one hand and any Yoruba subject on the other. As in 1888 it was again laid down that the alafin was not to give away any part of his territory or enter into any agreement with any other foreign power except with the agreement of the Governor of Lagos.

One may wonder whether the alafin knew what he was doing when he signed these treaties. This question has been raised by many African historians. It is quite clear that the alafin, like a number of other African rulers, did not always fully understand the meaning of the treaties. This was because the treaties were written in English and had to be interpreted. The British who drew up the treaties did not fully understand Yoruba; so they could not be sure that their interpreter translated the treaties accurately. The interpreter for his part, even if he understood the English of the treaties perfectly — and very few did — would be careful not to tell the ruler such things as were bound to annoy him and make him refuse to sign the treaty. So, everything considered, it is unlikely that, where the African ruler did not understand any English, and where the treaty was drawn up in that language only, the African rulers concerned understood the treaties they signed with European powers.

The other question that has to be asked is why did the alafin sign any treaties at all? The answer is fairly easy to find. The missionaries whom he had invited to Oyo were anxious that the alafin should be the friend of the British, for the British were seen by the missionaries as agents of 'civilization' and progress. The alafin himself must have thought he would get some benefits from friendship with the British. One thing is certain. Whatever treaties the alafin signed, he did not believe that his powers as alafin — as the ruler of his people — were in any way reduced. He certainly did not act as if they were. The other explanation for the alafin signing the treaties, especially that of 1893, was that the British had the power — the military power — to force him to sign. The year before the British had fought and defeated the Ijebu who had tried to resist European activities in their land. That incident was a great lesson to all the Yoruba. If the Ijebu could be so defeated, the alafin must have said to himself, what chances did he have if he stood against the British?

In the same year, 1893, the British got Ibadan to sign an

agreement by which Ibadan agreed to have European officers and British soldiers stationed in the town. Again, the Ibadan were not happy about this but they were made to understand that the British wanted it that way and if they did not co-operate willingly, they would be forced to do so. Following on this agreement, Captain R. L. Bower arrived in Ibadan at the end of 1893. Bower's full title was 'Resident of Ibadan and Political Officer in Charge of the Hinterland of Lagos Colony'. This 'hinterland of Lagos Colony' was usually interpreted to mean all of Yorubaland. Bower was thus placed in charge of all of Yorubaland outside Lagos. Governor Carter of Lagos stated that Bower's duty was to ensure that the Yoruba kept the terms of the 1886 treaty — that there were no petty quarrels, that trade routes were kept open, etc. To Ibadan with Bower came a certain Captain D. W. Steward and 100 soldiers. It was from Ibadan then that Bower began to interfere in the affairs of Oyo and so created the crisis which led to the bombardment of Oyo in 1895.

Two incidents gave Bower the chance he needed to bring the alafin under British control. At the time he arrived in Ibadan, the politics of the town of Okeiho were rather unsettled. Okeiho, a town under the alafin, was one of those towns that had grown up during the crisis that followed the break up of the Oyo empire. In fact, those who made up the town came originally from 11 different towns. Each of these towns, of course, had had its own ruler before. In the new town, they came to accept the authority of the onjo, who was originally ruler of the town of Ijo, largely because his town was a natural fortress to which people from the other towns moved. While the crisis lasted, the onjo's authority was accepted. But by the 1890s the other rulers were beginning to question why they should accept the onjo's authority. They wanted him to be no more than a nominal head. The onjos of the period refused to play this role. Consequently the other rulers kept deposing one onjo after the other. Usually, deposed onjos fled to the alafin, their overlord.

At the time of Bower's appointment to Ibadan, the Onjo of Okeiho was one Labiyi. Early in 1894, Labiyi was deposed by the other chiefs and one Ithanlu was put in his place. The alafin, who had already recognized Labiyi, was angry that the chiefs of Okeiho deposed Labiyi without consulting him. But he did not have the force to compel these chiefs to take Labiyi back. When Bower heard about the incident, he offered to help the alafin restore Labiyi to the throne. The alafin agreed, thinking that Bower was merely acting as his agent. But Bower was not acting as his agent. He was acting as the agent of the British. Anyway, Bower took a few soldiers with him to Okeiho and restored Labiyi.

Then the alafin stepped in and sent his men to demand the heads of the three principal chiefs in Okeiho who had been responsible for Labiyi's deposition. Actually the alafin was not expecting their heads. What normally happened was that such chiefs apologized for their misdeeds and bought their heads by sending presents to the alafin. Instead of doing this, however, the chiefs deposed Labiyi again and brought Itihanlu back from Iseyin where he had been sent by Bower. Once again the alafin was unable to get the chiefs to do his will, and once again it was Bower who secured the restoration of Labiyi and the arrest of Itihanlu. By the time this was done, it was quite clear that British rather than the alafin's power was responsible for the settlement.

The second incident was connected in a remote way with the above. When Bower was going to Okeiho for the purpose of restoring Labiyi the second time, he stopped at Iseyin where he asked the Okeiho chiefs to meet him. He did this because he wanted to look into a certain case there. This case concerned one Bakare who had been accused of having sexual intercourse with one of the wives of the ruler of the town. Acting according to custom, Bakare had been sent to the alafin where he was castrated. It should be pointed out that the punishment for this offence could be death. Castration was thus the lesser of the two possible punishments. The alafin had, therefore, done nothing new or against the custom of his people. It should also be pointed out that the alafin's action did not break any of the clauses of the treaties of 1886, 1888, or 1893.

Bower was obviously determined to use the Bakare case to seize political control of Oyo from the alafin. The Aseyin of Iseyin was so frightened of Bower that he lied to the latter that the charge against Bakare was false. Then he pleaded for forgiveness which he eventually got. Bower was not really interested in small fry like the aseyin. It was the alafin who interested him. So he sent to the alafin demanding that Bakare be handed over to him. The alafin sent word back that Bakare had escaped, obviously because he did not see what business Bower had to interfere in the matter.

On 7 November, Bower left Ibadan for Oyo to deal with the

alafin. He took with him 60 soldiers instead of the usual escort of 20. In Oyo meanwhile, the alafin and his priests were already worried by Bower's attitude and had begun to pray to their gods to prevent Bower from coming to their town. However, when Bower did arrive on 8 November, the alafin received him well and with respect. But Bower failed to show any respect to the alafin. In public he rebuked the alafin for sending men to demand the head of the chiefs of Okeiho and demanded to know where Bakare was. Still standing on his dignity as alafin, Adeyemi told Bower that he could discuss such matters only in private. But Bower would not listen. He demanded even more rudely still that Bakare and Kudefu, the principal messenger whom the alafin had sent to Okeiho, should be handed over to him at once. Of course, the alafin refused to do so. No one but Bower could expect the alafin to hand over an official of state for punishment when the official had done no more than carry out properly assigned duties. As for Bakare, he was killed before Bower arrived on the scene because the Oyo would not hear of him being handed over to Bower. So Bakare was nowhere to be handed over. Even if the alafin and his advisers were ready to hand over the men, the rude manner in which Bower addressed tha alafin was enough to change their minds.

After Bower left the palace to wait for the alafin's reaction, the alafin, advised no doubt by the missionaries, tried to make peace with Bower by writing to explain that he had done nothing against the law of his land. While the alafin was still thus prepared to engage in discussion, his chiefs began to prepare for war, for they saw Bower as one determined to fight. Next morning Bower took all his 60 soldiers with him as he went to see the alafin. When the people saw him with his soldiers going to their ruler, they quietly gathered, armed with guns and cutlasses, ready to resist Bower. But the crowd did not fire first. Rather it was Bower himself who opened fire and ordered his soldiers to get ready for battle. The firing on this occasion resulted in one man killed and eight wounded.

After this Bower withdrew and sent to Ibadan for reinforcements both of men and of artillery—one field gun and one maxim. When the reinforcements arrived, he repeated his demands, that Kudefu as well as the men who killed Bakare be handed over to him, that all arms and ammunition be surrendered, that the alafin should publicly prostrate before him in apology; that a British resident be allowed to stay at Oyo. No self-respecting ruler of the status of the alafin could possibly accept such terms. On 12 November Bower bombarded the town of Oyo. The people of Oyo put up such resistance as they could but there was really no hope. The alafin was forced to run away from his palace. By mid-day the affair was over. Oyo had fallen.

Although it has not been possible to give all the details of the Oyo episode, it is hoped that enough has been said to make it clear that the bombardment of Oyo cannot really be satisfactorily explained by the Bakare incident. Rather it was part of a general operation in the last ten years of the nineteenth century by which Nigeria gradually became a British colony. Both the governor in Lagos and Bower in Ibadan were anxious that Oyo become British. The Bakare incident was just a convenient excuse. Once Oyo had fallen the British went on to establish their rule over what used to be known as the Oyo province.

The other thing which must be said is that the fall of Oyo cannot be explained outside the politics of Yorubaland at the time. It was the situation in Yorubaland that forced Adeyemi I to welcome missionaries. It was these missionaries who made Adeyemi seek the friendship of the British in Lagos. It was this which, among other factors, led to the treaties of 1886, 1888, and 1893. These treaties provided the excuse for the British spreading their influence into the hinterland of Yorubaland. Out of this situation arose the stationing of Bower in Ibadan. And from Ibadan it was a short step to Oyo. No one can blame the alafin for the stand he took. It was better to be bombarded into submission than to accept the insulting terms demanded by Bower. Alafin Adeyemi I tried to stand on his dignity and was reduced to submission. But by so standing on his dignity he did both himself and his people proud.

BIBLIOGRAPHICAL NOTE

The most detailed treatment of the fall of Oyo is to be found in Chapter 2 of J. A. Atanda's *The New Oyo Empire*. Ayandele's article, 'The Mode of British Expansion in Yorubaland in the Second Half of the Nineteenth Century: The Oyo Episode', *Odu*, ii, 2 (1967) also discusses the episode.

EPISODE

4

The Fall of Ilorin

Today, Ilorin is capital of the Kwara State of Nigeria. Ilorin is also an emirate. The local government is headed by an emir. Ilorin thus looks very much like any of the Hausa-Fulani towns further to the north of Nigeria. There is no doubting the Muslim culture that exists in Ilorin. Yet Ilorin did not become Muslim till the first decade of the last century.

Until that time Ilorin was very much part of the Yoruba country controlled by the Alafin of Oyo in the heyday of the Old Oyo Empire. Ilorin became part of the Sokoto caliphate as a result of the jihad begun by Shaikh Uthman dan Fodiye. The initial move into Ilorin by Muslims was the result of an invitation by Afonja, the Ore ona Kakanfo (commander-in-chief) of the Old Oyo Empire. Afonja was at the time quarrelling with his alafin and needed allies to help him fight against his own ruler. The Muslims came down south, destroyed Old Oyo and forced the Yoruba to move further south. Then the Muslims turned against Afonja, killed him and his closest supporters, and took over control of Ilorin. From that time Ilorin became a Muslim emirate and instead of looking south towards the Yoruba began to look north towards Sokoto for leadership and direction.

During the Yoruba wars of the nineteenth century, Ilorin attempted to seize the opportunity of the wars to conquer other parts of Yorubaland. She gained some success until the year 1840 when Ibadan defeated her at the Battle of Oshogbo. After that Ilorin was unable to push down further south. But it continued to attack the Oyo and Ibadan areas from time to time during the rest of the nineteenth century. In fact one can say that there was constant emnity between Ibadan and Ilorin right from after the Battle of Oshogbo to the end of the nineteenth century. That emnity which led to occasional fighting between the two parties was important in bringing about the events that led to the fall of Ilorin to the British.

As is well known, the Yoruba wars came to an end in about

1886 when peace was signed between Ibadan and the Ekiti-parapo. The treaty which brought the war to an end was made possible by the missionaries, and the British Government established in Lagos since 1861 (see 'The Fall of Lagos'). The British in Lagos were very anxious to expand their trade in the Yoruba country. But the war made it difficult. Both the Ibadan and the Ekitiparapo were tired of war and wanted some third party that would help bring about peace. The British were only too glad to play the role of peacemaker.

By the time peace came to Yorubaland, the British were beginning to adopt a new policy towards Nigeria. Up to this time (1886) the British had engaged in trade with different parts of Nigeria. They had begun to interfere in the internal affairs of various Nigerian peoples. But, apart from Lagos, they had not tried to establish political control over any other part of Nigeria. However, as from the 1880s this policy began to change. France and Germany were beginning to have ambitions in Africa. Britain did not want to lose out to either of these two countries in the competition for empire in Africa. It was not therefore surprising that having helped to bring about peace in Yorubaland, Britain began to impose her rule on Yorubaland by force. In 1892 Ijebu was beaten to submission. Ibadan was quietly occupied by a British force in 1893. Two years later Oyo was bombarded and occupied. In the years that followed other parts of Yorubaland were gradually occupied. Similar activities took place in the Niger Delta and its hinterland.

With regard to what used to be known as Northern Nigeria the times were also beginning to change because of the activities of France and Germany. In the 1880s the Royal Niger Company represented the only British influence in Northern Nigeria. The company was directly interested in the trade of the Niger and Benue and had various stations along those rivers. But it also had trade relations with areas as far away as Sokoto. Indeed, because the emirates owed their loyalty to Sokoto, the Royal Niger Company had to create special relations with Sokoto. So far, however, all the agreements signed between the Company and Sokoto and other places were purely commercial treaties. One such area with which the Company had trading relations was Ilorin. However, these relations were not very close, for unlike what happened in some other places, the Company did not have a well-organized station in Ilorin. It certainly did not have a European agent there.

As has already been pointed out, Ilorin had been part of Yorubaland before the collapse of the Old Oyo Empire. Then it had become a Fulani emirate and had fought against the Yoruba during the Yoruba wars. The treaty of 1886 brought peace to the various Yoruba groups that had been fighting. But that treaty did not regulate relations between the Yoruba and Ilorin. Only a few years before the treaty was signed, Ilorin forces attacked parts of Oyo territory. After the signing of the 1886 treaty clashes continued to occur between the Ilorin and Oyo and between Ilorin and Ibadan.

As has also been pointed out, soon after the treaty of 1886 the British gradually occupied Yorubaland. The British government in Lagos would have liked to occupy Ilorin, especially as the Governors of Lagos always argued that Ilorin was part of Yorubaland. But the Lagos government could not do this because Ilorin was part of the territory which the British government in London had allowed the Royal Niger Company to control. The problem which now arose was what was to happen in a situation in which Ilorin continued to attack areas that were under the control of the British government in Lagos.

In 1894, following one of the usual Ibadan-Ilorin clashes, Captain Bower, British resident in Ibadan, was asked by the British governor in Lagos to travel to Ilorin to try and fix a boundary between Ilorin and Ibadan. Bower reported that he was insulted and badly treated by the Ilorin. Of course, the Ilorin had every reason not to treat Bower well. Bower was a foreigner with whom they had had no previous dealings of any sort. What right had he to want to negotiate a boundary between Ilorin and Ibadan? Naturally the governor in Lagos was angry about this alleged ill-treatment of Bower. He wrote an angry report to London and argued that it was quite clear that the Royal Niger Company had no real control over Ilorin. If the Company had proper control over Ilorin, the emir and his people would not have treated Bower so. And if the Company would not, or could not, keep Ilorin under proper control, argued Governor Carter, then the Lagos government should be allowed to occupy Ilorin and bring it under effective control — after all Ilorin was a Yoruba state before and ought to be restored to the Yoruba.

In 1895 the Lagos government again protested to London: the Emir of Ilorin had threatened that any messenger sent to him from Lagos would be killed. Then in 1896 Ilorin forces attacked a detachment of the Lagos constabulary force stationed at Odo Otin. The Lagos government cried for revenge. This time London informed the Royal Niger Company that action must be taken to bring Ilorin under control. If the Company could not take this action, then the Lagos government whould have to be asked to take it. Sir George Taubman Goldie, the head of the Royal Niger Company, was anxious to control the trade of the Ilorin area. Even more, he feared that the French, who were already interested in the Borgu area, might move into Ilorin and from Ilorin interfere with the Company's trade on the Niger. He therefore informed London that he would send a force to bring Ilorin under proper control. This was in 1896.

Although between 1895 and 1896 the Colonial Office in London had been putting a great deal of pressure on the Company to take military action against Ilorin, the Company did nothing to warn Ilorin that an armed conflict was likely to take place. Far from doing that, Goldie had even attempted to defend Ilorin against some of the charges brought against her by Lagos. In Ilorin itself, there was no doubting the fact that the anti-Lagos feeling was very high. In September 1895 the war leaders of Ilorin plotted against and killed Moma, the emir, because he was seen as being too soft with the Lagos Government. It was natural that the new emir, Suleiman, put on the throne by the war party, should adopt a noticeably hostile attitude to Lagos. This explains the message that all messengers from Lagos would be killed; this also explains why Lagos government troops stationed at Odo Otin were attacked by Ilorin forces. Ilorin was seeking to carry on the old Ilorin-Ibadan war; the British were determined that the war must stop.

Throughout 1895 and 1896 relations between Ilorin and the Royal Niger Company were friendly. The Company congratulated the new emir put on the throne in 1895. In 1896 after the Odo Otin affair, the emir wrote to Goldie to warn him that the situation in Ilorin was such that he would not advise any white man to visit the town. Goldie, in his reply to that letter, assured Ilorin that the Company was her loyal friend. Goldie was by that time deliberately deceiving the emir. For this was in 1896 when Goldie had already promised London that he would crush Ilorin. In fact, only a few months after the above exchange of letters, in February 1897, Goldie requested that Ilorin should submit peacefully to the Company. The Emir Suleiman was no

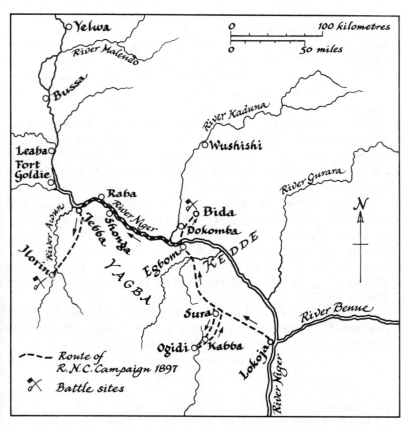

Map 6   The Royal Niger Company Nupe-Ilorin Campaign, 1897

doubt shocked at this request. He refused to submit.

In 1897 Ilorin was not in a particularly strong position to withstand an attack by the Royal Niger Company. There were divisions within between those who wanted war against the British in Lagos and those who were for negotiations. The emir was really no more than a tool in the hands of the baloguns (war leaders). Only in January 1897 an Ilorin force had been beaten in battle by a British force from Lagos. In that battle Ilorin had lost Balogun Adamu and some 150 men. In such circumstances the refusal of the emir to submit peacefully to the Company merely emphasizes how strongly Ilorin felt against being brought under British control.

The Company's forces arrived in Ilorin on 15 February. Even with the enemy forces outside his gate the emir refused to surrender. He would not even agree to hold discussions with Goldie. Fighting broke out on the 15th and lasted till the 16th of February when the Company's forces, very much better armed than Ilorin's seized the emir's palace and forced both the emir and baloguns to flee to the safety of outlying villages. The Ilorin fought very bravely, many advancing as close as 100 yards to the guns of the company's forces which mowed them down. The Ilorin lost a total of some 200 men in all. The bravery of the Ilorin was again not enough to meet the superior weapons of the British.

With the defeat of Ilorin in 1897, the Company was in a position to dictate terms. Goldie eventually sought out the emir and on 18 February signed a treaty with him and the baloguns by which Ilorin agreed to take directives from the Company as well as to accept a boundary with Lagos. On the face of it, Ilorin had lost everything for which she went to war. In practice, however, the situation at the end of the war was not too different from what it had been earlier on (except that Ilorin was now shy about taking a bold line). For on 19 February Goldie and his soldiers left Ilorin without setting up any kind of administration. This meant that the emir and his chiefs could continue to rule Ilorin as before. Naturally, Ilorin soon began to pursue her own interests once more. These interests did not always agree with the interests of the British government in Lagos which had forced Goldie to fight the war of 1897.

Soon after the departure of the Company's forces, the people of Ilorin began to show hostility towards the Company once more. They refused to supply labour for the construction of the telegraph line which the Company was building in Ilorin territory. This was because they saw the building of the telegraph as evidence that the Europeans meant to occupy Ilorin permanently. In August 1898 Ilorin attacks against territory claimed by the Lagos government began again.

Given this new show of hostility, the commander of the British troops stationed at Jebba sent a corporal and a few soldiers to the emir with a letter of warning. The messengers were very badly treated. The emir's servant to whom they gave the letter threw it on the ground. The emir himself warned the soldiers that if they ever returned to Ilorin·they would be killed. That Ilorin was able to behave like this despite the defeat in war of the previous year, shows how much the Europeans were hated.

Willcocks, the commander of the British forces, was naturally angry that his messengers had been so badly treated. On 28 September 1898 he sent yet another warning. But this time he sent the letter together with 50 soldiers commanded by a European officer named Somerset. The emir summoned a general meeting of his advisers. Many people in the town also crowded round. Somerset then presented the letter to the emir. In the presence of all his chiefs and many of the townspeople, the emir refused to take the letter from Somerset. Somerset felt deeply insulted. He warned the emir that if he did not behave, Ilorin would be bombarded. The emir ignored all the warnings. By October Ilorin was already preparing for war against the Europeans. The emir and his advisers decided during that month that no food should be given or even sold to Somerset's soldiers. The soldiers were warned that if any of them were found in Ilorin town proper they might be killed.

By this time (late 1898) it was already known by the officials of the Royal Niger Company that their home government meant to take over direct control of Northern Nigeria from the Company. Willcocks, the military commander who had been dealing with Ilorin during 1898, was not being paid by the Company but by the British government. The troops he commanded were to be used by the new authority which was to take over from the Royal Niger Company. Because of this situation the officials of the Company did not wish to co-operate with Willcocks in his dealings with Ilorin. When Willcocks had suggested that the Company should attack Ilorin in view of the latter's attitude to the Europeans, Watts, the agent of the Company, rejected the suggestion.

On 27 October 1898 this same Watts arrived in Ilorin. He posed as a friend of the emir and his people and was therefore well received. Then he proceeded to act as peacemaker between the emir and Somerset. At the end he agreed that the emir had behaved badly towards Somerset. He therefore decided that the emir should apologize to Somerset as well as pay a fine of £50. But Watts then offered to pay the fine for the emir. Somerset accepted this settlement and left Ilorin.

The Royal Niger Company now stationed a force of 50 men and one officer in Ilorin. The emir accepted this force because he regarded the Company as a friend despite the events of 1897. Had not Watts imposed a fine on him and then offered to pay the fine himself? He saw the force as a protecting force not an occupying force. What he did not know was that within a year the Company would lose its powers of administration and that the force which he now regarded as a protecting force would be transferred to the force commanded by his enemy Willcocks.

By this time it would appear that the emir was gradually coming round to the view that the only way he could survive was to be friendly with the Europeans. Not so his baloguns, led by Alanamu. The baloguns were really the men who decided policy. They were popular with the general mass of the people. It was they in fact who had made sure that the emir did not come to terms with Somerset till Watts stepped in as peacemaker. The baloguns thus became the real leaders of the opposition to British rule in Ilorin.

On 1 January 1900 Lugard took over from the Royal Niger Company and proclaimed the Protectorate of Northern Nigeria. One of his first acts was to send a proclamation to all the emirs as well as to the caliph in Sokoto informing them that he had taken over from the Royal Niger Company and had authority to rule all the white and black people in the caliphate. This proclamation was a great insult to the emirs but more so to the caliph. For what Lugard was saying was that the Muslims of the caliphate should accept him, an unbeliever, as their ruler. Lugard knew enough about Islam to know that no Muslim would willingly submit to rule by an infidel. He knew that the proclamation was tantamount to a declaration of war against the Sokoto caliphate.

What was the reaction of Ilorin to Lugard's proclamation? Emir Suleiman accepted the proclamation gladly. This was the best evidence that the emir had made up his mind that the only way he could survive as emir was to support the new authority. It is difficult to judge the emir. The baloguns and the mass of the people did not want British rule. Yet the experience of the past had shown that it was difficult to fight successfully against British troops who had much superior arms and were trained professional soldiers. Should Ilorin stand for her independence and so fight another battle which she was bound to lose? Or should she accept British rule as now unavoidable? The emir thought that the latter alternative was the only possibility. The baloguns thought otherwise. In the end Ilorin did not actually fight another battle but between 1900 and 1903 the baloguns and the people made things hard for the British.

The second half of the year 1900 was very difficult for the British. In May, Willcocks and 1,200 troops left Northern Nigeria for Ghana to help fight against the Asante who were then at war with the British. This fact became well known all over the caliphate. In Ilorin the reaction of the people was to flaunt the authority of the British. Lugard was at the time getting ready to fight against Bida and could not immediately afford to go to war with Ilorin. In July, however, he sent a small force of 30 soldiers to Ilorin to answer to the cry of the British resident, Carnegie, who told Lugard that the situation in Ilorin was becoming extremely difficult.

By August the situation became even more difficult. Bida was calling on Ilorin to join her fight against Lugard's soldiers. The emir refused to send help to Bida, but the baloguns and people were very eager to join Bida in her struggle against Lugard. In September, Balogun Alanamu tried but failed to expel the British resident and his policemen from Ilorin. After this failure the baloguns became more careful in their opposition to the British. They too gradually began to see that open opposition was not likely to succeed. As from that time they preferred merely to refuse to co-operate with the British, not to show any open signs of hostility.

In the end, what finally convinced Ilorin to give up any idea of military resistance against the British was the fact that other emirates which attempted such resistance were mercilessly crushed. First Bida, then Kontagora fell to the British. In

January, the defeated Emir of Bauchi was sent as an exile to Ilorin. Ilorin was deliberately chosen as the emir's home in exile for, from 1900, Ilorin had refused to accept the fact of British rule. The Emir of Bauchi had also refused to accept British rule, and so had been beaten in battle and deported to Ilorin. Ilorin was expected to learn a lesson from the fate of the Emir of Bauchi.

The British were not, however, so foolish as to think that the example of Bauchi was enough. A few weeks after the Emir of Bauchi arrived in Ilorin, British troops were sent into Ilorin from Lagos. The troops marched through the town of Ilorin to show to the people the might of the British Empire. Soon after this the Caliph of Sokoto wrote to the Emir of Ilorin asking the latter to create some disturbance in Ilorin so that British attention would not be turned towards Sokoto. This was the supreme test. Would the emir do his caliph's will or would he prefer to please the British? He tried to do both. He read the caliph's letter aloud to his people as custom demanded. But he then sent the caliph's messenger to the British resident thereby letting the British know what the caliph was plotting. It was quite clear that the emir was no longer able to do as he pleased. As if to let the emir know once and for all that he was now emir by the authority of the British and no longer by that of the caliph in Sokoto, the then British resident, Dwyer, presented the Emir of Ilorin with a new staff of office soon after the incident described above. Although the situation in Ilorin remained a little difficult for some time to come, there was no other major act of resistance. By the end of 1903 the British occupation of Ilorin had at last become a reality.

The fall of Ilorin to the British had to do, to begin with, with the rival claims of two British authorities — the British government in Lagos and the Royal Niger Company. Involved in the situation were also the old emnities built up during the Yoruba wars of the nineteenth century. For it was Ilorin-Ibadan wars which the British in Lagos used as the excuse for asking that Ilorin be attacked and brought under control. The attack on Ilorin by the Royal Niger Company in 1897 broke Ilorin's military power once and for all. Thereafter, although there was still a great deal of hatred for the white man in Ilorin, the Ilorin could not engage the British in any major war. The coming of Lugard in 1900 and his systematic battles against other emirates gradually convinced Ilorin that armed resistance would be fruitless. Passive resistance continued until 1903 and even later, but the British also' settled down and Ilorin, like other parts of the country, passed under British rule.

BIBLIOGRAPHICAL NOTE

The two readily available sources which deal with the British occupation of Ilorin are J. E. Flint's *Sir George Goldie and the Making of Nigeria* and R. A. Adeleye's *Power and Diplomacy in Northern Nigeria*.

EPISODE
5

The Fall of Brass

Brass was one of what, in the history books, are referred to as the city-states of the Niger Delta. Others include Kalabari, Bonny, and the Itsekiri kingdom. Have you ever wondered why these states were called city-states when today none of these centres faintly resembles a city? The answer lies in the great importance which these centres acquired from about the sixteenth century till the end of the nineteenth. These centres were great trading centres, some of the best known in all of West Africa. As a consequence of this trade both among themselves and with Europe, they became not only wealthy but also politically well organized.

A look at Map 7 shows that all of these centres named occupy the delta. The most remarkable feature of the delta is the thick mangrove swamp and the many creeks and streams which flow through it. In this kind of environment agriculture was, and still is, largely impossible as there was little farmland available. The peoples of the delta have thus never been able to produce enough food to feed themselves. How could wealthy and powerful states develop in this kind of surrounding?

It is easy for us of today to pity those who live in the delta and to say what a miserable life they have to lead. It is important, however, to remember a few facts. It is true that the peoples of the delta did not grow enough food for themselves. They did, nevertheless, have some extremely important commodities: salt, fish, and earthenware utensils of all sorts.

Salt is an extremely important commodity. In the days before European manufactured salt became readily available, it was the delta peoples who supplied salt to the peoples of the forest belt. They made this salt either by evaporating the sea water which flowed through their territory or from the shoots, roots, and leaves of the mangrove trees which abound in the delta and which absorb a great deal of salt from the sea water. Similarly the water provided them with fish. At all times the bulk of the delta population have been fishermen. Then there was the fact that various parts of the delta possessed the kind of clay with which earthenware utensils of various kinds were made.

If, therefore, the delta peoples did not grow enough food to feed themselves, they did produce commodities which they could exchange for food. Indeed, this was the basis of the internal trade. The peoples of the delta traded with the peoples of the forest belt for foodstuffs, exchanging for these salt, fish, and earthenware. There thus developed a south–north, north–south trade. But this was not all.

There was also an east–west, west–east trade: there was trade within the delta itself. For example, not all the delta peoples produced equal quantities of salt. Some areas specialized as producers of salt. Brass, the subject of this chapter, was one such area. Other areas specialized in making earthenware Gbaramatu in the western delta was, for example, known for this.

Then there was the means of transport within the delta itself — canoes. Canoes cannot be made from the mangrove tree: they can only be made from certain types of trees. Not all the delta was fortunate to have the right type of trees growing nearby. So again there were areas, like the Apoi area, known for the building of canoes. Indeed the trade in canoes was one of the most important aspects of the east–west, west–east delta trade. In general terms, then, the peoples of the delta traded among themselves in accordance with their own needs. Those who were specialized in salt making might need the earthenware utensils of another group and *vice versa*, while all needed the means of transportation. It was in this way that the delta peoples developed as great traders.

To this purely internal south–north, east–west trade was added the trade with Europeans from the sixteenth century. As is well known the slave trade became important from the latter half of the sixteenth century and the delta states became great slave trading areas. These states did not possess the kind of population that could support the trade in slaves. They obtained their slaves from the peoples of the forest belt, either by buying the slaves from the slave markets which developed, or by occasional raids for slaves. At any rate, those at the coast were able to obtain European goods, especially guns and ammunition, various types of alcoholic drinks, gaudy glass, textile goods, and the like, and then to cleverly use these to get the forest peoples to sell them slaves. Guns and ammunition given to the peoples of the hinterland were used for raids and wars from which slaves were obtained. The peoples of the delta made sure that the peoples of the forest belt did not themselves come down to the coast to trade direct with the Europeans. And the Europeans did not know the hinterland and so could not trade directly with those who lived there. This is how the peoples of the delta became the great middlemen of the trade.

With regard to the slave trade it is important to stress that the trade was made easier by the fact that the delta as well as the hinterland peoples already had well established lines of trade and contacts which the slave trade followed. It was not the slave trade which created these lines of communication. Usually each of the delta states had its own area of operation, its own markets which it sought to organize and control. Thus, although Brass traded with the neighbouring Ijo groups for foodstuffs and other delta products, her main customer was Aboh at the confluence of the delta.

Aboh was too far from the sea coast to trade directly with the Europeans, especially in the period before the 1840s. Yet Aboh was very well placed to control the trade of the Niger Valley. So she developed trade contacts with the Ukwuani peoples further to the hinterland, with Onitsha and with the Igala kingdom. From these customers Aboh got not only slaves but foodstuffs — yams, and cattle, and so on. These she sold to Brass traders with whose king the Obi of Aboh had special trading relations. So Brass traders bought the products of the hinterland from Aboh and gave the latter arms and ammunition and other European goods obtained from the Europeans in return for slaves and other Nigerian products. Both parties benefited from this arrangement which ensured profitable trade till the Europeans began to tamper with it in the nineteenth century, especially in the second half of that century.

For all of the delta states the nineteenth century brought important developments. In 1807 Britain passed a law against the slave trade. Thereafter she tried to get all of Europe and America to pass similar laws. While Britain had to persuade Europe and America to join her in the battle against the slave trade, she tried to force abolition on the peoples of Africa. Thus, not only did she encourage her traders to develop trade in commodities other than slaves, she stationed warships along the coast of West Africa to force the Africans to stop the trade in slaves. Sometimes British agents signed treaties with West African rulers by which Britain paid these rulers some small sum annually as compensation for giving up the trade in slaves. But, as in Bonny, it was not always true that the agreed compensation was paid. In the end Britain was able to succeed only because European and American slave traders were gradually forced to give up the trade in slaves. This was achieved partly through treaties with the European and American governments and partly through the use of the British naval squadron in West Africa.

The states of the Niger Delta reacted to the British pressure to stop the slave trade in different ways. Their reaction was dictated, among other things, by their geographical location. The British gunboats were the most effective agents for the suppression of the slave trade, so states like Bonny that could be easily reached by the gunboats could only secretly carry on the trade in slaves. However, Brass is situated in creeks which the gunboats could not reach. Thus, while Bonny and other places were forced to sign treaties suppressing the slave trade, Brass was able to refuse to sign such a treaty until the second half of the nineteenth century.

Brass had not been one of the great centres of the slave trade even in the golden age of that trade. Bonny and Kalabari were the more famous slave trade centres. However, between the years 1825 and 1850, Brass became quite famous as the great centre for the trade in slaves. This was because the British navy successfully blockaded the other rivers in the delta but not the Brass river. Consequently all the European and Brazilian traders who wanted to buy slaves found their way to Twon, the port of Brass. Bonny and other places shipped their slaves through the creeks to Brass where they were finally sold to European or Brazilian slave traders. So Brass engaged in very profitable trade right up to the end of the first half of the nineteenth century.

It should be pointed out, at this point, that alongside the trade in slaves, Brass continued to trade in the products of the delta and the hinterland as well as in the new trade in palm oil. So that when by about 1850 European and Brazilian slave traders virtually gave up the trade in slaves, Brass did not suffer very greatly. She merely increased her efforts in the palm oil trade.

The trade figures available show that whereas in 1830 Brass hardly sold any appreciable quantity of palm produce, by 1856, she was doing quite a reasonable amount of trade in this commodity, exporting a total of 2,280 tons of palm oil in the year 1856. This figure increased to 2,800 tons by 1864.

Up to 1864, then, one can say that Brass was still very much her old self. It is true that British influence was beginning to be gradually felt. But real authority was still firmly in the hands of the rulers of Brass. European traders who came to the Brass River still had to pay 'comey' or trade dues to the rulers before they could begin trading. If the traders wanted any piece of land they had to seek permission from the rulers. The rulers were able, throughout the 1860s, to prevent the European traders from going into the hinterland to trade directly with the producers of palm oil.

All of this changed from the 1870s. While Brass continued to keep a firm control over her own affairs, certain developments were taking place elsewhere which were to prove ruinous for her. Following the journey of the Lander brothers which showed that the delta was the mouth of the Niger, there was increased European activity on that river. Macgregor Laird organized a number of journeys in the 1850s and 1860s. Indeed by the 1860s a European trading station had been established at Aboh and by the 1880s Europeans were also established at Onitsha and Lokoja. As was pointed out earlier in this chapter, Brass had a trading arrangement with Aboh. Aboh, on her part, drew her trade from the Onitsha and Igala areas among others. Now that European trading stations were established at Lokoja and Onitsha, Aboh was not getting as much trade as before from these areas. What is more, even such trade as she managed to get, she could not control as before, because the European traders were doing all they could to impose their own terms on this trade. In fact this was the situation which gradually led to the decline of Aboh as an important trading kingdom by the end of the nineteenth century.

If the situation described above was bad for Aboh, it was worse for Brass. For Brass suddenly found that the Aboh market was suddenly lost to her. Most of her markets between the Brass River and Onitsha began to be less profitable because of the new competition from European traders. By 1876 the rulers of Brass were pleading that European traders should leave their markets

Map 7   State of Brass, showing trading contact both along the
Delta and the hinterland

to them. The plea fell on deaf ears.

As the century wore on, the situation became worse. In 1879 the United African Company (later the Royal Niger Company) was formed by George Taubman Goldie. The Company was formed by bringing together many of the smaller firms which had been competing against one another in the delta. Competition enabled the delta rulers to put up their prices. High prices for palm produce meant smaller profits for the European traders. Goldie's aim in bringing these firms together in one huge company was to reduce competition and increase profits — but it was not just a trading company. The Royal Charter which it obtained in 1886 gave the Company authority to have its own fighting force as well as authority to make laws for the improvement of its trading activities in the Niger Delta as well as the Niger proper. Nothing did more to bring about the fall of Brass than the activities of the Royal Niger Company.

At about the same time that Goldie was seeking a Royal Charter for his company, events in Europe were making Britain anxious to strengthen her position in the Niger Delta. This desire was no doubt one of the factors which led to the granting of a charter to Goldie. A British company of that type in the delta would be able to keep other European firms out of the area. And, indeed, Goldie went on to establish a trading monopoly on the Niger and most of the delta.

British interests were not, however, left completely in the hands of the Royal Niger Company. There were also the activities of the British consul who began signing 'protection treaties' with the delta states. We already know the usual provisions of these treaties and the objections which delta rulers had to some of the clauses. The rulers of Brass signed Hewett's protection treaty in 1884 for a period of only six months. In 1885 the treaty was renewed for another six months which expired on 1 August 1885. Why did Brass behave in this way? Brass was afraid of the growing British power in the delta. The Royal Niger Company was ruining her trade. This treaty sought to seize political power from her. So Brass tried to keep a free hand. Thus after 1 August 1885, the British did not really have any legal authority for claiming Brass as a Protectorate. But in the context of Afro-European relations in the 1880s it was not legal authority that counted. Britain had the naval and military power to declare the Niger Delta a British Protectorate. And she did so in 1885. From that time on, therefore, Brass became part of the British Protectorate of the Oil Rivers.

Between 1885 and 1891 nothing very much was done about governing this new Protectorate. There was still only one consul and a vice-consul to look after the entire delta. Consequently, although the delta was now, in theory, part of a British Protectorate, the rulers still enjoyed reasonable freedom of action. In Brass, for example, there was little difference between the situation before 1884 and that after the declaration of the Protectorate, except that between 1885 and 1891 Brass rulers no longer received all of the comey paid by the European traders. They received only half, while the other half went to the British Consul.

The major problem which Brass faced during this period was that of the decline in her trade. Between 1886 and 1889, there were increasing protests by the people of Brass against the trade monopoly of the Royal Niger Company. It is not often realized just how oppressive the Company was. It is therefore necessary here to state some of the conditions which the Company imposed on the people of Brass. According to the report of an official enquiry, any trader who desired to trade within the territories granted to the Royal Niger Company by the charter was 'required to pay a sum of 50 pounds for license to trade, with a further sum of ten pounds also yearly, for every station he traded at, and he would then be allowed to trade at such stations as had been declared open for that purpose, and nowhere else'. He would next be required to pay £100 annually if he intended to trade in spirits, 'without which . . . trade in the Delta is at present impossible'. This was not all. The Brass trader still had to pay a duty of two shillings per gallon of spirits (alcohol) at Akassa, where the station of the Company was. When the trader had finished his transaction, he was made to pay an export duty of 20 per cent on all the produce he sold. This was at a time when the government of the Protectorate itself did not charge any duties on export.

It was indeed a great pity that Brass was within the territories granted to the Royal Niger Company by the charter. No Brass trader could afford to pay the licenses, fees, and duties demanded by the Company. The only alternative left to the Brassmen was for them to engage in smuggling. And this they did with some success up to 1893. European firms, especially the

Liverpool traders not part of Goldie's set-up, encouraged the Brassmen in their smuggling because they too suffered from the difficult terms imposed by the Royal Niger Company.

Indeed, the Liverpool traders protested not only to the Company but to Parliament in Britain. It was as a result of the protests of both the delta traders and the Liverpool merchants that the British government sent out Major Claude Macdonald in 1891 to investigate the charges against the Royal Niger Company. Major Macdonald was also asked to make recommendations as to how the Oil Rivers Protectorate could best be governed.

The Brassmen as well as the Europeans made their grievances known to Macdonald who agreed that the terms imposed by the Company were excessive and oppressive. The Brassmen therefore expected that after 1889 things would improve for them. When Macdonald asked the rulers to choose between being governed by the Company and being governed directly by the Queen's agent, the rulers had no hesitation in saying they would prefer to be ruled by the Queen. After Macdonald submitted his report, the British government decided that the time had come to establish an effective government over the Oil Rivers Protectorate which, from 1893, became known as the Niger Coast Protectorate. Macdonald himself was appointed the Consul-General, that is, the head of the new government, in 1891.

By the time Macdonald was appointed Consul-General, the people of Brass had suffered under the injustice of the Royal Niger Company for more than ten years. They had complained to various British authorities. Before they signed the treaty of 1884, the rulers had asked Consul Hewett to ensure that their trade would be restored. Hewett could not give any assurance. Hence the treaty was signed only for six months. When the treaty was being renewed for another six months in 1885, the Brassmen had again pressed on Vice-Consul H. A. White to do something to relieve their suffering. White had promised to consult the government in Britain. In 1886 Consul Hewett announced that there could be no question of markets being reserved for special groups. Trade had to be free for all. The Brass traders accepted this. But that very year a charter was granted to the Royal Niger Company which proceeded to establish a monopoly and so destroy free trade. In 1889 the Brassmen had put their case before a special commission of enquiry. The Brassmen had thus done everything that anyone could expect them to do. So far nothing had come out of promises made by the British consular authorities. The Royal Niger Company had continued to operate unchecked.

In these circumstances, Brass had every reason to hope that Major (by 1891, Sir) Claude Macdonald would now look into their grievances and force the Royal Niger Company to stop its oppressive trade terms. But Macdonald's authority did not extend to the area covered by the Company's charter. There were, in fact, two separate British authorities in the Niger territories between 1886 and 1899. In fairness to Macdonald, he did try very hard to get the British government to do something about the complaints of the people of Brass. But nothing was done up to 1895 and the Brassmen continued to suffer.

It was said earlier on that, faced with the kind of conditions imposed by the Royal Niger Company, Brassmen were left with no alternative but to smuggle. But even smuggling was not easy because the Company had patrol boats which fired on Brass canoes engaged in smuggling. Not only were many canoes seized by these patrol boats, but a number of Brassmen lost their lives — killed by gun fire from the patrol boats. What is not often realized is that it was not only palm produce and other export commodities that the patrol boats seized. They even seized foodstuff. In other words, Brass was effectively stopped from trading for food with neighbouring Ijo groups. European traders in sympathy with the people of Brass could do nothing because of the vigilance of the Company. Then in 1893 came the final blow. The African Association, a Liverpool concern, had all along been an ally of Brass and had done all it could do to fight the Royal Niger Company's monopoly. In June 1893, Goldie succeeded in buying the African Association. With this the only remaining friend of Brass ceased to exist. The situation became unbearable and the people of Brass, as one of them put it, were reduced to eating sand.

It was against this kind of desperate background that the people of Brass decided that it was better to die fighting than to be starved to death. So Brass decided that the Company's depot and headquarters at Akassa must be destroyed. Most of the text books describe what happened on the morning of the 29 January 1895 at the Akassa Raid. The people of Brass certainly did not see themselves as going on a raid on that fateful January morning. They saw themselves as set to fight a war of survival. It is not easy to try and imagine how their minds must have worked. What did King Koko, who led the war, think the outcome was likely to be? Perhaps he thought that if the gods granted Brass success, the Company would be so surprised and angry that it would withdraw from the Brass area and so allow his people to carry on their trade as they had done before the Company came. Or perhaps he thought that even if he and his people failed on the battlefield, they would have shown Macdonald's government just how desperate they had become and so force that government to do something about their long-standing grievances. One thing is clear. By 1895 the people of Brass knew something already about British naval and military power. Only the year before the British had led an expedition against Nana and broken the power of that great middleman trader. So although they argued that it was against the Company, not the Macdonald government, that they were fighting, they must have known that the government was likely to get involved especially if they were successful. In other words the desperate nature of the venture was fully appreciated. Yet Brass chose to go on. That shows how hard pressed the people had become.

The preparations for the war with the company were carefully made. There was complete unanimity among all the settlements that make up the city-state of Brass. The usual sacrifices offered before Brass went to war were offered. Virtually all the important houses got their war canoes and fighting men ready. News of these preparations got to Flint, the company's agent at Akassa. Flint did not believe that the people of Brass would actually attack Akassa. Even when the vice-consul in Brass sent him a letter on the matter, he was still a little doubtful. That he did not expect anything serious is proved by the fact that he got only one gun mounted on the pier and got a launch ready for a quick getaway if this became necessary.

King Koko led his flotilla of war canoes out of Twon on the night of Monday 28 January 1895. The vice-consul, who was anxious to notify Akassa, did not know when the canoes left. Altogether 25 war canoes, each with at least one cannon, left Twon for the attack on Akassa. These 25 were met by others at an agreed point. Each canoe carried up to 60 fighting men. Thus most of the important men in Brass were present in this last stand against the oppression of the Royal Niger Company. If Flint had any doubt as to whether the people of Brass would actually attack his headquarters, these doubts were removed when, at 4.30 a.m., on Tuesday, 29 January 1895, the guns of the Brassmen began to boom.

The people of Brass were no fools. They chose their positions carefully in such a way that the one gun mounted by Flint could not be used against them. In fact they soon put that gun out of order. When Flint found that the gun had been put out of order, he escaped in the launch that he had got ready for an emergency escape. The Brassmen then moved in on Akassa. The other white employees were saved from death by the approach of a strange steamer which forced the attackers to withdraw temporarily. The white employees boarded the steamer and escaped. But the African staff paid the price of the oppression of their employers; 24 of them were killed by the attackers, and 70 were taken captive. Not only were buildings and other structures of the Company destroyed, there was also great looting of trade goods from the stores. From the treasury £2,000 was removed. Guns and ammunition were carried away, not to speak of drinks of all sorts. The Company's records—books of accounts, etc.—were destroyed. The attackers lost four men killed. The people of Brass thus took full vengeance on the Company.

If the people of Brass thought that they would be allowed to enjoy this victory, they were soon proved wrong. The Brass vice-consul, C. E. Harrison, cabled his boss, Sir Claude Macdonald, who arrived at the Brass consulate on 2 February 1895. The issue, as seen by Macdonald, was not whether Brass had been provoked by the Company. Macdonald had always agreed that Brass had a very good case against the Company. The issue was that Brass had attacked another British authority and had therefore taken the law into her own hands. It was convenient at this point for Macdonald to forget that the Brass people had sought through peaceful channels to obtain relief from oppression since the 1870s. British prestige had suffered as a result of the attack and victory. The shame of an African people successfully destroying a British company's station had to be wiped out.

Macdonald took the view on his arrival that Brass was at war with his own government. He therefore asked the rulers and people of Brass to surrender by 9 February. Brass replied that she had no quarrel with Macdonald's government but with the

Company. Meanwhile Macdonald began to concentrate troops in Brass. On her part, Brass too began to put herself in a state of defence. Scouts were posted at various points on banks of rivers and creeks and in the swampy forest. When on 6 February, Macdonald tried to have a look around the area with a view to deciding the best places for attack, he was surprised to find that his movements were followed by the Brass scouts. In fact he was later warned not to move around without telling the leaders of the Brass people, lest he run into unpleasant incidents with the men in the bush.

The warning was evidence that the people had no intention of harming Sir Claude himself. Even so, Macdonald went on to prepare for the showdown that was bound to come. Between February 19 and 23, various preliminary encounters took place between Protectorate forces and the Brass people. The major and final attack was mounted from 24–26 February 1895. It was not an easy affair for Macdonald and his men. The Brass people had prepared for what they knew would come sooner or later. Every chief's house was fully put in a state of defence and the British force had to take one house after the other. Macdonald himself put on record the great courage of the defenders. Many went on fighting until they were shot down at very close range. It was only when it became clear that all the chiefs' houses had been taken that the people began to run into the surrounding mangrove swamp from where resistance continued for many days after 26 February. Macdonald estimated that Brass lost about 300 men killed in the fighting.

After the events of 24–26 February Macdonald thought that enough punishment had been meted to the people of Brass, though the Royal Niger Company would have liked to see more destruction of houses and other property. He then proceeded to demand a surrender of all the war canoes used against Akassa in January as well as the return of all plunder. A fine of just over £500 was also imposed. The chiefs paid the fine and surrendered the war canoes and some other arms and ammunition. As for the loot it was difficult to surrender this as most of it was made up of perishable goods which had been consumed. So once again another Nigerian group, driven to the walls by an oppressive foreign régime, and anxious to reassert themselves, had been crushed by superior weapons.

Macdonald's strong views about the injustice done to Brass by the Company as well as protests from other parties in Britain led to an Inquiry being set up to look into the Brass grievances. Sir John Kirk who conducted the Inquiry was told once again about the grievances already discussed in this chapter. Like Macdonald, he agreed that the Royal Niger Company's terms were oppressive. However, Kirk blamed the British government which had given the Company a charter in the first place and so made it possible for it to enforce its oppressive laws on the Brass people. Brass did not benefit directly from the Inquiry. Four years after it, the charter of the Royal Niger Company was revoked and the Niger Coast Protectorate took over full control. By that time Brass was already ruined economically and the political structure that Sir Ralph Moor, the new head of the administration, was seeking to establish, left no doubt as to where real authority lay. Brass, as an independent and reasonably wealthy city-state had passed into history by the end of 1895. She has not, even now, really recovered from that blow, though other factors, which cannot be discussed here, have also contributed to this end.

The fall of Brass then was very much tied up with commerce and the activities of the Royal Niger Company. It was also the result of that growing European expansion in West Africa which alone explains why Macdonald, with his sympathies for the people of Brass, nevertheless mounted a punitive expedition. After all, Macdonald was an apostle of empire. His personal views had to give way to the larger aims of his employers, that is, the establishment of a British colony in what is now Nigeria.

BIBLIOGRAPHICAL NOTE

The old fashioned books like A. C. Burns's *History of Nigeria* and A. N. Cook's *British Enterprise in Nigeria* and others speak of the 'Akassa Raid' and give the impression that the attack by the people of Brass on the headquarters of the Royal Niger Company was a mere raid organized by a lawless people. These and other works written by former administrators turned authors and other Europe-centred scholars fail or refuse to see the issues which forced the people of Brass to go to war. Michael Crowder (1962) in *Story of Nigeria* points out that the people of Brass felt 'real bitterness' towards the Royal Niger Company. The full details of the enormity of the Company's cruelty to the people of Brass are to be found in E. J. Alagoa's *The Small Brave City State* (1964). Alagoa points out that so far as the Brass were concerned the attack on Akassa was not a raid: it was a major war of survival. Alagoa is thus the first scholar to put the episode here discussed fully into its proper historical perspective. J. C. Anene's M.A. thesis (1955) revised and published in 1966 as *Southern Nigeria in Transition* also deals with the subject from the viewpoint of Brass but Anene does not, because of the wider scope of his work, give as full a picture as does Alagoa.

EPISODE

6

The Fall of Benin

Before the nineteenth century, Benin had been a very important empire. With Benin City as headquarters, the empire included parts of Yorubaland, especially the Owo, Akure, and Ekiti areas, and a large part of the Midwestern State (recently renamed Bendel State). The empire was built largely through military conquest, and Benin is famous for its many wars.

The economy of Benin was based both on agriculture and on trade. Benin produced most of the food needed to feed her population. Her trade was widespread. She traded with the Yoruba country, with the Itsekiri to the coast, with the Nupe to the north and with Europeans. The most important item of trade which Benin got from the Yoruba country was probably cloth—Ijebu cloth. This passed from the Ijebu through the Itsekiri country to Benin. It may also have passed through the overland route.

Benin trade with the Europeans was very well controlled right from the time Europeans first made contact with Benin some time in the sixteenth century. Europeans did not go direct to Benin for their trading activities. The farthest they got was usually Ughoton on the Benin River (see Map 8), which was the port of Benin. At Ughoton the Oba of Benin had his trading agents who transacted business with the Europeans, and collected customs duties for the oba. The articles which Benin sold were pepper, ivory, cloth, and slaves.

Not only did the oba control the trade of all these articles through his agents, he also had agents trading on his behalf. For example the ivory trade was mostly the oba's trade, for any hunter who killed an elephant had to send at least one of the tusks to the oba. With the proceeds from his sales, the oba could buy arms and ammunition as well as other manufactured goods.

The Itsekiri served as middlemen for some of Benin's trade. They were well placed, for example, to trade with the Ijebu through the creeks, and some Ijebu cloth found in Benin no doubt passed through the hands of Itsekiri traders. Many Itsekiri

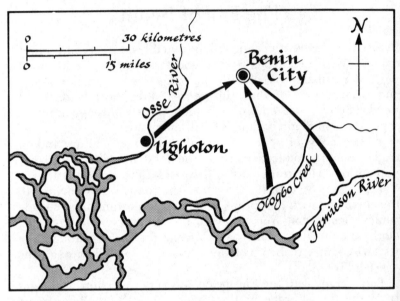

Map 8   The British invasion of Benin, 1897

were to be found at Ughoton where they traded with Benin traders and the oba's agents. Such Itsekiri had to pay the duties imposed by the oba and generally accept other terms imposed on Benin trade. It was, especially in the period before the nineteenth century, difficult for any group of traders — European or African, to break the terms of trade imposed by the Oba of Benin on the trade of his empire. At Ughoton, for example, were not only the trading agents, but soldiers stationed to protect the interests of the oba and of Benin generally. It was the wealth derived from this very well organized trade which enabled Benin to maintain her empire for centuries.

We do not intend here to go into details as to how Benin was governed. However, it is important to draw attention to certain aspects of Benin government if we are to understand fully the fall of Benin. Although the oba was a very powerful ruler, a near-god in the eyes of his people, he did not rule Benin alone. At the height of the empire, the oba had to work with his chiefs. There were, broadly speaking, two sets of chiefs — the town chiefs (eghaevbo n'ore) and the palace chiefs (eghaevbo n'ogbe). The former were chiefs who originally held their positions independently of the oba. Indeed, the oba used to be seen as only first among equals in his relationship with the Uzama chiefs. It is Oba Ewedo who is said to have tried with some success to establish the supremacy of the oba over the Uzama chiefs. It is important to point out here that the Uzama chieftaincy titles were not created by the present dynasty of obas. Thus five of the most senior titles (those of oliha, edohen, ezomo, ero, and eholo n'ire) existed before the present line of rulers appeared in Benin history. Indeed, the Uzama chiefs regarded themselves, at the beginning of the present dynasty, as kingmakers. It was partly because these chiefs saw themselves as independent of the oba that they became regarded as a kind of traditional opposition to the oba. It was these Uzama chiefs then who later became known as the *eghaevbo n'ore,* or town chiefs.

Oba Ewedo is also credited with the organization of the palace chiefs — the eghaevbo n'ogbe. This category of chiefs was divided into three associations. The senior of these was iwebo led by the uwangue. The iwebo were responsible for looking after the oba's regalia and wardrobe and later also kept an eye on the oba's finance and trade. The oba's personal attendants and domestic servants constituted the second association known as the iweguae, led by the esere. The third association was the ibiwe, responsible for looking after the affairs of the oba's wives and children. The leader of the ibiwe was the osodin. By controlling these three categories of palace officials, a wise and powerful oba ensured his own supremacy within the palace. However, a weak oba could very easily become a tool in the hands of his own ambitious servants.

Oba Ewuare is credited with having actually transformed the Uzama chiefs into the eghaevbo n'ore, led by the iyasere, who, by the seventeenth century, had already become the commander of Benin's fighting forces. The oba, by giving these chiefs a say in deciding state policy together with himself and the palace chiefs, sought to control a group that was traditionally hostile to him. Over the years these chiefs looked up to the oba for advancement and other favours just as the palace chiefs did. As the oba could create new titles and decide on the order of seniority, it became the practice for ambitious men to seek the favours of the oba. If the control of these chiefly associations could be, and was, a source of strength to the Oba of Benin, it could also be a source of weakness because pretenders to the throne could, by promising to advance people either within or outside these associations, build up a following for themselves hostile to the oba. The point that should be stressed here is that any Oba of Benin who wished to succeed had to play his cards very carefully, to build up the right kind of support from his chiefs. A happy relationship between the oba and the bulk of his chiefs was necessary for the well-being of the kingdom and empire.

The reader may begin to wonder why there is this kind of introduction to the story of the fall of Benin. The answer is that far too often the story of the fall of Benin is told as if that fall was brought about almost magically by the action of the British in 1897. The internal factors at work within Benin in the nineteenth century are often ignored with the result that the events of 1897 do not always make complete sense. It is proposed here to put the events of 1897 within their proper historical setting and so give new meaning to the story of Benin's fall.

As has been already stated, Benin's economy was dependent on a wide ranging trade with the Yoruba, the Itsekiri, the Nupe, and the Europeans. In the nineteenth century, something happened to disturb Benin's trade with every one of these groups. First the Yoruba. As is well known, the nineteenth century was for the Yoruba a century of wars. Although Benin was, for some time, able to profit from the wars by selling arms and ammunition to some of the Yoruba, the overall effect of the Yoruba wars on Benin was far from profitable. The overland route between Benin and the Yoruba country became in-increasingly unsafe, and trade through that route diminished. Politically, there was the rise of Ibadan as the most powerful state in Yorubaland. Ibadan succeeded, especially in the second half of the nineteenth century, in establishing control over most of western Yorubaland — Owo, Akure and the Ekiti country. These were some of the areas which Benin had controlled at an earlier period. Benin was unable to wage a successful war against Ibadan. So then, the Yoruba wars not only had a bad effect on Benin trade; they also led to the shrinking of the Benin empire.

The nineteenth century is also remembered for the suppression of the Atlantic slave trade by Great Britain. One way by which Britain achieved her end was to station what is known as the anti-slave-trade squadron along the West African coast. This squadron captured all vessels engaged in the slave trade and freed the slaves. One area where the presence of the naval squadron produced important consequences was the Itsekiri kingdom, one of the areas with which Benin traded. Until this time, the trade of the Itsekiri kingdom was done mostly along the Forcados River on which the capital, Ode Itsekiri, is situated. The Forcados River is notorious for its shallow bars which made navigation difficult. While traders were prepared to put up with the difficulty of shallow bars in normal times, they were not prepared to risk being caught by the anti-slave-trade squadron in a river where it was very difficult to turn their ships round and flee. Consequently European traders moved away from the Forcados River and began to concentrate their trading activities along the mouth of the Benin River. In fact all ambitious Itsekiri traders now began to move to the mouth of the Benin River. Ughoton, the port of Benin, was connected by creek to the Benin River, but it was so far from the mouth of the river that ships no longer went there. Benin trade, already badly affected by the wars in the Yoruba country, now suffered further from the virtual abandonment of Ughoton as a port. This meant that Benin trade now had to go all the way to the Benin River which was controlled by the Itsekiri. Earlier, the oba had dictated the terms under which trade was carried on at Ughoton; now it was impossible for him to do so. The greater distance which had to be covered by the journey to the Benin River meant reduced profits. What is more, with the overland route no longer safe, such trade as passed between the Yoruba and Benin had to pass through the creeks. The Itsekiri controlled the trade of these creeks. Everything considered, therefore, commercial developments in Itsekiriland had an adverse effect on Benin trade.

If the nineteenth century is famous for the Yoruba wars and the suppression of the Atlantic slave trade, it is also famous for the Muslim revival movement in the northern parts of Nigeria, otherwise known as the jihad. Like the Yoruba wars, the jihad, since it involved fighting, also tended to disrupt trade. With regard to Benin, the jihad had two notable effects. One, it reduced trade between Benin and the Nupe country. Two, the Nupe, in seeking to carry the jihad to the south, mounted a number of attacks on areas subject to Benin's control. So while the Yoruba wars led to the shrinking of the Benin empire in one direction, the Nupe attacks led to the shrinking of the Benin empire in another direction. Thus events within what became Nigeria had already created major economic and political problems for Benin before the British aggression which resulted in the sack of Benin in 1897.

It was not at all surprising that the events already described should have had some effect on developments within Benin itself. We do not yet know very much about events in Benin in the first half of the nineteenth century. The second half would appear to have been a period of troubles for Benin. When Oba Osemwede died in about 1850, there was a struggle among his princes as to who should become oba. We should perhaps at this point say something about succession to the Benin throne. By the nineteenth century, the practice had become established by which the eldest son of the oba was expected to succeed his father. It seems, however, as if there could be some disagreement as to which of the oba's princes was, in fact, the eldest, since the oba had many wives who might well have given birth at about the same time. In addition to the kind of confusion that could arise from this type of situation, there was the temptation for even princes who were clearly not qualified for the succession to want to fight for the throne. Hence, despite the theory that the eldest son of the oba succeeded him, the death of an oba, even in the nineteenth century, did tend to usher in a period of confusion and conflict.

Such a period of confusion and conflict followed the death of Oba Osemwede in about 1850. The princes fought themselves until Adolo, the younger of the two main rivals, emerged victorious and became the oba. But Prince Ogbewekon, who lost the struggle, remained dissatisfied and would not co-operate with the new ruler. He fled to his mother's town in Esan (Ishan) from where he organized rebellions against Benin till he died in 1880. Although we do not know all the details about these rebellions, it is said that thousands of men were involved in the fighting which lasted many years. This meant that a large number of men were prevented from engaging in agriculture, commerce, and other economic pursuits. It did not help matters that the Nupe launched a series of raids into Esan country at this time. It is easy to see how these events disorganized Benin politics and economy, especially in the second half of the nineteenth century.

Looking back at events now, one can say that it was unfortunate for Benin that at the time she had to cope with the type of internal problems and outside pressure described above, the British took the first step that was to prepare the way for British colonial rule in this part of Nigeria. European, largely British, traders had been trading in the Benin River throughout the first half of the nineteenth century. By the 1840s a number of British firms were established in the Benin River where they bought palm oil from the Itsekiri. Relations between the European traders and the Itsekiri were not always cordial. There were various factors which led to conflict, such as disagreement over prices and over the amount of debts outstanding. By 1850 armed conflicts had started to break out between the Itsekiri and the European traders. The details of these quarrels show quite clearly that both sides were equally to blame. But the Europeans always felt that they were right and that the Itsekiri were barbarous and so should be punished. However, the European traders could not punish the Itsekiri themselves because they did not have the means. This situation changed after the appointment of Beecroft in 1849. In 1851 Beecroft bombarded the Itsekiri settlement of Bobi; another consul imposed heavy fines on the Itsekiri in 1864 and again in 1866 even when the Europeans had been responsible for creating disturbance. The consul was able to do this because he always came in a warship which he used to frighten the Itsekiri people.

For some time Benin did not feel the new pressure of the British. Benin City is not on the coast and therefore could not be bombarded easily by the consul. Also the British were not doing trade directly with the Benin any more, since Ughoton was no longer functioning as a port. However, Europeans had heard about Benin since the sixteenth century when the first European visitors reached Benin. It was only natural, therefore, that European traders and the British consul should be anxious to get to Benin and establish some kind of relationship with the oba. The need for this kind of contact was the more necessary because the oba was regarded by all the neighbouring peoples with great fear and respect. The oba was regarded by these peoples as possessing supernatural powers. Indeed, he was regarded as a divine ruler, nearly a god in his own right. This being so, his influence was seen as very great even in this period when unfavourable circumstances were reducing the wealth and power of the oba.

At first Europeans had a very high impression of the civilization and culture of Benin. All the Europeans who visited Benin in the early period right up to the seventeenth century wrote very favourable reports. However, by the second half of the nineteenth century, Benin began to have a very poor reputation. Europeans began to speak about human sacrifice and other evils; Benin began to be referred to as the City of Blood. The people themselves were beginning to be described as barbaric uncivilized, and great rogues. These reports were without question great exaggerations. Benin, like other African kingdoms, no doubt indulged in human sacrifice. But nowhere in Africa was human sacrifice indulged in as a joke. Human beings were sacrificed to the gods and ancestors in moments of great crisis as a major atonement – as a plea to the gods and ancestors to forgive the wrongs of their children, to bring about favourable conditions. Also, when the oba or some other important person died, a number of his slaves were buried with him to minister to his needs in the other world. Already we have said that Benin was facing very unfavourable conditions during the first half of the nineteenth century. The rulers at the time may well have seen this as the work of the gods. To appease these gods they may have indulged in human sacrifice. Perhaps there were more such sacrifices than before. But the Europeans who reported about Benin did not understand why human sacrifices took place and so merely painted the people, and especially their oba, as barbarians.

No British consul visited Benin until Richard Burton did so in 1862. Burton was one of those Europeans who saw nothing good in the African. He went to Benin mainly because he thought he could get the oba to use his influence to keep the Itsekiri under proper control. The oba was, however, more interested in securing increased European trade for himself and his people. Burton was no doubt disappointed with his visit. But he took the opportunity of this visit to paint Benin in the blackest possible colours in Europe.

The consuls who came, after Burton inherited his prejudices. Virtually everything that happened in Benin was attributed to the oba's 'juju'. Thus, if the oba was unhappy with the trade situation and tried to get better terms for trade by stopping the flow of goods to the markets for a while, the Europeans reported that he was only able to do this because his people feared his supernatural powers. Even when the trade of other people, like the Itsekiri and Urhobo, was bad, European traders were quite ready to argue that the Oba of Benin's wicked influence was at work. In this way there was gradually built up an image of Benin as an unprogressive, economically backward, and morally corrupt state which could only be saved through the 'civilizing' influence of Europe, notably Great Britain.

However, Britain did not immediately take any action against Benin. It was not until the 1880s that Britain, in the age of the scramble for Africa, began signing treaties with the peoples of the Niger Delta. In 1884 the British signed a protectorate treaty with the Itsekiri but not with Benin. But Hewett, the British consul, saw the need to push on to Benin. So he sought permission from Britain to undertake a journey to Benin. This permission was granted. Hewett then asked his assistant, Blair, to go to Benin for the purpose of signing the treaty. Unfortunately Blair died of fever on his way to Benin. So Benin was, for the time being, saved from a British treaty. However, she was not saved from British influence because, when in 1885 the Berlin conference recognized the British protectorate of the Oil Rivers, the Benin kingdom was regarded by Britain as part of that protectorate. This being so, Britain could after 1885, take steps to ensure that Benin was brought under proper British control.

Three years after the Berlin conference, Oba Adolo died.

There was the usual confusion which attended the death of an oba. Various princes had various interests. This time there was no actual civil war before Idugbowa became oba with the reigning name Ovonramwen. But although there was no civil war, there were the usual divisions. The new oba found that his elder brother, Orokhorho, and a number of chiefs were very much against him. In an attempt to strengthen his position the oba killed many of the chiefs who were against him. While this may have frightened other chiefs, it could not make for that cordial relationship between the oba and his chiefs which, as was pointed out earlier, was needed for the political stability of Benin. Thus at the very time when the British were increasing their pressure on Benin, not only was there a new ruler in Benin, there was also a certain amount of disunity and suspicion within Benin's ruling class.

The next successful effort to visit Benin was made in 1892. But before that a number of developments had taken place. The British decided that their control over the protectorate, which they had declared in 1885, was not strong enough. In 1891 therefore they increased the number of British consular officers in what became known as the Niger Coast Protectorate. Apart from the consul and commissioner general, who was head of the protectorate, there were appointed vice-consuls to help him. One of these vice-consuls was stationed in the Benin River; another at Warri. Benin was placed under the Benin River vice-consul. This vice-consul together with his colleagues in Warri began to travel into the Urhobo and Ukwuani areas to try to bring these peoples under British control and also to get them to increase their trade with Britain. Similarly, they were anxious to do the same thing with Benin.

So in 1892 Gallwey, the Benin River vice-consul, decided to visit Benin. Three main factors were responsible for this decision. One, the Itsekiri traders, who made quite a profit as coastal middlemen traders, complained that Benin trade was not moving because the oba had imposed difficult conditions and had stopped trade in certain articles like palm kernels and rubber which he sought to monopolize. No doubt the oba, in doing this, was seeking to improve his own economic position. The British, getting their report mainly from the Itsekiri and others hard hit by the oba's commercial policy, argued that the oba was dislocating trade. Gallwey's visit to Benin was intended to get the oba to lift the 'ban' on trade.

Two, in 1890 Consul Annesley had visited Benin but the oba had refused to see him. This was regarded by Gallwey as a big disgrace. This time, Gallwey wanted to make sure that the oba did see him and so wipe off the 1890 disgrace.

Three, connected with the above, was the need, as Gallwey saw it, for the oba to accept British rule through the signing of the usual kind of treaty. Gallwey prepared thoroughly for the visit. Messages were sent to the oba about the intended visit. The oba finally agreed to receive Gallwey who accordingly left for Benin via Ughoton on 21 March 1892. Gallwey found that the oba already had guides waiting for him when he and his unarmed party arrived at Ughoton. But the journey from Ughoton to Benin took three days, the delay being deliberately arranged, it would seem, by the Oba of Benin. Finally, Gallwey arrived on 23 March.

Gallwey did not have audience with the oba till 26 March. The oba was clearly suspicious of the motives of the British and tried to put off actually meeting for as long as possible. But Gallwey threatened that unless the oba received him in audience he would go away and would not return as a 'friend'. When the meeting finally took place, the treaty was explained to the oba and his chiefs and then they were required to sign it. The other chiefs signed but the oba refused to actually 'touch the pen' on the grounds that he was engaged in certain religious rites which forbade his so doing.

Although it is quite clear that the oba and his chiefs were suspicious, the signing of the treaty was tantamount to accepting British rule even if, as is quite obvious, the oba and chiefs did not see it as such. Henceforth, the vice-consul could use the treaty as an excuse for interfering in the internal affairs, political as well as economic, of Benin. Some of the provisions of the treaty were fundamentally opposed to the whole social, economic, and political set up in Benin. Articles IV and V made it compulsory for the Oba of Benin to accept the advice of the consul in matters of internal and external policy. Article VI laid down that the trade of Benin was to be thrown open to everyone. Yet the oba was anxious to impose his own trade terms. Article VIII made it compulsory for Benin to accept Christian missionaries. In every way then the treaty was against the interests of Benin. Yet the treaty had been signed by the chiefs even though the oba himself had refused to 'touch the pen'. The ground was thus very well prepared for future conflict between the British and Benin.

Between 1892 when the treaty was signed and 1896 when a crisis developed, the reports of traders and the vice-consul were always against the Oba of Benin. For one thing, treaty or no treaty, the oba continued to control Benin trade in the usual way. The Itsekiri had to pay their trade tax or else face stoppage of their trade in Benin territory. Naturally they complained to the vice-consul. The oba continued to place a ban on trade in articles of royal monopoly. This continued to annoy the British. In addition there was the general British view that the oba was only able to act in this way because his subjects feared the 'juju' for which he was famed. So the British began to argue as early as 1893 that in order to improve the trade of this part of the protectorate, the power of the oba of Benin must be destroyed. Gallwey, who in 1891 was opposed to the use of force against the oba, gradually began to come round to the view that force might be the only answer. In fact the crisis had to wait till 1896 largely because the British were busy with Chief Nana in 1894 and with Brass in 1895.

The British action against Nana frightened the oba, who did all he could to avoid contact with the British. Ralph Moor, who was in charge of the protectorate during the expedition against Nana, was determined that an expedition should be sent against Benin. But Sir Claude Macdonald, the consul who had been on leave, forbade military action and pleaded that peaceful means be tried. So fruitless efforts were made to get the Oba of Benin to toe the British line. When in April 1896 the oba stopped all trade with the Itsekiri on the grounds that the Itsekiri were cheating his subjects, Ralph Moor, who had succeeded Macdonald as consul, thought that here, at last, was a good excuse for bringing the oba under control. But then he soon went on leave to Britain.

The man who acted for Moor was a certain Phillips. He visited the Benin River in November 1896 and according to his own account found that all the markets in the oba's territory were closed. The oba had asked the Itsekiri to give him 1,000 sheets of corrugated iron before he would open trade. Phillips tried through Itsekiri chiefs to get the oba to open trade and to allow a British officer to be stationed in Benin. The oba replied that he was engaged in religious ceremonies which would last four months and that he could not receive any white officer until that time.

Phillips now wrote to Britain for permission to visit Benin with a view to deposing and removing the oba. Although Ralph Moor supported Phillips's proposals for military action against the oba, the British government refused to allow such an expedition in 1896. Phillips was asked to postpone action for one year.

Phillips never got the instructions from London to postpone action for one year. By the time the telegram actually left London Phillips was already dead — killed in an ambush on his way to Benin. Phillips had apparently decided to visit Benin late in 1896. He sent messengers to inform the oba accordingly. The oba sent back a message that Phillips should wait for a month to enable him finish the *agwe* festival and that at that time Phillips could come with one Itsekiri chief, not the eight or nine other white men he (Phillips) said he would bring. Phillips probably felt that the oba was playing his usual tricks to avoid meeting with him, so he determined to go on to Benin. Itsekiri chiefs who knew the oba and Benin customs well warned him not to go to Benin. But the foolhardy Phillips decided to go on with the visit. Perhaps he thought the fear of the white man would ensure his success. He should have known from previous experience that the Oba of Benin had his own ideas about the white man.

The British party — 7 officials, 2 traders, and more than 200 carriers — arrived at Ughoton on 3 January 1897. The party was not armed though some arms were packed away in a box. We will never know for sure what happened inside Benin when the news that the British were at Ughoton reached the palace. What is clear is that the oba summoned his chiefs to consult with them. There is also some evidence that the oba was anxious that Benin should not fight the British even though he feared that the British party meant no good. It would seem that the oba was unable to persuade his chiefs not to fight. The majority of the chiefs were apparently satisfied that the British were coming to fight them and so decided that they would take the initiative and fight the British. No one can blame these chiefs. Their oba had told the white man not to come for one month. The white man had refused. Would a friend treat the oba like that? If the white man chose to insult their oba in this way, then he must be prepared for the consequences. And so it was that the Benin chiefs laid an ambush for Phillips and his party and killed all the white men, except two who managed to escape, and many of the carriers. This is what the old text books refer to as the Benin massacre of 1897.

It was quite clear that the British would avenge the death of their men. By February a force of 1,500 men (including the sailors who were to man the boats) had been assembled and the attack began on 10 February 1897. The very size of the attacking force was meant to strike fear not only into Benin but into all the surrounding peoples. The force was divided into three. The main force operated from the Ologbo creek, moving northwards from roughly the region of Sapele. Another force struck from Ughoton. The third attacked from the Jamieson River area. Of these, the one which really did havoc was the one which moved north from the Sapele area. Although the Bini fought doggedly, they could not hold back this force. The Ughoton group met with really stiff opposition, no doubt because the Bini expected the main attack to come from this route and so must have defended it with the best of their forces. In fact, so successful the Bini resistance on this route that the British force was unable to contribute anything much to the fall of Benin City. However, the British had superior weapons and, ultimately, through the success of the Sapele force, gained victory over Benin. It was thus that on 17 February 1897, Benin fell to the British after a heroic defence.

After the fall of the city, resistance continued for a long time. The oba, with a large number of his chiefs, fled the city, and it took a long time before these chiefs were finally persuaded to accept the fact that Benin had become British territory. Oba Ovonramwen, for example, did not submit till 5 August 1897. With him came ten of his chiefs. As is well known, Oba Ovonramwen was tried and deported to Calabar where he lived in exile till he died in 1914.

Such then is the story of the fall of Benin. It is quite clear that although in the accounts of European writers much emphasis is laid on the question of human sacrifice, that was not really the major issue in the conflict between the oba and the British. For the oba, the issue was one of survival at a time when Britain was determined to seize his territory by force if he would not (as which ruler would?) give up that territory peacefully. It is important to see that in all of this clash it was the British who were being aggressive even if they did not use guns. The treaty of 1892 was, in so far as it destroyed Benin's independence, an act of political aggression. The attempt to force the oba to give up his time-honoured ways of controlling the trade of his dominion was economically, an act of aggression. Itsekiri chiefs who complained about the oba's trade restrictions were paid subsidies in lieu of the duties they used to impose on European trade. The Oba of Benin was offered nothing as compensation. Yet he was expected to allow the British to have their way. If the killing of Phillips and his party was a massacre, the expedition against Benin by the British was an even greater massacre — indeed that, not what happened in January, should be regarded as *the* Benin massacre.

One other point requires to be stressed. The events of 1892-7 must not be seen in isolation from those developments in Benin throughout the nineteenth century to which attention has been drawn in this episode. This is because the oba was acting within a certain situation. Events within the country had weakened Benin's power both politically and economically. Not only had the Benin empire shrunk as a consequence of the events in Yorubaland and Northern Nigeria, the home front was also far from easy. How could Oba Ovonramwen who had killed a number of chiefs at the beginning of his reign really hope to have the full confidence of his council of state? Is it surprising, therefore, that he was not able to persuade his chiefs about the best way to act in the crisis situation of January 1897? All these developments must be taken into full account if we are to properly understand Benin's attitude to the British. The coming of the British was, in fact, no more than just another adverse circumstance. The difference this time was that the British happened to be technologically superior to the Edo and so, when the final trial of strength came, the British won.

BIBLIOGRAPHICAL NOTE

For people like Burns and those who take after him, the fall of Benin resulted from a logical reprisal for what has gone down as the 'Benin Massacre' meaning the attack on Phillips and his band. In books like *The Benin Massacre* (1897) by Alan Boisragon and *Benin, The City of Blood* (1897) by R. H. S. Bacon, two survivors from Phillips's band, written in the years just after the event, the impression is given that the Bini were a bloodthirsty lot whose attack on the British party was typical of their normal pastime. There now exist works which appraise the situation more critically. These include J. C. Anene's *Southern Nigeria in Transition* and A. F. C. Ryder's *Benin and the Europeans* (Longman 1969). Ryder's work is particularly useful in giving the most detailed account presently available of nineteenth-century Benin such that the events of 1897 are seen against the larger background of the history of Benin during the century rather than as a sudden, isolated episode. Dr P. A. Igbafe has also done work on Benin and has in two articles questioned the old theories and provided a more satisfactory analysis of the situation. P. A. Igbafe's 'Oba Ovonramwen and The Fall of Benin', *Tarikh* II, 2, 1968, 'The Fall of Benin: a reassessment', *Journal of African History,* XI, 3, 1970. Igbafe also devotes the second chapter of his forthcoming book on *Benin under British Administration 1897-1938* (Longman) to the same subject.

EPISODE
7

The Fall of the Aro

By the end of the nineteenth century most of the coastal parts of Southern Nigeria had fallen to the British. In the Yoruba country the British were already establishing themselves in the hinterland. Across the Niger the hinterland of the eastern delta was occupied by the Igbo and Ibibio. These were the peoples on whom the coastal traders depended for the products they sold to the Europeans — be these slaves or, since the suppression of the overseas trade, palm produce and other products of the forest belt. By the end of the nineteenth century the British had also begun the push into this Igbo-Ibibio hinterland. However, not much had been achieved. British influence in the Igbo and Ibibio country was still very limited, for only a few towns and villages rather near the coast and along the rivers had been visited. Some of these visits in the years between 1896 and 1899 were of a peaceful nature. Others were small military expeditions designed to teach the groups concerned the efficiency of the maxim gun.

Of the Igbo and the Ibibio groups the most famous was the Aro group. As is well known, the Igbo and Ibibio are organized on a clan basis — using the term clan in the sense of a group of villages which trace their origin to a common male ancestor. Usually there was the clan centre where the founder of the clan first settled. From that parent settlement new settlements sprang. All such new settlements, however, recognized their blood ties with the parent settlement. Each Igbo or Ibibio village was an independent unit subject to the control of the village elders who were the link between the ancestors and the present generation. Age, however, was not the only criterion for wielding influence and authority. Some of the Igbo and Ibibio groups boasted secret societies which, because they could only be joined by the wealthy, tended to enjoy special influence in village and clan. Proven success in various fields — war, hunting, farming, trading, and so on, also conferred special respect and enabled a man to play a leading role within his community.

161

The fragmented nature of Igbo and Ibibio society meant that the area within which the writ of any particular authority ran was limited. Disputes which arose between individuals had to be settled within the village. When inter-village disputes arose, a third village was often called in to arbitrate. There was no central Igbo or Ibibio political authority to which appeals could be made. This meant that the people had to be content, most of the time, with the decision of their elders. There were, however, occasions when the decisions of the elders did not satisfy one of the parties to a dispute. In the absence of a central authority with which an appeal could be lodged, the Igbo and Ibibio had recourse to the supernatural. This was not surprising, for these peoples, like all peoples in Africa and elsewhere, were deeply religious. In fact, the respect which their elders enjoyed was the result of the fact that these elders were the priests of their people. Each lineage head owed his authority to the fact that he was the custodian of the *Ofo*, the 'spirit' of the lineage handed down from lineage head to lineage head. He propitiated the departed ancestors as well as the deity of the lineage or the village and so ensured the well-being of his people.

With a people like this, it need not surprise anyone that the supernatural was brought into the settlement of disputes between individuals and between groups. Thus it was that various oracles became famous in Igbo and Ibibio land. However, by far the most famous of these oracles was the Ibinokpabi oracle, better known to history as the Long Juju of Arochukwu. To Arochukwu came people from far and near to have their disputes settled. The Aro put the fame of their oracle to good use economically. Astute traders themselves, the awe of their oracle insured them against attacks by other peoples as they travelled across Igbo and Ibibio land plying their trade. Aro trade spread through the entire Igbo and Ibibio country reaching quite close to the coast. Along these many routes Aro traders settled to do their trade. Aro traders settled among other Igbo and Ibibio groups played the role of informants to the priests of the Long Juju so that the priests were often quite well informed about the details of the cases referred to them, and so usually gave fair verdicts. This enhanced the reputation of the Long Juju and further guaranteed the safety of the long-distance Aro trader. The Aro did not depend only on the supernatural to ensure that the verdict of the Long Juju was obeyed. Rather, they had mercenaries in the Abam whom they armed with guns obtained from the coast. Those who failed to carry out the verdict of the Long Juju were visited by the Aro mercenaries—physical sanctions thus being applied to ensure respect for, and obedience to, the divine!

Before the suppression of the overseas slave trade by the British, the main commodity of Aro trade was slaves. Although certain criminals convicted before the Long Juju were sold as slaves, it is unthinkable that such victims of justice alone could have furnished the Aro with all the slaves they are reputed to have sent down to the coast—for the Aro were the great slave suppliers of Eastern Nigeria. Rather, the Aro bought their slaves all over their areas of commercial activity, the Long Juju playing its role as guarantor of their personal safety and as a supplementary source of slaves. When the British suppressed the overseas slave trade the Aro turned their attention to the new trade in palm produce and, just as they had been the main suppliers of slaves, they quickly also became the main suppliers of palm produce.

It was as middlemen of the hinterland that the Aro made their name as traders. They bought slaves and later palm produce from the other Igbo and Ibibio peoples and supplied to the coastal states. They did not themselves get to the coast but neither did the coastal traders come right up into the hinterland. A gentleman's agreement was reached by which the Aro brought their wares to a point near the coast like Itu where the agents of the coastal traders bought from them. This arrangement also enabled the Aro to be the main suppliers of European goods to many of the Igbo and Ibibio groups in the hinterland of the delta states. It is easy to see therefore how the Aro dominated the commercial life of the Igbo hinterland. Let it be said at this point that the Aro at no time sought political dominion over the other Igbo and Ibibio groups. Their main interest was trade and if they came to blows with any of the other groups it was usually because such groups threatened their commercial interests.

By the end of the nineteenth century the British had succeeded in gaining control of the delta states. While the delta states must have resented the loss of their political authority, they probably resented even more the determination of the British to penetrate the hinterland and deal directly with the oil producers. As is well known the delta states developed on the basis of their middleman

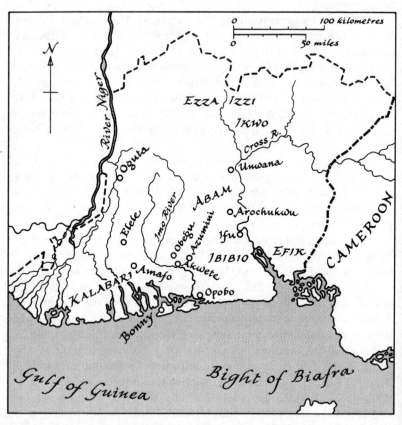

Map 9   Map of Southern Nigeria, showing Arochukwu and surrounding settlements

monopoly of the trade between the hinterland and the Europeans. Their fall to the British was accompanied by a determination by the latter to trade direct with the hinterland. The coastal trader, gradually being displaced from his role as a middleman trader in the old style, began to want to accompany the British into the hinterland so that he could, as it were, develop a new way of playing the old game. If any group in the hinterland stood to lose by this new development it was the Aro, the great middlemen traders of that hinterland. Hence the conflict which developed between the British and Aro can really only be understood against this essentially economic background.

The British military attack on the Aro did not take place until December 1901. The four years which preceded that date were, however, years of continual conflict between the British and the Aro. Having occupied the coastal states, the British began to push into the interior as from about 1896. The Aro immediately began to organize to frustrate this push. The British were pushing in from two centres, the Cross River area and the Atlantic seaboard with Bonny, Opobo, and Kalabari as bases. The Aro ensured that they worked out peacefully or by force a system of alliances with various groups designed to obstruct British penetration. Thus, in the Cross River zone they instigated the Ikwo, Ezza, and Izzi clans to resist British penetration in 1898. A military expedition sent into the area was not sufficiently powerful to break the resistance of these people who made no secret of the fact that they were acting as allies of the Aro.

In 1899 the British had a similar experience from the Bonny, Opobo, and Kalabari end. The Aro forced the villages north of the Azumini river to resist British advance. British political officers were told by informants that left to themselves some of these villages like Ihafu, Elele, Amafo, and so on would have been prepared to deal with the British, but that the Aro had warned all and sundry that any group who co-operated with the British would receive condign punishment when they, the Aro, had inflicted a crushing defeat on the British. Further into the hinterland, the Aro carried out various acts of terrorism, attacking villages and killing some of their occupants. The aim behind these attacks was not mere lust for blood but a demonstration that the Aro would not tolerate the British attempt to upset the old trading system and that any group that toyed with the idea of receiving the British must regard itself as an enemy of the Aro.

Aro fears about future prospects for their trade was not brought about only by the attack on their middleman role in the hinterland. As was said earlier, the fact that the Long Juju served as a court of appeal for many groups even outside Igbo and Ibibio countries played an important part in promoting the trade of the Aro. As agents of the Long Juju people were not only afraid to lay hands on them, but went out of their way to court their friendship. This was good for Aro trade. Now, however, the British had started establishing Native Courts in the areas which they had occupied. British political officers as well as missionaries preached against the age-old judicial and other institutions of the Nigerian peoples. British occupation would thus mean not only loss of the middleman position in the interior enjoyed by the Aro, it would also ultimately remove that supernatural sanction which did so much to promote Aro trade. The Aro thus had yet another reason for opposing the extension of British influence.

In a sense the British misunderstood the reasons for Aro hostility. They assumed, wrongly, that the Aro were the political leaders of the Igbo and Ibibio and that their hostility stemmed from their unreadiness to yield that leadership to the British. Consequently the British were satisfied that once they had been able to overcome the Aro there would be no further resistance and that the entire hinterland of the eastern delta would be theirs for the taking. Partly because of this misconception and partly because Aro activities in the period 1898-1901 had shown them to be inveterate enemies of the British, Sir Ralph Moor, the head of the British administration, made elaborate preparations for the Aro Expedition. He would have liked to act earlier than he did but was prevented from doing so by the fact that Nigeria had to contribute troops to the British war against the Asante which did not end till early in 1901.

The force which was ultimately got together was placed under the command of Lt Colonel H. F. Montanaro, pompously entitled Officer Commanding Aro Field Forces! The force consisted of 87 officers, 1,550 rank and file, and 2,100 carriers. There were four columns taking off from Oguta, Akwete, Unwuna, and Itu. Political officers as well as medical doctors were attached to each column. The commanding officers, obviously thinking that this was a major war, issued detailed directives to the sectional commanders. Ralph Moor briefed the political officers as to how to win the people over. At the same time he made it clear that the political officers were not to interfere with the soldiers when the latter came across any hostile towns. Hostile towns were defined as those whose inhabitants resisted the troops going through their towns or which evacuated their people on the approach of the British. Moor anticipated very tough opposition and the Aro Expedition was conceived of as one of the grandest the British would undertake in Nigeria. The officers were to stick to their orders. No radical departure from the plan was to be made without consulting the consul-general himself.

While the British were thus busy writing memoranda and issuing directives, the Aro struck. In a raid against the town of Obegu, the British reported that the Aro killed 400 people. Obegu was a government centre with a rest house which the Aro burnt down. Some stores had also been kept there for the soldiers; the Aro destroyed these too. Undoubtedly, then, the Aro knew that an attack was under way and they thought they might at least make one themselves on a pro-British town. This action, however, had the effect of preventing any further delays and the British forces set out on 28 November 1901.

The actual expedition turned out to be an anti-climax. Although the reports speak of the great resistance put up by the Aro, there really was not much fighting. Aroland is savannah country. The people had no chance in such country against rifles and the maxim gun. Most villages were abandoned before the British arrived. Those who stayed behind were sensible enough to surrender. The only worthwhile action was perhpas the blowing up of the shrine of the Long Juju with Montanaro himself leading the operation. The expedition was soon over. The Aro had been overthrown and the British could begin — only begin — to spread their influence into Igbo and Ibibio country.

The fall of the Aro did not mean, as the British had hoped, the fall of the other groups. However, it taught other groups that the might of the British was irresistible even though a few groups still challenged that might even after the Aro experience. There can thus be no questioning of the fact that the fall of the Aro was a major breakthrough in the British conquest of the hinterland of south-eastern Nigeria. It should be clear from all that has been said that Aro attitude to the British was determined by their desire to preserve the old socio-political and economic arrangements in that part of Nigeria. The destruction of these arrangements was, however, in the logic of the British imperial thrust. The conflict described above thus falls into focus.

BIBLIOGRAPHICAL NOTE

The British attitude to the Aro is discussed fully in J. C. Anene's *Southern Nigeria in Transition*. Anene also has an article on the Aro in *J. H. S. N.*, *11*, (1965). A. E. Afigbo, 'The Aro Expedition of 1901–1902' *Odu* (New Series), *7* (April 1972) states clearly and briefly what were the main issues in the Aro-British confrontation and Afigbo fits the Aro into the wider framework of Igbo resistance to the British in his 'Patterns of Igbo Resistance to British Conquest', *Tarikh*, *4*, *3* (1973). Elizabeth Isichei's *The Ibo People and the Europeans* also discusses the subject.

EPISODE

8

The Fall of the Tiv

British occupation of the Tiv country was spread over many years. Although the first clash between the two parties occurred as early as 1900, it cannot be said that British occupation was complete or effective until about 1914. The explanation for this lies in the fact that the Tiv are a decentralized or fragmented society organized on a lineage or clan basis. There were thus very many Tiv groups and villages each of which was independent of the next and each of which had to protect itself against any possible encroachment by the next group.

Like many other societies similarly organized, it was not unusual for quarrels between villages to result in fighting. Also the groups situated immediately on the banks of the Benue engaged in some piracy, attacking the canoes of enemies who might be passing by and seizing whatever they could. A look at Map 10 will reveal that the Tiv were outside the Sokoto caliphate. As is well known, one of the most important nineteenth-century events in what became Northern Nigeria was the jihad of Uthman dan Fodiye. The leaders of the jihad and their successors did their best to spread Islam to most of Northern Nigeria. The Tiv were among those who were not converted into Islam as an immediate consequence of the jihad. To say this is to say that the Tiv successfully organized themselves for survival in the face of militant Islam. They could only do this because they were tough fighters who acquired a reputation for maintaining their independence against all comers for most of their history.

It was not enough to keep Islam out of their country. The Tiv also had to be able to withstand the slave raids organized by the various emirates against their infidel (non-Muslim) neighbours. The evidence available suggests that the Tiv were able to do this. Various factors — the logic of their socio-political institutions and the menace of their neighbours, especially the Sokoto caliphate — thus made the Tiv into redoubtable warriors known for their poisoned arrows and their courage.

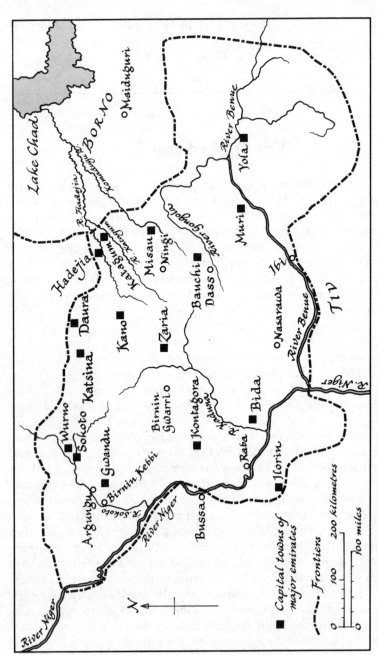

Map 10   The Sokoto caliphate before the British conquest

The British clashed with the Tiv in the very first year of their administration of Northern Nigeria. This need not surprise anyone, for Lokoja, the first headquarters of the British administration, was quite close to Tiv territory. Before Lugard took over from the Royal Niger Company, the Company had started the construction of a telegraph line from Lokoja to Ibi. Lugard, who was anxious to lay out lines of communication for his new administration, decided to carry on with the building of this line already begun by the Company. The first clash of arms between the British and the Tiv occurred as a consequence of the British crossing of Tiv territory for the purpose of constructing this telegraph line.

Lugard sent a telegraph construction party under a military escort into Tiv territory. Existing works on the British conquest of Nigeria never sufficiently stress the shock and irritation that our peoples must have felt at the violation of their territories by the imperialists. Take the Tiv for example. To have suddenly observed strangers surveying their land, to have seen these backed by soldiers armed with rifles or even more deadly weapons must have filled them with great anger and fear. Lugard apparently thought that since in January 1900, he had proclaimed a British protectorate over Northern Nigeria, there was no need for him to get in contact with the various peoples for the purpose of explaining to them why certain things — like the construction of a telegraph line — had to be done. After all was he not the representative of Her Britannic Majesty? For the Tiv, a people with a reputation for fiercely maintaining their independence, Lugard's act was tantamount to a declaration of war. They responded by launching an attack on the telegraph party, killing three and wounding Captain Easton, the commanding officer, and ten others. Captain Easton was forced to retreat. Lugard explained that the retreat became necessary because the maxim gun was jammed and so the British party was handicapped. The truth may well have been that the Tiv, taking advantage of the bushes, fell upon the British party so unexpectedly that Easton had to retreat to save the lives of his men.

Lugard was not the man to allow what was obviously a blow on 'British prestige' to pass unrevenged. He organized a counter-offensive. The force which he now sent against the Tiv was commanded by Lt Colonel Lowry Cole, one of the most senior officers available in Northern Nigeria at the time. Under him were Captains McClintock, Easton, Cubitt, Carroll, Cockburn, Wilkinson, and Robertson, two lieutenants, ten non-commissioned officers, 306 rank and file armed, in addition to rifles, with five maxim guns and one rocket tube. It is clear from the composition of the force that Lugard regarded the encounter with the Tiv as a major one. The British fought the Tiv on and off from 4 January to 9 March 1900. The report of the war showed that the British engaged in indiscriminate burning of whole villages as part of their offensive. Lugard, who must have derived great satisfaction from the success which his soldiers, armed with rifles and maxim guns, scored against the Tiv armed with spears and bows and arrows, nevertheless wrote to London, 'I cannot but express my sense of regret at the very great loss of life among these ignorant savages and the burning of scores of villages with their food. The Munshis, however, are a most intractable people, and nothing except extremely severe chastisement of this sort will prevent them from lawless murders and looting of canoes, or induce them to allow the telegraph to be constructed through their country.'

To further justify his action Lugard argued that because the Tiv had no 'recognized chief' they were 'continually fighting among themselves. They have a character for extreme lawlessness and disregard for life and are reputed as treacherous and thieves.' He related how in 1885 and again in 1886 the Tiv had attacked and looted the trading stations established in their country by the Niger Company. It was characteristic of Lugard not to explain why the Tiv had attacked the Niger Company stores. It was equally characteristic of him that he made no effort to understand why the Tiv were warlike. His concern was clear: to prove to his employers that the Tiv could understand no other language than that of force. If indeed he knew this to be true then it is the more reprehensible that he chose to send an armed party through their country without establishing prior contact. The Tiv responded to his act of disregard by killing three and wounding eleven. His soldiers had reacted by causing 'very great loss of life' and 'burning scores of villages with their food'. It is easy to see which side was behaving more like 'savages' in the situation.

From Lugard's report we get some picture of the nature of Tiv defences and war methods. Tiv towns were not walled like those of the Hausa-Fulani. The Tiv did not, therefore, always have to fight from within their towns. On most of the occasions described by the commander of the British forces, the Tiv moved out of their towns and took advantage of 'dense forests' which hid their numerical strength and gave them the element of surprise. Their weapon was the poisoned arrow. When hard pressed they fled to their towns. The British reported that in one such town they discovered that the Tiv had dug a trench eight feet deep and ten feet broad right round. The only way across the trench was 'a bridge of eight logs only'. In traditional warfare it would have been difficult for the enemy to cross such a bridge. The British with their maxim guns had no difficulty in doing so.

The next encounter took place in May 1901, at a time when Lugard was away on leave and Wallace was acting as High Commissioner. If the 1900 episode had the Tiv attack on the telegraph line to explain it, the 1901 episode had no other explanation than the determination of the British to reduce Northern Nigeria to obedience. The British force, led by Captain Eckersley and made up of Lieutenant Wilkin, two sergeants and 150 rank and file, were in Tiv territory for some five weeks in the months of May and June. As in the previous year this expedition was marked by the burning of villages, cattle, and food crops. Wallace, like Lugard, justified these barbarities. 'It is important', he pleaded with the Colonial Office, 'that severe punishment be meted to these savage tribes when we first come in contact with them.' Yet no evidence was adduced by Wallace to justify the accusation of savagery on the part of the Tiv, unless refusal to yield up a people's independence can be construed as savagery.

In a sense the events of 1900 and 1901 were but the prelude to the major British push into Tiv territory which took place in the years 1906-8.

In January 1906 Lugard sent this telegram to the British Colonial Office: Munshi tribe has destroyed Royal Niger Company's depot Abinsi. Navigation of Benue closed making necessary preparations for strong military expedition.' The background to the events which led to the telegram was a quarrel which broke out between some Hausa and Jukun in Abinsi, apparently within the precincts of the Niger Company's trade store. In the fighting which resulted from the quarrel the Jukun were coming off worse. They therefore called on their Tiv neighbours to come to their aid. The Tiv, who probably saw the Hausa as rivals in trade anyway, welcomed the opportunity to join the affray. This support ensured the success of the Jukun against the Hausa. During the fighting the Niger Company store was looted and then razed to the ground.

The records are silent on what was the role, if any, of the Niger Company's agents during the fight. Lugard, in what may well have been an exaggerated report, claimed that hundreds of people including women and children were driven into the Benue where they drowned, while many more headless corpses were left on the scene of fighting. The truth as to the actual number of dead will never be known, let alone details as to how many of the dead were Tiv and Jukun and how many were Hausa. For Lugard these details were not important, for he was not seeking permission to punish all the parties that had been engaged in the fighting. He was looking for some excuse to carry on the British occupation of the Tiv territory.

The Colonial Office reaction to Lugard's telegram was one of caution. That office was worried that Lugard had not indicated which particular section of the Tiv were involved in the affray. The officials feared, quite correctly, that Lugard meant to seize the opportunity to launch an attack against all of 'the Munshi country' which 'we know . . . is a large one'. Another minute questioned the wisdom of sanctioning expeditions 'of indefinite character and considerable extent without any substantial information'. It was noted that if the peace and order of the colony depended on a vigorous offensive then Lugard had to be supported. At the same time, however, the Colonial Office was worried about the 'chronic bloodshed' in West Africa brought about by incessant military expeditions. In the end the Colonial Office telegraphed Lugard that it could not sanction a large expedition without more detailed information and that Lugard had better therefore limit the operations to what was necessary for opening the Benue to navigation and protecting life.

While the officials in London were busy writing minutes, Lugard was busy getting his force ready to move into Tiv territory. As finally composed the 'Munshi' expeditionary force consisted of 26 officers, 2 medicals, 13 N.C.O's, 642 rank and file, 850 carriers, and 4 maxim guns — all to be commanded by Colonel Hasler, Acting Commandant of the Northern Nigeria

Regiment of the West African Frontier Force. As was the case with his handling of the conquest of the emirates, Lugard did not always wait for instructions from London. Quite often he delayed giving information until he had made up his mind what to do. In this case he had already sent the force into the field before the telegram from the Colonial Office reached him. His reaction to the telegram was again typical. He replied by telegram as follows:

'600 corpses remain at site of Abinsi, numbers drowned carried off, unknown . . . Propose to follow offenders, inflict punishment, recover property, captives and afterwards traverse Munshiland . . . It seems to me favourable opportunity for settlement of the question once and for all. Request you to inform me at once, whether you order cancellation of expedition.'

Lugard knew that he held the trump card in the fact that the expedition was already under way. The Colonial Office would never order its recall, knowing that to do that was to expose the British in Northern Nigeria not only to ignominy but to possible attack by the Tiv and other peoples. The Colonial Secretary was forced to cable back that it was not his intention that the expedition be recalled. Lugard had had his way, and was able to report in March 1906 that the expedition had been completely successful. He noted that the Tiv offered little resistance to the expedition; yet villages in which loot or captives were found were fined, or burnt, or both. Lugard's only regret was that the outbreak of the Satiru rebelluon in Sokoto prevented his taking advantage of the success of the expedition to reduce all Tivland to obedience, as the troops were needed to deal with the Satiru affair.

In view of Lugard's regret that the Satiru rebellion forced him to postpone reducing all Tivland to obedience in March 1906, it was to be expected that the issue would be re-opened once that rebellion was successfully crushed. This was exactly what happened, except that Lugard himself had left Northern Nigeria by the time the next move was made. In November 1906 Wallace wrote to the Colonial Office seeking permission to send an expedition into the Tiv country to continue the work already begun. He argued in support of his case that the Tiv were becoming 'more truculent and daring'. This time the Colonial Office was not prepared to let Wallace have his way. The

Secretary of State for the Colonies wrote, 'I desire that no outrage or aggression .on the part of the natives should be tolerated but that your government should also abstain from any action which may constitute an aggression or a cause of grievance to native tribes'. The Colonial Office was satisfied that Wallace had brought forward no justifiable reasons for a military expedition against the Tiv. While that office was quite prepared to allow steps to be taken to establish trading stations and prevent inter-village fights and so on, it would not sanction military expeditions just for the sake of 'teaching the natives the efficacy of the maxim'. The Tiv were thus spared any further military expeditions in the process of the British occupation of their territory.

This is not to say that British occupation was thus completed. Far from it. All that had happened after the 1906 expedition was that a government station was opened at Katsena Allah. From there it was now proposed to push gradually inland. The policy was for political officers escorted by a small military force to move into the Tiv interior and gradually open up the country to British trade and influence. The Colonial Office was determined that this had to be done peacefully, not through war. Percy Girouard, who succeeded Lugard as High Commissioner, carried out this policy faithfully. He was lucky to have in Resident Ruxton, who was in charge of the Tiv country, a man fully committed to the policy of peaceful penetration.

Lugard and Wallace had been inclined to paint the Tiv in lurid colours to justify a policy of aggression. In doing so they blinded themselves to the fact that Tiv reaction to the British was determined by a long tradition of independence and a natural objection to indiscriminate traversing of their country by Europeans — whether traders, missionaries, or soldiers. The people of the Niger delta opposed British penetration for similar economic reasons. The Tiv were very keen traders as even Wallace had to admit. Their determination to keep the British out of their country was determined partly by fear of losing their trade. Girouard took full cognizance of this fear. While urging gradual penetration he made it quite clear that European influx into Tiv country must be strictly controlled. Supporting Ruxton's policy, he quoted from the latter's report:

'This country (Tiv country) is certainly not ripe for the unrestricted advent of Europeans and still less so for missionaries.

I fear that neither the European nor the coast native would appreciate the slenderness of our hold, and realize the free and independent character of the Munshis.'

Wallace, who remained second in command to Girouard, had to toe the official line. He was clearly amazed that Ruxton was able to pursue a policy of peaceful penetration. 'Few thought', he wrote, that Ruxton, 'would succeed in carrying out the policy laid down and that he has done so reflects greatly to his credit for I know from my own experience with the Munshi that it requires greater courage to negotiate with him than to open fire on him.' It is quite clear from his own attitude that Wallace did not possess this 'greater courage'.

, So, then, for the Tiv a policy of *festina lente* (hasten slowly) was pursued from 1907 right up to the end of the decade. By that time their brothers who belonged to Southern Nigeria were similarly 'pacified' and the British occupation of Tiv country was complete, even though many details of administration had yet to be worked out.

BIBLIOGRAPHICAL NOTE

There are very few published works on the Tiv. The picture here presented has been based very much on the primary sources and is essentially based on my research note, 'The British Pacification of the Tiv', *Journal of the Historical Society of Nigeria, 7, 1* (December 1973).

EPISODE

9

The Fall of Borno

In late August 1973 the President of the Democratic Republic of Sudan, Sayed Gafar Mohammed Numeiri paid an official visit to Nigeria. One of the states he visited was the North-Eastern State with Maiduguri as capital. Speaking on the occasion of the visit the Shehu of Borno, Umar Ibn Abubakar Garbai El-Kanemi recalled what he described as the historic links between Borno and the Sudan. He recalled how some of the earlier rulers of Borno had passed through the Sudan on their way to the holy pilgrimage. He recalled how even now many people of the state find hospitality in the Sudan as they undertake the *haji* every year. He spoke of a fusion of cultures arising from a common religion — Islam. 'We do not hesitate to affirm that in this part of our country we regard the Sudanese as one of ourselves.'

What the learned shehu did not recall was that between 1893 and 1895 one, Rabih Fadlallah, whose career began in the Sudan had conquered Borno and assassinated Hashimi, the then shehu. The fall of Borno to the British cannot be fully understood except within the context of the activities of Rabih and his son after him, as well as the response of France and Germany to these activities.

Rabih was originally in the service of Zubeir Pasha, an adventurer in the Eastern Sudan (present Democratic Republic of Sudan) who made a name as a great slave raider. Zubeir Pasha fell out with the Egyptian authorities (until the rise of the Mahdi in 1882 the Sudan was under Egyptian control) who accordingly waged war against him. Rabih, as one of Zubeir Pasha's commanders, fought against the Egyptian forces led by one Romolo Gessi. In 1878 Romolo Gessi laid a trap which, had it succeeded, would have resulted in the destruction of Zubeir Pasha's forces. Rabih got wind of this trap and escaped westwards. As a soldier of fortune he fought his way through the areas along his escape route. By 1893 he had overrun Wadai, Dar-Kuti, and Baghirmi and was on the outskirts of Borno. His already large and well armed force was strengthened by the alliance of Hayat b. Said, a rebel member of the family of the Shaikh Uthman dan Fodiye. Hayat believed in the Mahdist movement, which the caliphate officially disapproved of. Even before Rabih's arrival in Borno, Hayat had made himself a threat to the internal security of the Sokoto caliphate by his raiding activities in the Adamawa region. He joined forces with Rabih Fadlallah because he believed that Rabih, like himself, was a Mahdist.

Rabih's forces fell on Borno in 1893 and very rapidly conquered it. Kukawa the capital was sacked and the shehu was forced to flee to Zinder. Rabih caught up with the shehu there and had him assassinated. Thereafter, Rabih set himself up as ruler of Borno and even threatened to overrun Katagun, Zinder, Kano and Sokoto. Between 1893 and 1900 Rabih ruled Borno.

The death of the shehu in 1893 led to a dispersal of the royal family. Some went to Zinder, some to Kano, some to Damagaram. Among those who fled to Damagaram was Umar Sanda Kura Ibn Ibrahim. The activities of the members of the Borno royal family between 1893 and 1900 are rather confused. Some went to stay with Rabih, their conqueror, in Dikwa. Others, like the group led by Umar Sanda, resented their conquest by Rabih and sought the alliance of the French operating in the Zinder area to get rid of Rabih. The French were by this time active in the Lake Chad region and were genuinely afraid of the possible consequences for themselves of Rabih's activities. They were, therefore, only too glad to accept the overtures of Umar Sanda and his group. In January 1900 the Bornoans installed Umar Sanda as the Shehu of Borno, with a French military expedition watching. The idea was to demonstrate that they did not accept Rabih as their ruler. Although the French did not, on the occasion of this installation, promise the overthrow of Rabih, they took Umar Sanda with them as they marched towards the Chad. Ultimately a joint French-Bornoan force succeeded in killing Rabih at a place called Kusseri on 22 April 1900.

Rabih's son, Fadlallah, took over his father's mantle. The French therefore carried on the war against Fadlallah. Although Fadlallah had a fairly large force and was himself not a bad soldier and leader, he realized that he could not withstand the French. He knew that the British were already organizing the conquest of what was to become Northern Nigeria, and so he sent a message to the British requesting that the latter should recognize him as the ruler of Borno.

Meanwhile, the French fell out with Umar Sanda. After the defeat of Rabih, the French asked the shehu to pay them the sum of 30,000 Maria Theresa dollars for their services in bringing about the fall of Rabih. The shehu was inclined to do this. But to get the money he had to send his troops into Borno to raise the taxes from his people. While he was doing this, the French further demanded that all the Shuwa Arabs living west of Lake Chad should be driven away into the Chad region. Although Umar Sanda hated the Shuwa Arabs because they had given their support and loyalty to Rabih, he was not prepared to drive them from Borno territory. The Shuwa Arabs were great pastoralists and were very wealthy in cattle and sheep. To drive them away was to impoverish Borno, and it was quite clear that the French, who were establishing their control over the Chad region, would be the gainers by the suggested action. So Umar Sanda refused the French demand. For that, the French got him deposed and exiled to the Congo in October 1900. They then installed as shehu his younger brother Abubakar Garbai, father of Umar, the shehu mentioned at the very beginning of this chapter who died in August 1974. It was this Abubakar Garbai who had to deal with the British.

Fadlallah's request to the British for recognition as ruler of Borno was well received by Lugard. It did not seem to worry Lugard, the advocate of legitimacy (or was he?) that Fadlallah had really no historic claim to the throne of Borno. What must have weighed most with Lugard was the fact that British recognition of Fadlallah would deter the French from wanting to fight Fadlallah. Accordingly, Lugard sent an emissary to Fadlallah. The emissary reported favourably and recommended that Fadlallah be appointed Shehu of British Borno without any further delay. Unfortunately, Lugard was on leave by the time the recommendation was made and Wallace who was acting did not feel able to take such a far reaching decision.

Fadlallah's efforts at getting the British to recognize him as the Shehu of Borno was, of course, a direct challenge to Abubakar Garbai who also sent an emissary to the British pleading to be recognized as the Shehu of Borno. Unfortunately, this emissary failed to make contact with the British. Fadlallah reacted to Abubakar's challenge by sending troops against him. Abubakar could not withstand the forces of Fadlallah and so fled to the French whom he asked for military aid. The French responded favourably and a joint force of French troops and troops of Abubakar Garbai set out against Fadlallah, drove him out of Dikwa and killed him at a battle near Gujba on 23 August 1901.

Lugard returned from leave to discover that Fadlallah, whom he was anxious to install as shehu, was dead. He was of the opinion that the French, in crossing over into what was clearly British territory and killing Fadlallah, had insulted British prestige. So he sent an expedition to Borno to find a chief whom the British could install as the ruler of Borno in place of Fadlallah. Apparently Lugard was not anxious at this point to recognize Abubakar Garbai as the Shehu of Borno or was perhaps not even aware that he had been so installed by the French.

Colonel Morland, Commandant of the West African Frontier Force, who led the expedition, eventually made contact with Abubakar Garbai. At the time Abubakar was in Dikwa where the French held him until he paid the remaining sum of 65,000 dollars demanded by the French for their assistance against first Rabih and then Fadlallah. Morland succeeded in getting Abubakar released and then asked the latter to accept appointment as Shehu of British Borno. Abubakar accepted, whereupon Morland gave him a letter of appointment similar to that which had been given to the Emirs of Yola and Bida to which reference was made in the first part of this book. It can thus be said that Borno had become British territory in 1902. The matter was, however, not as simple as that.

Abubakar Garbai in accepting appointment as Shehu of British Borno apparently meant to carry on ruling his people as before. He gave evidence of this quite soon after his appointment. The British wanted him to rebuild Kukawa his traditional capital. For various reasons, including sentiment, Abubakar Garbai was quite willing to do this. Meanwhile, however, the British asked him to establish a temporary headquarters at Maifoni where the British resident and garrison were to be stationed. Abubakar refused and preferred to live in Monguno which had neither a British garrison nor resident. He did not intend to live under the shadow of British guns and resident.

Another respect in which Shehu Abubakar Garbai showed his

independence was in the realm of taxation. He sent his servants
to collect tax in the time honoured way. The British did not object to the Shehu collecting tax, just as they did not prevent the
Emirs of the Sokoto caliphate from collecting tribute from their
erstwhile subjects. In Borno as elsewhere, however, the British
objected to methods which they regarded, usually with a touch of
exaggeration, as tantamount to looting. The British resident
protested to the shehu but the shehu would appear to have been
unwilling to curb the activities of some of his servants. It has been
suggested by one authority on this subject that what the shehu
was probably doing, was deliberately punishing, through heavy
exaction, those of his peoples who had aided Rabih and his son.
In other words the shehu was seeking to act very much as he
would have done had the British not been there. The British, for
their part, were anxious that the shehu should not act in a
manner which would give the Bornoans the impression that
nothing had changed, despite the British presence.

To leave the shehu in no doubt that the old order had to
change, the British forced him to arrest his own servants, whose
tax collecting methods the British found objectionable. One of
these, Mala Bukar, described as 'a much trusted slave of the
shehu' was publicly hanged because he had caused the death of
one man in the course of his activities. Next the British ordered
that the Bornoans must hand in all firearms. For a people who
had been fighting for survival against Rabih and then Fadlallah,
the possession of firearms was more than a token of manliness.
To surrender them would be to admit that they were no longer
responsible for their own security, their own survival. It was a
bitter realization. But the Bornoans had no choice. The
reluctance to hand in firearms was demonstrated by the fact that
it took two years before the order was fully complied with
(1902–1904).

The British also had difficulties with the shehu over the
question of moving to Kukawa. Somehow the shehu did not wish
to move under the supervision of the British. Apparently, both
the shehu and his people believed that the British would not stay
permanently in Borno. At a time when both Britain and other
European nations had become committed to the building of
empires in Africa such a belief was not particularly
defensible. Perhaps the fact that the British had been willing to
deal with both Rabih and Fadlallah gave the shehu the

impression that the British did not particularly care about Borno. He did not bestir himself to rebuild Kukawa until Resident Hewby threatened that he would burn his house in Monguno. Kukawa was finally rebuilt and occupied in 1903. There, on 30 September 1904, Lugard formally presented a staff of office to the Shehu Abubakar Garbai. The presentation of office was preceded by the taking of an oath of loyalty to the British. Abubakar Garbai only took this oath after he had been assured that the British had no intention of tampering with the religion of his people.

The final act in the drama which ended with the British occupation of Borno thus took place on that fateful 30 September 1904. One fact which should have emerged from this admittedly simplified narrative should be emphasized. The conditions which prevailed in Borno from 1893 onwards were not such as could have enabled Borno to put up the kind of fight against the British which Kano or Sokoto put up. Yet this was not because the people of Borno had no fight in them. They had spent their force against Rabih and Fadlallah before the British arrived to claim their territory. In a sense they looked on the British as providing some deliverance from further fighting. In a period of peace, the shehu hoped that it would be possible for him to re-establish his authority and to reconsolidate the heritage of his fathers. But the times were out of joint; it was the age of aggressive imperialism. So the shehu had to yield to the inevitable. In doing so, however, he stood on his dignity to the very last.

BIBLIOGRAPHICAL NOTE

Existing works on the British conquest do not devote much attention to Borno largely because such works tend to concentrate on the Sokoto caliphate. Thus, Adeleye does not fully discuss the subject in his work; nor does Margery Perham. The account here given is based on Mahmud M. Tukur's paper (as yet unpublished) 'Shehu Abubakar Garbai Ibu Ibrahim El-Kanemi and the Establishment of British Rule in Bornu, 1902-1914' presented to the Ahmadu Bello University (Zaria)

History Department's Bornu Seminar in May 1973. For a nineteenth-century background account of Borno, see R. Cohen and L. Brenner, 'Bornu in the Nineteenth Century' in J. F. Ade Ajayi and Michael Crowder (eds), *History of West Africa Vol. 2*, (Longman 1974).

EPISODE
10

The Fall of Zaria

It is difficult to say exactly when Zaria fell to the British. This is because the fall of Zaria was different from, say, the fall of Kano or Sokoto. In 1899 Bishop Tugwell led a C.M.S. missionary team into Northern Nigeria. The missionaries wanted to establish a centre in Kano. On their way to Kano, they stopped at Zaria. According to the missionaries, the Emir of Zaria received them very well. The same missionaries say that the emir received them well because he was, at that time, not on very friendly relations with Caliph Abdul of Sokoto. He therefore thought it wise to show friendship to the Europeans. We do not know the full story about relations between Zaria and Sokoto. Some say that the unfriendly relations began because the caliph did not at first want to approve of the emir's appointment. Others that the pro-Sokoto elements in the town of Zaria were troublesome and that at the time of Tugwell's visit, the situation was so bad that a civil war could not be ruled out. Whatever the truth, there is no doubt that the Emir of Zaria welcomed the missionaries for some good reason of his own.

When the missionaries left Zaria they went on to Kano. The Emir of Kano refused to have the missionaries in his domain. Tugwell and his group were therefore forced to leave Kano. They went back to Zaria. The Emir of Zaria was not so sure what to do this time. Kano had expelled the white missionaries obviously because the emir did not want Christians to preach their religion in his emirate. Could Zaria, also a Muslim centre, receive the missionaries? If Zaria did, would this not be seen as working against brother Muslims? On the other hand, Zaria was not as powerful as Kano. If she refused to welcome the missionaries this time, might they not bring other Europeans to fight against and conquer her? The emir knew that to the north, the French had conquered a number of Muslim rulers; he knew that once it came to fighting he was no equal of the British. So he tried to please both sides. He refused to let the missionaries establish themselves in Zaria. But he let them settle at Girku to the south of Zaria. This was in 1899.

On 1 January 1900, as has already been described, Frederick Lugard declared what used to be known as Northern Nigeria, a British protectorate. As we already know, the Sokoto caliphate refused to accept Lugard's declaration. Consequently the only way by which British rule could be effectively established in Northern Nigeria was through military conquest. One of the first places to fall to the British was Kontagora which fell in 1901. However, the Emir of Kontagora, Ibrahim, was able to escape from the town. Zarian-British relations from the date of Kontagora's fall were determined very much by the activities of the fugitive Emir of Kontagora as we shall soon see.

Zaria's first contact with the new British presence in the caliphate was early in 1900. Perhaps the fact that Zaria had welcomed the Tugwell missionary party impressed the British and made them anxious to establish friendly relations with the emir. Early in the year 1900, therefore, Colonel Kemball, the Commandant of the West African Frontier Force, visited Zaria and informed the emir that he had come to offer him the friendship of the British. He wanted peaceful relations between Zaria and the British. The emir received Kemball warmly and it looked as if there would, in fact, develop peace and friendship between the two parties. But even this first contact revealed the basic conflict which existed between the new British authority and the emirates of the caliphate. This was that the British were offering friendship and peace but only on their own terms. Thus, even on this visit, during which Kemball offered friendship and peace, he nevertheless burnt down two towns in Zaria emirate, Remo and Kaje, for obstructing his passage to Zaria. Not only did he burn down these towns, he boasted that all of Zaria emirate would soon become British territory and that slave trade and slavery had to stop. In the circumstances it became quite clear that there could be no true friendship between Zaria and the British. In fact, by the time Kemball left Zaria, the emir was already afraid of what the British might do to him.

It was this fear that led the emir to write to Lugard. He told Lugard in this letter that he could not on his own allow his territories to become British or agree to stop slave trade and slavery as he was no more than an agent of the caliph in Sokoto. He further drew Lugard's attention to the fact that Kemball's actions and threats were contrary to the promise of peace and friendship which he had made. A copy of this letter was sent to the caliph in Sokoto. The year 1900 thus ended with relations between Zaria and the British being very uneasy.

In 1901 the British took Kontagora, and forced the emir, Ibrahim, to flee. Ibrahim fled with a very large following. The question of how to provide for this large following soon became a problem for Ibrahim. He found an answer in raiding villages in the neighbouring Zaria emirate. The Emir of Zaria appealed to him to stop ravaging his territory but to no avail. The caliph himself instructed Ibrahim to stop raiding the territories of a brother emir but was ignored. Apparently Zaria was unable to meet force with force and so push Ibrahim out of Zaria territory. So Ibrahim's raids continued. It was this situation that forced Zaria into the hands of the British once more.

The British had been watching Ibrahim's activities with great interest. For one thing they were anxious to capture Ibrahim, who had managed to escape from their hands when Kontagora had fallen. For another, Ibrahim's activities and Zaria's inability to meet force with force provided a good opportunity for the British to step into the situation as friends of Zaria. In fact, for most of 1901 the British were constantly asking the Emir of Zaria to accept their assistance against Ibrahim. Unable to dislodge Ibrahim himself and with no help coming from Sokoto, Zaria at last agreed to accept British help. In March 1902 the British took the field against Ibrahim. This time he was unable to offer any major resistance. He was captured and sent in chains to Lokoja for trial.

But the British did not then move away from Zaria territory. Rather they established a garrison near Zaria town itself and in April one Captain Abadie arrived as British resident of what was now described as Zaria Province. Both the emir and his people were surprised at the attitude of the British. They had asked for British help against Ibrahim but not British occupation of their territory. Besides, the situation which existed made Zaria look disloyal to Sokoto. In fact Zaria was so worried by this aspect of the matter that the emir told Captain Abadie that if the caliph were to order him to expel the British from his emirate, he would have no choice but to carry out the instruction. This was a clever way of telling the British that he did not approve of their presence.

It was not only Sokoto that Zaria had to reckon with. There was also Kano. Kano became extremely hostile to the British once they were established in Zaria. This was because Zaria territory is next door to Kano's and Kano feared that the British would cross over into Kano territory from Zaria. The British for their part were very anxious to occupy Kano and saw their occupation of Zaria as a necessary first step towards the occupation of Kano. So Zaria became a kind of British military base. British troops from Bauchi and other areas began to be moved into Zaria in readiness for an attack on Kano. The Emir of Zaria protested against this action but in vain. Unable to do anything effective, the emir wrote to Sokoto and Kano telling them of his plight and warning that the British meant to advance on Kano when they were through with Zaria.

The emir's position was extremely difficult. From the Ibrahim affair, it was quite clear that he did not have an effective fighting force. But even if he had the British concentration of forces in Zaria was such that he could not hope to take the field against them with any success. The only way left open to him through which he could show his disapproval of British occupation of his territory was to flee from Zaria. And if he fled, the bulk of the population of Zaria would join him because there was no doubt that the people too were unwilling to be subjected in this way to British rule.

The British realized that flight was the only avenue open to the Emir and they took steps to ensure that such a flight did not take place. Such a flight would create a disturbed situation inside Zaria itself. What was more, if the emir fled and was joined by a large following, he was most likely to go to Kano and so strengthen the Kano force that would ultimately fight the British. Hence, in August 1902 the British put patrols on the Zaria–Katsina, Zaria–Bauchi, and Zaria–Kano roads. These patrols had orders to arrest the emir if he tried to escape; they were also asked to prevent any reinforcements from other emirates reaching Zaria. A number of clashes occurred at this stage between these patrols and groups of Zaria warriors, but no major fighting took place. As for the emir, he merely showed his non-acceptance of the situation by refusing to co-operate with the British by supplying them men for the building of roads, etc, and by refusing to hand over runaway criminals to the British.

In this situation the British decided that the emir must be removed from office. In August Lugard sent more soldiers into the town. Captain Abadie then asked the emir to get ready to meet Lugard himself. The emir must have suspected that if he went to this meeting with Lugard he would either not return or be given impossible terms under which he was to remain emir. So he refused to meet Lugard, arguing that he did not recognize either Lugard or the British government but the Caliph of Sokoto alone. The British immediately took control of all the gates of Zaria. Then British soldiers marched in the emir's palace and arrested the emir whom they took away from the town. Another official, the Galadima Suleiman, was asked to take over the functions of emir. In this rather quiet way Zaria finally fell to the British.

The fall of Zaria was very different in nature from the fall of Kano and Sokoto which are discussed in the next two episodes. Indeed it can be said that the process began with the fall of Kontagora which forced Ibrahim to move into Zaria territory and so forced the Emir of Zaria to appeal to the British for help. The activities of Ibrahim also raise the question of what kind of relationship existed between the different emirates. If all the emirs owed allegiance to Sokoto as they obviously did, why did Ibrahim have to attack the territories of a brother-emir?

The answer to this question is that common loyalty to Sokoto did not exclude hostility between those who gave this loyalty. We have to realize that relations between the various Hausa states of the period before the jihad were carried over to the period after the jihad. So there were enmities which a common loyalty to Sokoto did not necessarily remove. But the more important factor in the situation in 1901 was that the coming of the British into the caliphate created a new situation in which every emirate was concerned chiefly with survival. The Emir Ibrahim ravaged Zaria territory because he had to have the wherewithal to feed himself and his followers in order to survive. In order to survive, the Emir of Zaria was quite prepared to welcome British aid. That aid ensured the expulsion of Ibrahim from Zaria's territory at the same time as it paved the way for Zaria's fall.

EPISODE
11

The Fall of Kano

The fall of Kano is perhaps the best known episode in the British conquest of Northern Nigeria. Partly this is because Lugard, who planned the attack on Kano, made such noise about it. More importantly, however, Kano had a reputation of its own long before the jihad and the establishment of the Sokoto caliphate of which it became a part. Kano was a major commercial centre long before the events of the nineteenth century. It was, without doubt, the wealthiest emirate in the Sokoto caliphate. In addition, it was reputed to be militarily strong. For the British, therefore, the conquest of Kano was seen as a major concern, to be carefully planned. In fact, for Lugard, Kano and Sokoto were the most important centres in the caliphate.

It also happens, however, that Kano and Sokoto lay far away from Lugard's initial headquarters at Lokoja or even his later headquarters at Zungeru. If Kano and Sokoto were to be successfully tackled the 'southern emirates' had to be dealt with first. In the first part of this book we saw how Lugard proceeded to deal with these southern emirates. Their conquest merely emphasized the need to deal with Kano and Sokoto, for many of the defeated fled in the direction of Kano, while even occupied areas still looked to Sokoto. In the last chapter we saw how Zaria was influenced by the attitude of Kano. Lugard's resolve to deal effectively with Kano was strengthened by the influence which he knew Kano exerted on other parts of the caliphate, influence which, in part, was owed to Kano's leading role among the Hausa states in the pre-caliphate era. All the time, therefore, that Lugard was dealing with the southern emirates, he had his mind on the coming struggle with Kano. As from May 1902, Lugard was certainly planning war with Kano.

Kano for its part also began to make preparations for war as reports of British intentions reached there from other emirates. The walls of Kano were rebuilt during the year and fitted with very strong gates. Other towns within the emirate were asked to similarly rebuild their walls and generally strengthen their defences. Taking advantage of links with North Africa through the trans-Saharan routes, Kano bought large quantities of arms. This is perhaps the best point at which to say something about the walls of Kano. The whole of Kano was at this time surrounded by a wall, which, as has been said, was rebuilt in 1902. At the time of the British attack it was said that this wall was 11 miles in perimeter. The wall was broken at intervals by gates — 13 in number in 1902. British accounts claim that the walls were 30 to 50 feet high and about 40 feet thick at the base. The walls had slits in them through which, in wartime, the Kanawa (the people of Kano) could observe what was going on outside the walls and through which they could fire at the enemy. In addition there was a great moat all round the city. The British were very impressed by Kano's defences which were probably the most impressive in all of the caliphate.

Lugard heard about these preparations and began to write to his employers in London to the effect that Kano was seeking to provoke war against the white man. One may ask why Lugard did this. The fact is that the Colonial Office in London was anxious that Lugard should not go to war with the caliphate unless this was absolutely unavoidable. Lugard had, however, made up his mind that Kano and Sokoto must fall if the British were to establish themselves effectively in the caliphate. He therefore had to build up some case against these places which would justify his war policy: he had to make it appear that war was being forced on him.

Fortunately for Lugard, events played into his hands. While he was busy making preparations for war against Kano so as to ensure success, a British officer, Captain Moloney, was killed at Keffi in October 1902. The details of the actual incident do not concern us here but the Magajin Keffi, who ruled the town on behalf of the Emir of Zaria, was charged with the murder. It is not clear whether Moloney was actually killed by the magajin. However, even if he did not personally kill Moloney, he, as the ruler of the town, had, in some degree, to take responsibility. As often happened when a British citizen died at the hands of Africans, an expedition was immediately sent against Keffi. The expedition sacked the town. The Magajin Keffi with a large following fled and made his way to Kano where the emir, Aliyu, gave him a hero's welcome.

Lugard thus got the excuse for war which he had been waiting for. He reported the incident to London, taking care to add that it was unthinkable for the life of a European to be taken with impunity. This would ruin the prestige of his government and make all other officers insecure. It was Lugard's view that a ruler who shields the murderer of a European officer had virtually declared war. For his part, he was determined to ensure that the Magajin Keffi was arrested wherever he might be. And so it was that Lugard gave orders for the expedition against Kano.

As was typical of Lugard, he gave his orders before he actually informed London that he was already at war with Kano. This was because he feared that the Colonial Office might instruct him not to proceed. Once the troops were on the march it would, for prestige reasons, be difficult for the Colonial Office to order a withdrawal. One thing, however, was important: Lugard could not afford to fail. The British had suffered humiliations at the hands of the Zulu in South Africa only a few years back and the Boers had given the British an extremely difficult time in the war of 1899-1902. Lugard knew that these facts made the Colonial Office extremely touchy about going to war. If he failed, he knew that he would most probably be recalled in disgrace. So he had to ensure success. He did this by ensuring that the force which was to attack Kano was sufficiently strong in terms of numbers, and arms, and ammunition. He also saw to it that Sojoto was prevented from sending aid to Kano by stationing a British force of 250 men in Argungu to keep an eye on Sokoto.

The force which was sent against Kano consisted of 24 officers, 12 N.C.O.s, two medical officers, and 722 rank and file. In addition to individual arms and ammunition the force took four 75 millimetre guns and four maxims. The officer commanding was Colonel T. N. Morland. The force moved off from Zaria towards Kano on 29 January 1903.

Lugard in the meantime tried to divide the people of Kano. He sent a proclamation in Hausa to Kano. In it he said that the British had no quarrel with the Kanawa or any other people except with Magajin Keffi and those who had received him with honour in Kano. The British force which was marching into Kano would not fight anyone but those who chose to fight it. Lugard probably sent this proclamation because he had earlier claimed that he had been informed that the Kanawa were not anxious to fight against the British and that it was only the emir who was hostile. We do not know for sure whether the proclamation had any effect on the Kanawa.

In Kano the situation which developed at the time of the British expedition was unsatisfactory. The emir had requested the towns on the route through which the British force was likely to pass to fortify their walls and oppose the British by force of arms. It would appear, however, that although Aliyu knew that British intentions towards him and Kano were hostile, he did not know or believe that the attack would be launched at the time it was for on 2 January he left Kano for Sokoto 'with all his principal officials and the headmen of the western districts of the emirate and their forces'. The trip to Sokoto was apparently to pay homage to the new caliph, Attahiru, and to pray at the grave of his mother who was from Sokoto. Whatever the actual reason for the trip to Sokoto, it is evident that by removing himself and his principal officials as well as forces from the western part of his emirate, Aliyu greatly reduced the total strength with which Kano faced the British force.

The British force met its first resistance at Bebeji which opposed the passage of the British troops. The town was sacked. Thereafter none of the other towns which had been instructed to obstruct the British forces put up any fight. The British therefore continued their march peacefully till they encamped outside the walls of Kano. On the morning of 3 February 1903, Morland led his forces against Kano. Kano was apparently in a state of watchfulness, for 800 yards outside the city walls, a Kano scouting party exchanged gun fire with the British force. The British chose the Zaria gate as their first target. But one hour of shelling failed to break down the gate or the wall. Meanwhile the Kano defenders at the gate kept up a steady though inaccurate fire against the British force.

Morland must have been rather dismayed at the strength of this gate and the wall. He chose to try another gate, the Kowbuga gate, to the west of the Zaria gate, while he left some troops to keep an eye on the Zaria gate. The force which attacked the Kowbuga gate was about 450 strong. After some shelling, the British succeeded in making a small breach. Then the British force rushed the gate and forced their way into the city, some using ladders to climb over the wall. Once the gate was successfully rushed, the Kano defenders withdrew from the walls and effective resistance to the British inside Kano was at an end. The party which opposed the British was said to be about 800

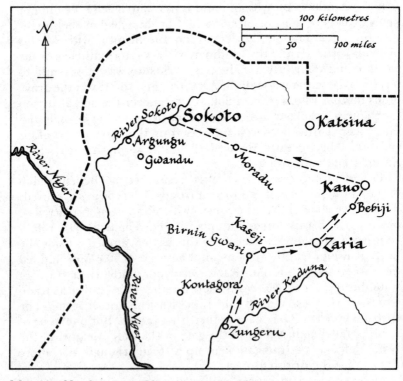

Map 11   North-western Nigeria, showing the approximate route
of Lugard's march on the Kano-Sokoto campaign of 1903

cavalry and 5,000 foot. Of these, some 300 were said to have been
killed. On the British side 14 only were reported wounded.

If the Kanawa who defended the gate and walls did not show
much heroism, the Sarkin Shanu, Muhammad, put up a gallant
fight when the British arrived at the emir's palace to take it over.
With only a handful of men he refused to give up his master's
palace and died defending it.

Kano had fallen. The British declared Aliyu deposed. Henceforth the British would appoint the emir. The bearing of firearms was prohibited. Slaves were told that they could complain to the British officer if their masters maltreated them. The Kanawa could not be expected to accept the new order with any enthusiasm. It was clear that if they appeared to be well disposed to the British, it was only because there was little choice immediately open to them.

Meanwhile Aliyu was on his way back to Kano. Near Kaura Namoda he heard that Bebeji had fallen. At a town called Birnin Goga, he was informed that Kano had fallen though he refused to believe it. News that the emir was returning to Kano must have given some of the Kanawa a new spirit. A large number of people fled from Kano meaning to join forces with their emir who would lead them in an offensive against the British in Kano. The British quickly got to know what was happening and sent out a force with instructions to prevent the people from Kano linking up with Aliyu's forces.

As events turned out, Aliyu did not lead any force in an effort to take Kano from the British. At dawn on 24 February, the emir, with only a handful of followers, deserted his forces. It is difficult to explain the emir's action. The likelihood is that once he became satisfied that Kano had fallen, he feared for himself and preferred to escape rather than be caught by the British and humiliated. He must have heard that the British had already declared him deposed. Or it may be that he accepted the Muslim teaching which enjoined Muslims to flee from their country rather than allow infidels rule them. Whatever the explanation for his escape, there can be no doubt that his action greatly demoralized all those who looked to him to lead them against the British in Kano.

Not all the emir's officials were ready to give up without a fight. The waziri stepped into the position vacated by the emir and rallied the remaining force, about 3,500 strong, for a march against Kano. The British were determined that the Kanawa must not be allowed to reach Kano and mount a major attack. So British parties were sent in different directions to try and intercept the Kanawa forces. On 25 February a British party commanded by Lt Wright engaged the Kanawa in a fight. The Kanawa lost some 50 killed. Then the Kanawa force retreated. The next day, however, the two forces met again near the town of Kotorkwoshi.

This was easily the most heroic engagement in which the Kanawa took part in their effort to hold their own against the British. A fierce battle took place between Lt Wright's party and the Kanawa. Wright drew up his men in square formation. The Kanawa led by the Wazirin Kano charged this square formation many times in face of accurate fire. Lt Wright's account shows that even though their colleagues fell, the Kanawa kept charging until their leader was killed. It was a most heroic last stand during which the Kanawa showed great courage, going within 15 yards of the British guns in their attempt to break the square formation. However, their courage was not an adequate answer for the fire power of the British. With their leader and ten of his immediate lieutenants killed, the Kanawa retreated in what must have been an extremely sad and demoralized mood.

The battle near Kotorkwoshi on 26 February 1903 marked the end of serious resistance on the part of the Kanawa. The survivors of the battle now decided to surrender to the British. Led by the Wombai of Kano, Abbas, they found their way to Kano where they surrendered on 6 March. The party which the Womban Kano led in on this day were some 2,500 cavalry and 5,000 foot. These figures show how many were those who had left Kano either with Aliyu on his trip to Sokoto, or who had fled the city after the British attack on 3 February 1902. The party was made to give up all their guns. That the Kano fighters were quite poorly equipped in firearms was shown when this large party could hand over only 120 rifles. Obviously most of the Kanawa had had to fight with their traditional weapons — bows and arrows. With the surrender of this party, the Kano-British confrontation came to an end. Abbas was appointed emir by Lugard and Kano got ready to see what future British rule held out to her.

The fall of Kano, regarded as the caliphate's strongest military power, was a major victory for the British. It is easy to see that the fall was due to the depletion of Kano's forces caused by the emir's journey to Sokoto as much as it was due to superior British arms. The Kanawa showed in those months of February and March that superior force does not necessarily conquer men's spirits. As Muslims, many went to their deaths rather than submit to rule by white unbelievers. Those who survived bowed to the inevitable and accepted British rule, though the future was to show that they devised new ways of fighting the old battle.

BIBLIOGRAPHICAL NOTE ON

EPISODES 10, 11 & 12

These three episodes are taken together because they are treated in the same works as part of the Sokoto caliphate. The works most readily available are Margery Perham's *Lugard: The Years of Authority* about which comments have been made in the bibliographical note to Chapter V; C. Orr, *The Making of Northern Nigeria*; H. A. S. Johnston, *The Fulani Empire of Sokoto*. D. J. M. Muffet *Concerning Brave Captains* and 'Nigeria — Sokoto Caliphate' in Michael Crowder (ed.) *West African Resistance* and R. A. Adeleye *Power and Diplomacy in Northern Nigeria*. I. F. Nicolson's *The Administration of Nigeria* does devote some space in a general way to Lugard's methods in the conquest of the Sokoto caliphate but does not deal in detail with the subject. Of these works Adeleye's *Power and Diplomacy* best puts the events of the British conquest in their overall historical perspective.

EPISODE
12

The Fall of Sokoto

After the fall of Kano, it was perhaps logical that the British should next move on to Sokoto, the headquarters of the Sokoto caliphate. In fact, it is only because Sokoto was so far away from the first base of the British in Northern Nigeria, and because the British were busy with other emirates, that Sokoto survived until March 1903.

From the beginning, Lugard knew that Sokoto would have to be taken. But he may have hoped that it would be possible not to go to war against Sokoto. In fact he tried to achieve the fall of Sokoto through diplomatic moves. However, each such move was, whether Lugard knew it or not, a major affront to the caliph. Lugard's very first act in Lokoja on 1 January 1900 was to hoist the Union Jack and to declare 'Northern Nigeria' a British protectorate. Who was he to lay claim rulership over the land which the ancestors of the caliph had brought under their rule? Indeed Lugard's declaration was, from the caliph's viewpoint, an act of aggression.

As if that was not bad enough, Lugard actually wrote to the caliph informing him of what he had done and asking him to accept it. He made matters worse by reminding the caliph in his letter that in other parts of the world the British had established their rule over Muslims and that as it was in those parts, so it should be in the Sokoto caliphate. To say this to the head of Muslim society in all of Northern Nigeria was to declare himself (Lugard and with him the British) Public Enemy Number One. It is not surprising therefore that the caliph did not reply to the letter.

Lugard's next act was to attack and conquer Kontagora, Bida, and Yola in 1901 and Bauchi in February 1902. All of these were places which owed loyalty to the caliph; their rulers paid annual tribute to Sokoto. It is easy to see what their conquest must have meant to the caliph in Sokoto. The importance of Sokoto in the lives of these emirates was proved by the fact that even after they had been conquered by the British, they continued to pay tribute to Sokoto. Lugard was worried by this, for it showed that these emirates did not yet regard him as the final authority in the land, and made him even more determined to bring Sokoto itself under British control.

If Lugard did not march against Sokoto early in 1902, it was only because he was not yet ready. After the conquest of Kontagora and Bida, he wrote to the caliph to report what he had done. He told the caliph that the emirs of Kontagora and Bida had been oppressing their people, engaging in slave trade, attacking traders, organizing stealing parties, and generally making life difficult for all the people around. He wrote, 'Because of these evils of theirs, I have taken their crowns from them and banished them.' The caliph had approved the appointment of these emirs in the first place, and now, without consultation with him, Lugard, an uninvited guest, had removed them and felt able to tell the caliph so. Surely this was the age of 'might is right'.

But that was not all. Lugard invited the caliph to select a ruler who would replace the deposed Emir of Kontagora. By doing this, he was no doubt trying to make the caliph feel that he still recognized him as head of the Muslims. Yet Lugard had not consulted the caliph before he deposed the rulers. Even in asking that the caliph should select another ruler, he still made it clear that it was he, Lugard, who would put this new ruler on his throne. And it was he, Lugard, who would decide whether the ruler was good enough to remain on the throne. If the new emir did not satisfy him, he, Lugard, would remove him from the throne. Naturally the caliph refused to reply to this great insult. Then Lugard, in reporting to his employers (the Colonial Office) in London, used the refusal of the caliph to reply as evidence of his unfriendly and hostile attitude to the British.

In March 1902 Lugard again wrote to the caliph. This time it was to report that he had heard that the caliph had written to the Emir of Bauchi to stop oppressing his people, but that the emir had not heeded the caliph's advice. Therefore, Lugard made it clear, he would have to remove the emir and appoint another one in his place. He also informed the caliph in this letter that the Emir of Kontagora who had been in flight had been captured and that he, Lugard, would try him. Every single act of Lugard's was thus an attack on the powers and position of the caliph — a clear way of telling him that if he was wise he had better submit

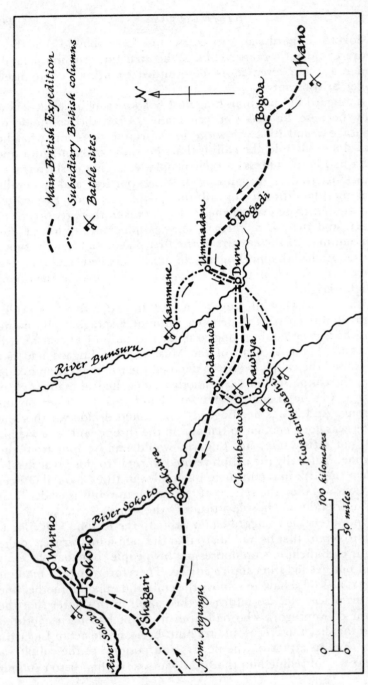

Map 12 The routes of the Kano-Sokoto expedition

tamely to the British.

The caliph did not receive Lugard's letter of March 1902 before he wrote to Lugard the famous letter in which he said that between him and the British there could be only one kind of relationship — war. When he received the letter of March 1902 he again wrote to Lugard. In order to show quite clearly how the caliph felt, we reproduce in full the caliph's letter to Lugard:

'In the name of God.

The Governor Lugard. To continue, know that we did not invite you to put right [affairs in] Bauchi or anywhere else, not to speak of your interference in putting [the affairs of] the country and districts in order. We do not request help from anyone but from God. You have your religion and we have our religion. God is our sufficiency and our excellent agent. There is neither might nor strength except in God, the exalted, the almighty. This and peace.'

The two letters which the caliph wrote to Lugard leave no doubt as to the latter's total rejection of the British in Northern Nigeria. That he wrote both letters in May 1902 after Bida, Kontagora, Yola, Bauchi, and a number of other places had already been conquered by the British shows the kind of spirit which Islam gave him. He would not willingly give up his position, not even when faced with the military might of the British.

This was roughly the situation up to the end of 1902 except that Lugard had begun to prepare for what he now knew would be war against Sokoto, by stationing British troops at Argungu and Gwandu. Early in 1903 came the Kano expedition. After Kano, Sokoto. It will be remembered that before the war against Kano, Lugard tried very hard to build up a case against Kano in Britain, so that the British people would believe that it was Kano that forced Lugard into war. In the same way Lugard tried very hard in 1903 to paint the caliph and indeed all the emirs of the caliphate in the blackest colours possible.

On 15 January 1903 he wrote to London. He said that those in London who did not support war in Northern Nigeria were ignorant of the true situation. They did not know how corrupt the foreign Fulani rulers were; they bought and sold their own citizens; they took bribes; they oppressed their people; they mutilated their citizens for very minor crimes. In Bida, Kontagora, and other places where the British had used their military might to seize power, these evils had already been stopped; similarly would they be stopped in Kano and Sokoto once these places were occupied by the British.

On 23 January he wrote again. This time it was to say that a number of emirates, notably Katsina, were refusing to reply to his letters which called on them to accept British rule. This refusal he rightly interpreted as refusal to accept British sovereignty. He wrote 'The time has come when [the British] Government must declare its Sovereignty and assert its right to send officials without molestation to any place within the protectorate.' That was not all. He told his employers that the rulers did not have the sympathy of their subjects because of the former's tyranny. He even went as far as stating that the subjects were in open revolt against their rulers — and that this was the more reason why Britain must step in and seize power. He wrote, 'The population are on our side and I believe welcome our advent as a deliverance from misrule.'

In sending this type of report home, Lugard was telling deliberate lies as he often did whenever he had to build up a case like this. Some reason had to be found for waging war against a people who did not desire one. Many times he informed not only Sokoto, but other emirs that he and his government meant to respect Islam and would not tamper with this religion. Yet virtually every step he took was a challenge to Islam and an abuse on the leader of the Muslims in Northern Nigeria. This indeed was the crux of the matter, in addition to a people's natural unwillingness to give up their independence and become a colony. Hence, when Colonel Morland wrote to the Caliph after the fall of Kano the Caliph would not, even then, accept British rule. In a late reply he informed the British that he had called in his councillors and district heads to consider the situation and would write back after he received their advice.

The situation in Sokoto just before the British attack deserves to be looked at. The Caliph, Abdal-Rahman, with whom Lugard had been dealing since 1900, died on 9 October 1902. As so often happens in Muslim countries, there was some struggle about who should succeed him. Thus, although Attahiru I was installed as caliph in November, there was a group within Sokoto that had only unwillingly given up the struggle for the throne. There was no guarantee therefore that in the face of this external threat Sokoto could put up a united front.

The other important problem was that opinion was divided about how Sokoto was to meet the British challenge. One group advised that Sokoto should make peace with the British, as Katsina had done at the last minute. This group argued that Sokoto could not hope to fight successfully against the British. Another party was for war despite the fact that all who had so far fought against the British had been beaten. A third party, to which the caliph himself belonged, advised that the people should migrate from Sokoto rather than submit to being ruled by the infidels. But no group succeeded in convincing all the others. There was thus no agreement as to how to prepare against the British. In Kano there was no doubt that war was the only way. The walls were repaired and strengthened. As we saw earlier even the towns on the route which the British were likely to take were ordered to strengthen their defences. In Sokoto the walls were left unrepaired. If anything, it seems as if the majority were actually getting ready to move away from Sokoto: donkeys, mules, camels, and other necessaries were being got ready not more munitions of war. As it turned out, even these preparations were not ready before the British attack came on 15 March 1903.

In Sokoto, the news that the British were on their way led to the giving up of the plan to emigrate. Rather, hasty preparations were made for war. True to their religious convictions, the people engaged in prayers for their success as well as in the making of charms against bullets. There was even disagreement as to whether they should stay within the walls like the people of Kano had done and defend the city from within or go outside the walls and face the British in the open. For some reason not at all clear, Sokoto decided to face the British in the open, outside the city walls. Whatever chance of putting up a good fight Sokoto had was thrown away by this decision. Sokoto just could not face the British in open battle.

The clash took place on the morning of 15 March 1903. The British force which advanced on Sokoto was made up of 25 officers, 5 N.C.O.s, 2 medical officers, 1 medical N.C.O., 68 gunners, 656 rank and file, 400 carriers, four maxims, and four 75 mm guns. While this force was armed with modern rifles, in addition to the maxims and millimeter guns, the Sokoto force, which the British estimated 2,000 horse and 4,000 foot, were armed with spears, bows and arrows, and old guns. The Sokoto had very few rifles. With this kind of difference in arms and ammunition, the Sokoto army, commanded by the caliph himself, had really no chance of success against the British. As the British advanced, the Sokoto put up a fight. But by the time 100 of them had been killed, there was little reason for them to carry on. The caliph and some followers fled towards the east. Other commanders and their followers fled in various directions. The whole battle lasted only some 90 minutes. Sokoto, the very seat of the caliphate passed into British hands.

The Sokoto resistance was not particularly tough. But even so it produced its heroism. When the Sokoto army marched out of the city walls to await the British they took with them the flag of the caliph. The main body of the army was already in flight within half an hour of the beginning of the battle. However, a small group stood its ground to defend the flag, the symbol of the caliphate. The British were themselves amazed at the courage and devotion of this small group. One British source describes how, as the British opened fire on the group, one after another of the defenders fell dead. But as soon as one fell another took over the flag and held on to it till he in turn was shot down. And so it continued until the last of the group, the fiftieth as one British source says, fell dead and the flag fell on him. The British thereupon captured the flag. But such was the importance of the flag to the people, that someone managed to steal it and take it back to the caliph in flight. Few Nigerians of today would defend their flag with such courage — particularly to the death.

The flight of the caliph and of a large number of important Sokoto officials was, as it were, a going back to the idea of a *hijra* — emigration from infidels. But not everyone could go with the caliph. True, Sokoto was, by the time the British marched victoriously in, almost completely deserted. But most of the people looked for some kind of direction and leadership. Many of these grouped round the wazir or prime minister of Sokoto. The wazir was in a difficult position. He consulted the *ulama,* as Muslims learned in Islamic theology and law are called. These learned mallams advised that the Sheikh Uthman dan Fodiye, the man who had led the jihad early in the nineteenth century, had laid it down that it was permissible for Muslims to make friends with unbelievers when the Muslims were forced to live in fear of such unbelievers and could not successfully fight against them. The only condition that dan Fodiye attached to this permission was that this forced friendship was not to be deep: the

Muslims had to wait till they were strong enough to fight back and regain their independence.

It was in this way that it came about that on Thursday, 19 March 1903, the Wazir, Muhammad al-Bukhari, led a large crowd back into Sokoto where they surrendered to the British. The British for their part guaranteed the Muslims freedom of religious worship: they promised that they would not tamper with Islam. On 20 March, Sokoto officials met and chose Muhammad al-Tahir b. Ali b. Muhammad Bello as the caliph. He took the title Attahiru II. This was the same man who had earlier on contested the title with Attahiru I. Lugard approved this choice and, on 21 March, Attahiru II was duly installed. The British thus settled down to try to rule a people who had only accepted their rule because they had failed on the battlefield.

One problem, however, remained for the British to solve. The Caliph Attahiru I was in flight. The people of the caliphate regarded Attahiru I as the proper caliph. They knew that Attahiru II was a British created caliph who had been put on the throne only because Sokoto had been beaten in war. And the caliph (Attahiru I) represented the symbol of the people's religion as he was their imam, their high priest. The people saw his flight as a continuation of his struggle against the British. They saw it as an attempt to uphold the teaching of Islam which forbade Muslims to submit to unbelievers. Indeed, the *hijra* of Attahiru I was a direct challenge to all those who had accepted defeat and, as a result, British rule. Emirs and people alike responded to this challenge either by joining the caliph or by sending him assistance in the form of food, clothing, and other necessaries. The British suddenly discovered that Attahiru in flight was more dangerous to them than Attahiru in Sokoto.

To overcome this danger and to stop people flocking to join him, the British decided to pursue Attahiru I and capture him. They did not find this at all easy. They were never sure where the caliph was at any given time. For example, after the fall of Sokoto, the caliph left for Gusau. Soon afterwards Lugard left Sokoto for Katsina. But the Emir of Katsina, even though he had submitted peacefully to the British, sent to the caliph twice to warn him that Lugard was in Katsina. He even sent presents to the caliph. In other words even those who accepted British rule still knew that the caliph was doing the right thing. The emirs and people knew where their caliph was and what routes he was

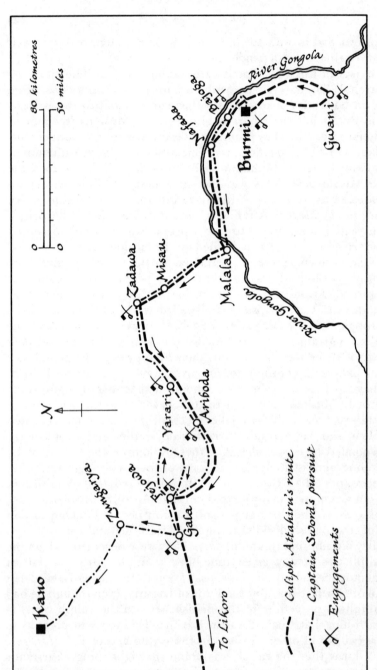

Map 13   The flight and pursuit of Attahiru I

using. The British often did not know.

Despite this difficulty, however, the British quickly organized themselves for the pursuit. The first encounter between Attahiru's supporters and the British took place on 22 April near Bebeji, the place where the British had been opposed on their march to Kano. Although the caliph's supporters suffered heavily, they forced the British party to send for reinforcements. The commander of the British party, Crozier, was himself knocked unconscious during the encounter. Between 22 April and 6 May six other encounters were fought, with neither side winning any major victory but with the caliph still at large.

The next major event was the First Battle of Burmi. This took place on 13 May 1903. By this time the caliph was on his way to Gwani. Captain Sword and a party of British soldiers were in pursuit. When Sword got to Burmi, he thought that the caliph was there and so attempted to take the town. It was the wrong town to choose to attack, for the people of Burmi were full of religious zeal and full of hatred for the white man. Their ruler, Musa, and his people did not tell the British that the caliph was not in their town. Rather, they gave battle. It was a very fierce battle. The British reported that they fired over 10,000 shots. The people of Burmi lost 250 killed and many wounded. Musa, the ruler of the town died in the battle. But despite this heavy loss Burmi continued bravely to fight. People from surrounding towns flocked into Burmi to give added support to these valiant Muslims as they stood their ground against British conquest. In the end the British force accepted defeat and Captain Sword had to retreat at night. The British suffered the loss of 2 soldiers killed, and several officers and many men wounded. By their own records, not only was this the first defeat suffered by the British since they began the conquest of the Sokoto caliphate, the casualties were also the heaviest.

The above defeat forced the British to redouble their efforts to capture the fleeing Caliph Attahiru I. At the time of the First Battle of Burmi, there were three different British military parties chasing the caliph from different directions. The number of troops engaged in the chase was now increased. The Colonial Office in London was so frightened about what might happen in Northern Nigeria that they asked the Governors of Sierra Leone, the Gold Coast, Lagos, and Southern Nigeria to get ready to send troops to Northern Nigeria. This shows how seriously the British took the situation that had developed. As for the caliph, two months of flight had begun to tell on his followers. Many had returned to their homes. Many had died in battles against the British. Although those loyal to him continued to send food and water, there was never enough for this was still the dry season.

After the First Battle of Burmi, the caliph was encouraged to move into that town. He was enthusiastically received. It was there that he took his final stand against the British. For most of June and the first week of July Burmi was engaged in various encounters with British forces which were gathering round the town in order to surround it, and prevent help from other towns reaching it. The final attack on Burmi — the Second Battle of Burmi — took place on 27 July 1903. By this time the British force available was made up of 25 officers and 500 rank and file, with four maxims and two 75mm guns. The second battle was even fiercer than the first. It went on from 11 in the morning right up to 6 in the evening, the longest battle in the British conquest of the Sokoto caliphate. The caliph, who was in the mosque when the attack on the town began, came out and led the group which drove back the first British party that attempted to enter the town. He continued to fight until he fell dead. On top of him fell about 100 other supporters many of them officials who had either fled with him from Sokoto or joined him later. Altogether over 600 were killed by the British during this battle. Those who died came from all over the caliphate — Sokoto, Kano, Gombe, Kontagora, Nupe, Katagun, Missau, Bauchi — showing thereby how devoted the people were to their religion and to the caliph who was the symbol of that religion. On the British side too, the casualties were heavy. For the first time the British lost an officer — Major Marsh — who was killed by a poisoned arrow. Four other soldiers were killed and many wounded. But the victory was clearly theirs and with that victory, the military resistance to the British conquest of the caliphate came to an end.

It is clear that although the British had succeeded in conquering the caliphate, they did not find things very easy. The resistance of the caliphate had very much to do with the religion of Islam which forbade Muslims to submit tamely to rule by unbelievers. In very few places did rulers or people submit peacefully. Even when they did they continued to show resentment to the British and loyalty to Sokoto. However, as Islam was the strength of the resistance so also was it a source of weakness. Islam did not lay down only one way of responding to attacks of this nature by unbelievers. Muslims were required by their religion to fight against unbelievers who tried to rule them. But they could also go on a *hijra* when fighting looked hopeless. They could even surrender and give half-hearted friendship. With this kind of choice, it was not always possible for the Muslims to be of one opinion when an attack threatened.

The other source of weakness was that the caliphate was not centrally organized for war. Each emirate fought its own wars. Emirs might seek help from brother emirs but there was no central army which the caliphate could send to assist a particular emirate at war. This explains why the British were able to take the emirates one after the other.

The main reason why the British were victorious was, of course, that they had more modern weapons of war—rifles, maxims, and so on. In addition they had an army that had been drilled and taught how to fight. As against this the bulk of the armies which opposed them were ordinary farmers who took up arms to fight for their fatherland. And for most of them the arms they took up were bows and arrows and spears. Even those who had old guns, or the few with rifles, were not expert at how to use them. The opposing armies were therefore never equally matched. In the circumstances it was a great wonder that the armies of the caliphate fought with such determination. As was pointed out earlier, this determination was closely tied up with their religious convictions.

Finally one has to remember that the emirates had never before fought against European-trained armies. All their war tactics were determined by their experience in fighting against neighbouring peoples. So they really did not know how to oppose the British effectively. The British on the other hand had, after their first few battles, become familiar with how the Muslim armies fought. Hence they knew what to expect.

This then, explains how it was that the British were able to conquer the caliphate. One should say, however, that though conquered, the people did not immediately accept the British. For years after the actual conquest they continued, in their own way, to show that the British were not welcome; that their loyalty to the British was forced loyalty. This was why British forces were stationed at various points in the caliphate for some time even at the end of active military resistance.

Conclusion

This history of the British conquest of Nigeria has been designed to highlight certain features. One such feature is that although the actual military conquest or political occupation took place in the closing decade of the nineteenth and the opening decade of the present century, the grounds for, and the nature of, British conquest, as well as the reaction of Nigerian rulers and peoples to this conquest were determined by events and developments which took place much earlier in the nineteenth century. This is particularly the case in Southern Nigeria where the problems of suppressing the overseas slave trade, the advent of Christian missionaries, the nature and problems of the palm oil trade, and the rise of consular power played their various roles in determining relations between Europeans and Nigerian peoples in the age of scramble and partition. Thus the bombardment or blockade of Nigerian coastal or riverain towns either in the interest of the suppression of the slave trade or the pursuit of the new trade in forest produce highlighted the imbalance in fire power between Nigeria on the one hand and Britain on the other and helped to demoralize our forebears long before the conflicts of the new imperialism were fought out. Missionary activity in certain parts of Southern Nigeria undermined or helped to undermine the effective sovereignty of some rulers and groups long before the age of Macdonald, Moor, or Egerton. Hence, for a proper understanding of the fall of Nigeria to British imperialism these antecedents are just as important as the events of the era of partition.

Another feature to which attention needs be drawn is the character of the prevailing situation in Nigeria and the nature of inter-group relations. It is impossible, for example, to explain Egba enthusiasm for Christian missionaries outside the context of the Yoruba wars and the struggle for survival in that part of the country. Yet missionary activity in Egbaland played an important role not only in determining relations between the Egba and the British but also in determining the British attitude to other parts of Yorubaland. Nor is the nature of the final

British push into Yorubaland intelligible except in the context of that war weariness which characterized most of Yorubaland by the mid-1800s. As to why the Yoruba did not, despite a common language, unite in opposition to the British, the answer is easy to find. Not only did the Yoruba at the time not constitute a single political entity, but the interests of each group differed and often conflicted. Thus Ibadan and Abeokuta were anxious to open up relations with coastal Lagos especially in order to obtain a regular supply of firearms for the wars of survival then going on. Ijebu on the other hand, anxious to play the role of middleman, would do anything to block Ibadan's route to Lagos. Such divergent interests proved difficult to submerge in the interest of joint and, presumably, more effective opposition to a common ˙enemy. Besides, it was not always that the British were recognized as a common enemy. Group rather than common interests dominated the thinking of the various Yoruba groups — group interests which, given the war situation, sometimes saw the British as lesser dangers than other Yoruba groups.

In the Niger Delta and Calabar the social and political aftermath of the suppression of the overseas slave trade and the desire to succeed in the palm oil trade led to competition between houses (as highlighted especially in Bonny) and between states. This competition in turn affected the ability or inability to mount meaningful resistance against the British. That same competition and the conflict attendant thereon explains the role of certain groups within certain states which appeared willing to side with the British against their rivals for economic or political power. While it is true that by siding with the British such groups aided British imperialism, it is important to appreciate the fact that they did not necessarily see themselves as saboteurs or collaborators. As one historian of Tanzania has put it, and as the present writer has argued elsewhere, such groups or individuals were merely seeking to use the British as allies for the promotion of their own interests. What, of course, they did not fully realize was that the British were also using them for the promotion of their own specific interests and that when the chips were down such British interests and their own (African) interests were fundamentally incompatible.

Perhaps this is the place to make another point related to that made above. Although considerations of space have not allowed detailed comments on the British occupation of the Niger delta hinterland, one feature of that occupation which is worthy of note is the role played by those described in the colonial records as British Political Agents. These agents were usually delta middlemen traders who were used by the British for various purposes. They served as intelligence officers for the British; they were often sent to the hinterland to prepare the ground for the visits of British political officers; they invariably accompanied British military expeditions and served both as guides and as interpreters. As paid agents of the British, they were expected to persuade the hinterland peoples to accept British rule. It is easy to see in people like Dogho, Coco Bassey, Daniel Kalio, Sam Ogan, and Henshaw—to name only a few of such agents—men who, for considerations of personal gain, had no scruples in aiding the British in their conquest of Southern Nigeria. It is important, however, to be clearly aware of the context in which these men acted. One of the consequences of the British overthrow of indigenous authority at the coast and their gradual penetration of the hinterland was the undermining of the middleman role of the delta traders. In the new situation there was the need for a reconsideration of trading patterns and partnerships. In becoming political agents and going into the hinterland with the British, these men were, whatever else they may have been doing, taking advantage of their new positions to forge new trading partnerships and generally improve their economic lot which the coming of the British had undermined. They were clearly among the most wealthy traders of the early colonial period even if some of this wealth was 'filthy lucre'. For the political agents then, as indeed for other delta traders who though not British agents sought to accompany the British into the hinterland, the issue at stake was how to make the most of the new situation—how to play the old game in a new way.

With regard to Northern Nigeria, it is necessary to draw attention to certain facts without a proper awareness of which the British conquest and the reaction to it can hardly be adequately understood. It is not generally remembered that although the jihad succeeded in establishing a caliphate, it failed to achieve complete success even within that caliphate, let alone in all of what became Northern Nigeria. In a number of the emirates, notably Gombe and Bauchi, there were many peoples who for most of the nineteenth century held out against militant Islam.

In Bida there were groups, especially south of the Niger, who rejected Islam.

An emirate like Kontagora was not, in fact, established until the 1850s. This meant that in the second half of the nineteenth century Kontagora was still busy consolidating its position. Consolidation meant on-going war just as the presence of pockets of Islam-resisting peoples within or outside the borders of other emirates meant occasional raids. In other words, it can be argued that although the major wars of the jihad may have been fought by the 1820s there continued to be fought, long after that period, a number of minor wars in the interest of furthering the aims of the jihad.

The point discussed above is important for the British conquest of Northern Nigeria in at least two ways. Firstly, it means that many of the emirates were, during the nineteenth century, preoccupied with internal rather than external affairs and that most of the wars they fought were fought against those whom Adeleye calls their traditional enemies using the traditional weapons with which they were familiar. For these emirates the wars against the British were unfamiliar wars fought against an enemy with infinitely more sophisticated weapons and strange war tactics.

Secondly, the wars and raids in which the emirates engaged, yielded slaves. As was pointed out in the last chapter, Lugard made a great deal of this issue of slave raids. Bida, Kontagora, Bauchi, and other emirates were great slave raiding and slave trading centres whose rulers deserved to be smashed so that these raids could be stopped. Kontagora alone was said to be taking, in 1900, 8,000 slaves a year in these raids. True, no detailed work has been done on slave holding in the Sokoto caliphate but demographers would no doubt wonder what the population of the area was which yielded 8,000 slaves a year. The fact, of course, was that the slave raid issue was a convenient weapon to seize upon at that point in time. It gave Lugard and his minions the opportunity to adopt a moral tone in their dealings with Africans while conveniently ignoring the question of the morality of imperialism. In Southern Nigeria Nana and the Oba of Benin were also accused of slave trading and human sacrifice; so also in Asante and elsewhere. The would-be imperialists had to find proof of the 'depravity' of the African peoples whom they were anxious to subjugate and 'civilize'! Yet they would have been the first to reject that same argument, for the Muslims could argue that they only engaged in raids against non-Muslims in order to convert the latter and shower on them the blessings of Islamic 'civilization'. Lugard knew quite well that he was not conquering Northern Nigeria in order to free its peoples from slave raids. If Bida and Kontagora had to fall, it was because they refused to let Lugard construct telegraph lines through their territory or to set up military posts without permission. To admit this was to weaken his case against these two rulers; so a more persuasive explanation had to be found.

With regard to the Sokoto caliphate it is also possible to ask the question why the caliphate did not fight against the British as a united entity. The answer to this question lies in the nature of the caliphate. The caliphate was essentially a confederacy made up of emirates which enjoyed a large measure of autonomy. The defence arrangements were such that the emirates were expected to defend the caliphate by defending their own immediate borders against enemies. While the emirates might send contingents to Sokoto to augment Sokoto's forces for a specific assignment, there was no caliphate army as such. While it is easy to point to the deficiences in such an arrangement, it is equally germane to remember that that arrangement served the needs of the caliphate for nearly a whole century. That being so, it is easier to appreciate why no fundamental change was effected even in the face of the new danger from British arms. The emirs wrote or otherwise sent messages to their brother emirs warning them of the coming of the British. The caliph enjoined the emirs not to welcome the British but rather to resist them. Nothing more was done in the nature of joint planning or joint defence. The British found this most convenient as it enabled them to take the caliphate piecemeal. Past usage thus contributed in no small way to the relative ease with which the Sokoto caliphate fell.

In discussing the caliphate's resistance to British conquest, a prominent place is usually given to the role played by Islam. There is good reason for doing so. Islam forbade Muslims from willingly submitting themselves to infidel rule. Because of this injunction the Muslims of the Sokoto caliphate felt they had a duty to resist the British push. The correspondence which passed between the caliph and Lugard leaves one in no doubt that the former was acting within the context of this injunction. In the circumstances the clash of arms was all but inevitable. Having said that, however, it is also necessary to point out that the variety of opinion within the body of Islamic law, could and did constitute a weakness in the caliphate's reaction to British conquest. Thus, for example, Islam provided a number of alternative reactions to threat of infidel conquest — resistance through fighting, resistance through emigration, acceptance of infidel conquest 'with the mouth' but not 'with the heart' while waiting to fight when strong enough. It was not always clear which of these alternatives it was best to take when faced with imminent British attack. As indicated in Episode 12, valuable time was sometimes spent on debating which alternative to adopt instead of spending such time on military preparation. Hence, while not doubting that Islam provided a zeal to fight, it also raised questions of decision. Finally, in this connection, the point must be made that it is easy to over-play the role of Islam in the reaction of the Sokoto caliphate to the British. True the caliphate reacted within a certain religio-political context. But the reaction of the Ijebu, the Tiv, Kosoko, Nana, Brass, and Benin all show that the crucial issue was the peoples' basic refusal to lose their freedom without a fight. Besides, Lugard's methods were, in most cases, deliberately calculated to provoke conflict. Hence, although Islam undoubtedly affected the attitudes of the rulers and peoples of the caliphate, the issue was sufficiently basic to have led to stout resistance even without the tenets of Islam.

It remains to say a few words about the pattern of resistance of Nigerian peoples. As would have become clear some people took up arms in defence of their cherished sovereignty, others did not. Quite often those who took up arms were virtually forced into doing so by the provocative policies of the British. In the south, Lagos, Nana, Benin, the Brass men, the people of Asaba, and the Ijebu were all forced by the British to fight or else accept extremely degrading humiliations. In the north, Lugard's measures, as already indicated, were not such that any self-respecting people would have accepted without protest. To suddenly discover white men building military posts or erecting telegraph lines in their domains without previous negotiation was not the kind of action that rulers like those of Bida and Kontagora could condone. The decision to fight against the British in such circumstances was often spontaneous. Yet once it became a matter of war, the outcome was a foregone conclusion given the disparity in armaments and drill.

There were those who accepted British rule without a fight. Some of these, like the Efik, had lost the will to fight by their own internal wranglings which had made them increasingly the victims of British encroachment. Others, like the Egba and the Ibadan were not only war-weary, but witnesses of British military exploits against Lagos, Ijebu, and Oyo. Yet others, like Zaria, were unable to fight because of prevailing internal problems which forced them to see the British as lesser dangers than their own immediate neighbours.

In the final analysis, British occupation whether it came as a result of military confrontation or not was a bitter pill to swallow. No Nigerian people, as indeed no people in the world, welcomed imperial rule. In the years immediately following conquest and occupation various groups were to demonstrate their non-acceptance of British rule by revolts and other manifestations of discontent. By that time, however, there could be no question of reversing the tables: the British had dug themselves in and meant to stay whether our peoples liked the idea or not. By that time, the British conquest of Nigeria had, indeed, become a reality.

Appendix I

Treaty with Chiefs of Itsekiriland, 1884

Her Majesty the Queen of the United Kingdom of Great Britain and Ireland, Empress of India, &c., and the Chiefs of Jakri being desirous of maintaining and strengthening the relations of peace and friendship which have so long existed between them;
Her Britannic Majesty has named and appointed E. H. Hewett, Esq., Her Consul for the Rights of Benin and Biafra, to conclude a Treaty for this purpose.
The said E. H. Hewett, Esq. and the said Chiefs of Jakri have agreed upon and concluded the following Articles:-

ARTICLE I
Her Majesty the Queen of Great Britain and Ireland, &c., in compliance with the request of the Chiefs, and people of Jakri, hereby undertakes to extend to them, and to the territory under their authority and jurisdiction, Her gracious favour and protection.

ARTICLE II
The Chiefs of Jakri agree and promise to refrain from entering into any correspondence, Agreement, or Treaty with any foreign nation or Power, except with the knowledge and sanction of Her Britannic Majesty's Government.

ARTICLE III
It is agreed that full and exclusive jurisdiction, civil and criminal, over British subjects and their property in the territory of Jakri is reserved to Her Britannic Majesty, to be exercised by such Consular or other officers as Her Majesty shall appoint for that purpose.
   The same jurisdiction is likewise reserved to Her Majesty in the said territory of Jakri over foreign subjects enjoying British protection, who shall be deemed to be included in the expression 'British Subject' throughout this Treaty.

ARTICLE IV

All disputes between the Chiefs of Jakri, or between them and British or foreign traders, or between the aforesaid Kings and Chiefs and neighbouring tribes, which cannot be settled amicably between the two parties, shall be submitted to the British Consular or other officers appointed by Her Britannic Majesty to exercise jurisdiction in Jakri territories for arbitration and decision, or for arrangement.

ARTICLE V

The Chiefs of Jakri hereby engage to assist the British Consular or other officers in the execution of such duties as may be assigned to them; and, further, to act upon their advice in matters relating to the administration of justice, the development of the resources of the country, the interests of commerce, or in any other matter in relation to peace, order, and good government, and the general progress of civilization.

ARTICLE VI

The subjects and citizens of all countries may freely carry on trade in every part of the territories of the Kings and Chiefs parties hereto, and may have houses and factories therein.

ARTICLE VII

All ministers of the Christian religion shall be permitted to reside and·exercise their calling within the territories of the aforesaid Kings and Chiefs, who hereby guarantee to them full protection.

All forms of religious worship and religious ordinances may be exercised within the territories of the aforesaid Kings and Chiefs, and no hindrance shall be offered thereto.

ARTICLE VIII

If any vessels should be wrecked within the Jakri territories, the Chiefs will give them all the assistance in their power, will secure them from plunder, and also recover and deliver to the owners or agents all the property which can be saved.

If there are no such owners or agents on the spot, then the said property shall be delivered to the British Consular or other officer.

The Chiefs further engage to do all in their power to protect the persons and property of the officers, crew, and others on board such wrecked vessels.

All claims for salvage dues in such cases shall, if disputed, be referred to the British Consular or other officer for arbitration and decision.

ARTICLE IX
This Treaty shall come into operation, so far as may be practicable, from the date of its signature, except as regards Articles VI and VII which are to be left for negotiation on a future occasion.

Done in duplicate on board H.B.M.S. *Flirt* anchored in Benin River this sixteenth day of July, 1884.

(Signed) Edward Hyde Hewett.
(There followed the marks of:
Nana (Governor), Chanomie (Tsanomi), Dudu, Numa, Ogree, Fragonie, Nafomie, Etchie, Mudwa, Brigby, Awalla, Peggy.)
Witness to above signatures:

(Signed) Theo. Hilliard
Chairman of Court of Equity.

NOTE
The above treaty is a sample of the 'Protection' treaties signed by the delta states and other Nigerian groups. The point which was made in Chapter 3 is that while most of the delta states refused to sign the treaty until Clauses VI and VII were struck out, they failed to see the significance of Clauses II-V which were probably never properly translated since the concepts embodied therein were unknown in the ordinary usage of our forebears.

Appendix II

Treaty conceded by the Shaikh of Bornu 'Umar b. Muhammad al-Amin al-Kanemi, to the British Government, 5 August 1851

What God wishes suffices.   [Seal]
The help of the slave is
with God: 'Umar b. Muhammad
al-Amin al-Kanemi.

In the name of God the merciful and the beneficent. Praise be to God, Lord of all peoples, the peace of God be upon our Lord, Prophet and master, Muhammad, the best of all prophets and messengers, and upon his family and his companions all. To continue, the document of the state of the English [i.e. England] containing stipulations which shall be mentioned in this legal document, has reached the revered exemplary of leaders, the flower of leaders, the celebrated, the most glorious, the eminent, the most happy, the shining light of the Kingdom of Bornu and the happiness of these Islamic regions, the most mighty, the most famous, the most fortunate, the dazzling Imam, the illuminating lamp of his time and a perfect jewel. He is in his place; my master, the Shaikh Umar, son of the one who knows God well; my master, the Shaikh Muhammad al-Amin al-Kanemi. May God surround him with his gracious help. This sublime Imam has considered the stipulations of the documents and his disposition to its contents. He has ordered one of his scribes to write down his stand on each of the six stipulations which came from that state. [England]. The answer is, in reality, according to the stipulation of the *Hanifi* (Islamic) religion. We shall set down the stipulations and answer them according to the principle of the accepted *shari'a*.

The first Stipulation

That the English shall not be prevented from entering the land of Bornu and all its territories and from journeying in them. That their settlers shall be as friends of its [Bornu territory] people as long as they remain in it and that their persons and their property shall not be endangered. They shall also not be prevented from travelling at the time they wish and the same condition shall apply to [the movement of] their possessions. The answer to this is: They shall not be oppressed and their persons and property shall not be endangered by any one. They, with their possessions, shall not be hindered from journeying and leaving at the time they desire.

The second Stipulation

That the subjects of the English Queen [Sultana] shall be equal with the people of Bornu with regard to all the goods they may wish to buy or sell throughout Bornu territories and that the ruler of Bornu shall ensure to them that no preference shall be given to any trader of other races. The answer to this is: they shall not be hindered from buying and selling whatever is legal for them according to the *shari'a* of Muhammad (the peace of God be upon him). But with regard to illegal things such as slaves, copies of the Qur'an and the like, no. However, with regard to there being no preference between them and other races, if those others are Christians, they shall not be given preference over them since the religion of all Christians is one and the same religion to us and as such [they are entitled to] the same protection [*dhimmi* status]. This is the answer.

The third Stipulation

That the roads shall be safe throughout the land of Bornu, and the English traders shall not be prevented from carrying their goods from one town to another nor from roaming about in the country and moving from one town to another and that other traders shall not be prevented from passing through and trafficking with them. The answer to this is: They shall not be hindered from all this if there is no disobedience of the pure *shari'a* involved.

The fourth Stipulation

That the English Queen [Sultana] shall have the right to appoint an agent to live in the land of Bornu to see to the welfare of the English on the basis of the stipulations. That the agent shall be honoured and protected and his words shall be heeded and that the safety of his person and whatever belongs to him shall be guaranteed. The answer to this is: She shall have the right to install this agent and his safety and whatever belongs to him shall be guaranteed. But other than this, he shall be treated according to what is enjoined on us by the *shari'a* since it will not be proper for us to exceed its limits.

The fifth Stipulation

That the ruler of Bornu, my master, the Shaikh 'Umar al-Kanemi, shall expend his energy in the matter of the correspondence of the subjects of the English Queen which may be sent to them and which they may send to their country. The answer to this is: This is an easy thing which does not call for his expending his energy. There shall be no occurrence of losses with regard to this or anything you will find distasteful.

The sixth Stipulation

That the ruler of the land of Bornu shall make a law and give an indication about the conclusion of these conditions and that he shall publish them [i.e. make them known] from the time of their conclusion and throughout their duration. The answer to this is: We shall give an indication according to the condition of the country and the locality and in line with the manner in which we have conceded these stipulations to you.

This is the sum-total of what we wrote down with regard to the stipulations. Indited in the morning of Tuesday the 7th of Shawal 1267 A.H.* May the kindness of God be with its writer, Amen.

*Tuesday 5 August 1851. According to Dr Barth (vol. iii, p.473), the Shaikh signed the Treaty on 31 August 1851. This would imply that the Treaty was handed over to him on the 31st. The final conclusion of the treaty, i.e. after the approval of the British government, took place on 3 September 1852 (see A. A. Boahen, *Britain, the Sahara and the Western Sudan*, p.205).

Appendix III

Treaty granted to the British Government
by the Amir al-Mu'minin, Aliyu, of Sokoto, 2 May 1853.

To continue, the Sultan [sic] of the state of the English [i.e. England] whose name [lit. his name] is Victoria, wishing to conclude a treaty (*amana*) of buying and selling [i.e. commerce] with the sultan of the Muslims, sent 'Abd al-Karim, Henry Barth. The Emir of Sokoto, 'Ali-the Amir al-Mu'minin—having heard and understood the discourse of 'Abd al-Karim, the messenger of the Queen of England, gave his consent and granted to the English a treaty of commerce of the following conditions:

Traders from England shall travel under safe-conduct throughout the territories of the Amir al-Mu'minin, 'Ali, with their children, their property and their mounts and they shall lose nothing not even a tether — as they come and go at their good pleasure. Neither in speech shall they hear that which may be loathsome to them nor shall any oppressor harm them.

No Governor in the territories of 'Ali shall lay hold of them nor shall any danger befall them. They shall return safely with their property and their honour inviolate.

If any one indebted to them delays payment, Amir al-Mu'-minin 'Ali shall recover the debt for them from the debtor.

If any of them 'i.e. the English traders' dies, the Amir al-Mu'minin shall extract the tenth (*'ushr*) from his property and the remainder shall be in the custody of the Amir al-Mu'minin until the nearest to his territory among the agents of England 'i.e. consuls' sends for it.

They shall traffic in everything except slaves for the Amir al-Mu'minin will not allow them to purchase slaves. This is all. Peace.

Date of Inditement
23 Rajab 1269 (2 May 1853).

Note Appendices II and III have been taken from R. A. Adeleye's *Power and Diplomacy in Northern Nigeria*, pp 331-4.

SELECT BIBLIOGRAPHY

BOOKS

ADELEYE, R. A. *Power and Diplomacy in Northern Nigeria 1804-1906,* Longman, 1971

AJAYI, J. F. A. *Christian Missions in Nigeria 1841-1891,* Longman, 1965.

AKINTOYE, S. A. *Revolution and Power Politics in Yorubaland 1840-1893,* Longman 1971.

ALAGOA, E. J. *The Small Brave City State,* Ibadan University Press and Wisconsin University Press, 1964.

ANENE, J. C. *Southern Nigeria in Transition 1885-1906,* Cambridge, 1966.

ATANDA, J. A. *The New Oyo Empire,* Longman, 1973.

AYANDELE, E. A. *The Missionary Impact on Modern Nigeria 1842-1914,* Longman, 1966.

CROWDER, M. (Ed) *West African Resistance,* Hutchinson, 1971 (see Chapters on Ijebu, Ebrohimi and Sokoto Caliphate).

DIKE. K. O. *Trade and Politics in the Niger Delta,* Oxford, first published in 1956.

FLINT, J. E. *Sir George Goldie and the Making of Nigeria,* Oxford 1960.

IKIME, O. *Merchant Prince of the Niger Delta,* Heinemann, 1968.
. . . *Niger Delta Rivalry,* Longman, 1969
. . . *The Isoko People,* Ibadan University Press, 1972.

ISICHEI, E. *The Ibo People and the Europeans,* Faber and Faber, 1973.

JOHNSTON, H. A. S. *The Fulani Empire of Sokoto,* Oxford, 1967.

MUFFET, D. J. M.	*Concerning Brave Captains*, Andre Deutsch, 1964.
NAIR, K. K.	*Politics and Society in South Eastern Nigeria 1841-1906,* Frank Cass, 1972.
NEWBURY, C. W.	*The Western Slave Coast and Its Rulers,* Oxford, 1961.
NICOLSON, I. F.	*The Administration of Nigeria 1900-1960,* Oxford, 1969.
OLIVER, R.	*Sir Harry Johnston and the Scramble for Africa,* Chatto and Windus 1957.
ORR, C.	*The Making of Northern Nigeria,* Frank Cass, 1965.
PERHAM, M.	*Lugard: The Years of Authority,* Collins, 1960.
RYDER, A. F. C.	*Benin and the Europeans 1485-1897,* Longman, 1969.
TAMUNO, T. N.	*The Evolution of the Nigerian State,* Longman, 1972.

ARTICLES

ADERIBIGBE, A. B.	'The Ijebu Expedition, 1892: An Episode in the British Penetration of Nigeria Reconsidered'-*Historians in Tropical Africa*, Salisbury, 1962.
AFIGBO, A. E.	'The Aro Expedition of 1901-1902', *Odu*, New series, 7 (April 1972). 'Patterns of Igbo Resistance to British Conquest', *Tarikh*, IV, *3* (1973).
AJAYI, J. F. A.	'The British Occupation of Lagos, 1851-61: A Critical Review', *Nigeria Magazine, 169,* (August 1961).
ALAGOA, E. J.	'Koko: Amayanabo of Nembe', *Tarikh* 1, *4* (1967).
ANENE, J. C.	'The Protectorate Government of Southern Nigeria and the Aros, 1900-1902', *Journal of the Historical Society of Nigeria* (hereinafter *J.H.S.N.*), I, *1* (December 1965).
AYANDELE, E. A.	'The Mode of British Expansion in Yorubaland in the Second Half of the Nineteenth Century: The Oyo Episode', *Odu*, II, *2* (1967).

IGBAFE, P.   'Oba Ovonramwen and the Fall of
                     Benin', *Tarikh*, II, *2*, (1968).

IKIME, O.   'Sir Claude Macdonald in the Niger
                     Coast Protectorate: A Reassessment',
                     odu, New series, *3* (April 1970).

. . .   'Colonial Conquest and Resistance in
                     Southern Nigeria', *J.H.S.N.*, **VI**, *3*
                     (December 1972).

. . .   'Colonial Conquest and African
                     Resistance in the Niger Delta States',
                     Tarikh, **4**, *3* (1973).

. . .   'The British Pacification of the Tiv',
                     J.H.S.N., **VII**, *1* (1973).

. . .   'The British in Bauchi, 1901–1908: An
                     Episode in the British Occupation and
                     Control   of   Northern   Nigeria',
                     J.H.S.N., VII,*2* (1974).

TAMUNO, T. N.   'Some Aspects of Nigerian Reaction to
                     the   Imposition   of   British   Rule',
                     J.H.S.N., III, *2* (1965).

Index

The abbreviation RNC *is used throughout for the Royal Niger Company*

Kalabari, 12, 25, 41, 43, 130, 133, 165
    War against (1853), 25
Kalio, Daniel, 212
Kanawa peoples, *see* Kano *below*
Kano: 86, 179, 185, 187-8, 190-6
    -Sokoto campaign, map of, 194, 200
Katagun, 179
Katsena Allah (Government Station), 176
Katsina, 188, 205
    Emir of, 86, 202
Kebbi, 73
Kede rebellion (1882), 65
Keffi, 191
    Treaty with, 70
Kemball, Colonel, 81, 186
Kirk, Sir John, 143
Koko, King, 140
Kontagora, 69, 78-82, 127, 186-9, 198-9, 213-15
    see also Ibrahim, Emir
Kosoko, Oba, 93-100, 215
Kotorkwoshi township, 195-6
Kudefu, (a messenger), 117
Kukawa township, 179-83
Kurunmi, 112
Kusseri, 179
Kwana, 71
Kwara State, 119
Kwarra, 66
Kwassau, 73

Labiyi, Onjo, 115-16
Lagos, 5, 9-11, 53-7, 93-101, 215-16
    Oba of, 93-4
Laird, Macgregor, *see* Macgregor
Lander Brothers, 7
Leaba, 68
Livingstone, 28-9
Lokoja, 12, 30, 32-3, 64, 77-8, 80, 134, 171, 187, 190, 198
Long Juju of Arochukwa, 162-3, 166-7
Lowry, Cole, Colonel, 77, 171
Lugard, Lord (Frederick), 4, 58, 76-8, 80-3, 126-8, 171-6, 180-1, 183, 186, 188-9, 190-2, 198-9, 201-2, 205, 213-15

Macdonald administration, 43-4, 46, 110, 140
Macdonald, Sir Claude, 43-4, 47, 49, 67, 70-1, 110, 138-9, 141-3, 156
Macgregor Laird, 7, 12, 30, 32, 108
McClintock, Captain, 172
Madu, Regent of Opubu, 20
Magajin of Keffi, 191-2

Maiduguri township, 178
Makum, The, 69-70, 81-2
Maliki, Emir, 68
Manilla Pepple, house of, 28
Maps:
    Niger Delta, 19
    Southern Nigeria, 38
    Ebrohimi, 48
    Northern Nigeria, 79
    Nigeria, the 12 States of, 90
    Nupe-Ilorin campaign, 123
    Brass State, 135
    Benin City, 146
    Arochukwu expedition, 163
    Sokoto Caliphate, 170
    Kano-Sokoto campaign, 194, 200
    flight of Attahiru I, 206
Marafar revolt (1891), 73
Marsh, Major, 208
Missionaries:
    growth of activity of, 7-12, 96-7, 112, 155, 185
Missionary Impact on Modern Nigeria (Ayandele), 12
Mizon, Mons., 71
Moloney, Governor, 56, 113, 191
Moma, Emir, 122
Monguno, 181, 183
Montanaro, Lieut-Colonel H. F., 166-7
Moor, Sir Ralph, 44, 46, 49-50, 143, 156-7, 166-7
Moore, C. B., 58
Morland, Colonel, 77, 83, 181, 192-3, 202
Muhammad al-Bukhari, Wazir, 205
Munshi peoples, 172-7
Muri, Treaty with, 70-1, 73
Musa, Ruler of Burmi, 207
Muslims, *see* Islam

NAC (National Africa Company), 30-3
    see also United Africa Company *and from 1886* RNC (Royal Niger Company)
Nana:
    Chief, 156, 213
    fall of town of, 44-7, 140, 215
Nassarawa, Treaty with, 70
National African Company, *see* NAC
Navy, British Royal, activities of, 6
Ndomi region, 30
Niger, 66
Niger Coast Protectorate (1893), 22, 138, 154
Niger (River) Delta, map of, 19
Nigeria, map of 12 States of, 90